CAMBRIDGE TEXTS IN THE
HISTORY OF PHILOSOPHY

# *Locke on Toleration*

# CAMBRIDGE TEXTS IN THE HISTORY OF PHILOSOPHY

*Series editors*

## KARL AMERIKS

*Professor of Philosophy at the University of Notre Dame*

## DESMOND M. CLARKE

*Emeritus Professor of Philosophy at University College Cork*

The main objective of Cambridge Texts in the History of Philosophy is to expand the range, variety, and quality of texts in the history of philosophy which are available in English. The series includes texts by familiar names (such as Descartes and Kant) and also by less well-known authors. Wherever possible, texts are published in complete and unabridged form, and translations are specially commissioned for the series. Each volume contains a critical introduction together with a guide to further reading and any necessary glossaries and textual apparatus. The volumes are designed for student use at undergraduate and postgraduate level, and will be of interest not only to students of philosophy but also to a wider audience of readers in the history of science, the history of theology, and the history of ideas.

*For a list of titles published in the series, please see end of book.*

# Locke on Toleration

EDITED BY

## RICHARD VERNON

*University of Western Ontario*

TRANSLATION OF *A LETTER CONCERNING
TOLERATION* BY

## MICHAEL SILVERTHORNE

**CAMBRIDGE**
UNIVERSITY PRESS

CAMBRIDGE UNIVERSITY PRESS
Cambridge, New York, Melbourne, Madrid, Cape Town, Singapore,
São Paulo, Delhi, Dubai, Tokyo, Mexico City

Cambridge University Press
The Edinburgh Building, Cambridge CB2 8RU, UK

Published in the United States of America by Cambridge University Press, New York

www.cambridge.org
Information on this title: www.cambridge.org/9780521764193

First published 2010

Printed in the United Kingdom at the University Press, Cambridge

*A catalogue record for this publication is available from the British Library*

*Library of Congress Cataloguing in Publication data*
Locke, John, 1632–1704.
Locke on toleration / [edited by] Richard Vernon.
p.   cm. – (Cambridge texts in the history of philosophy)
Includes bibliographical references and index.
ISBN 978-0-521-76419-3 – ISBN 978-0-521-13969-4 (pbk.)
1. Religious tolerance–History–17th century.   I. Vernon, Richard, 1945–
II. Title.   III. Series.
BR 1610.L826 2010
261.7′2–dc22
2010021888

ISBN 978-0-521-76419-3 Hardback
ISBN 978-0-521-13969-4 Paperback

# Contents

*Acknowledgements*                                          *page* vii

*Introduction*                                                    viii

*Chronology*                                                    xxxiii

*Further reading*                                               xxxvi

*Note on the texts and translation*                            xxxix

### Locke on Toleration

Locke: *A Letter concerning Toleration*                              3

Locke: From the *Second Treatise* (in *Two Treatises of
    Government*, 2nd edn, 1698)                  47

Locke: From *An Essay concerning Human Understanding*
    (4th edn, 1700)                              50

Proast: *The Argument of the Letter concerning Toleration, Briefly
    Considered and Answered* (1690)              54

Locke: From *A Second Letter concerning Toleration* (1690)          67

Proast: From *A Third Letter concerning Toleration in Defence
    of the Argument of the Letter concerning Toleration, Briefly
    Considered and Answered* (1691)               108

Locke: From *A Third Letter for Toleration* (1692)                 123

# Contents

Proast: From *A Second Letter to the Author of the Three Letters for Toleration* (1704)     164

Locke: From *A Fourth Letter for Toleration* (1704)     170

*Index*     178

# Acknowledgements

I am indebted to my colleague Dennis Klimchuk for critical comments on a draft of the Introduction, to Sarah Bittman for excellent assistance in making selections from Locke's and Proast's texts, and to Desmond Clarke, Roger Emerson, Mark Goldie, and Michael Silverthorne for helpful advice. Wolfson College, Cambridge extended hospitality to me while preparing this volume, and the staff of the Rare Book Room of the Cambridge University Library provided exemplary assistance.

# Introduction

*A Letter Concerning Toleration* is an English translation of a Latin work, the *Epistola de Tolerantia*, that John Locke wrote towards the end of the year 1685, while living – often in hiding – in the Dutch Republic. The *Epistola* was not however published until 1689, after Locke's return to England, and the English translation followed very shortly after. It soon met with a critical reply, in a pamphlet written by the Oxford chaplain Jonas Proast, which was to launch a polemical exchange in the course of which Locke wrote three further defences of his argument for toleration. Unlike the *Epistola/Letter* (hereafter: *Letter*), which is intense and compactly expressed, these defences are lengthy and often repetitive. But they comprise Locke's most fully elaborated statement of his case; they are valuable, too, because the pressure of controversy led him to clarify the priorities among his arguments.

Locke's period of exile in the Dutch Republic is very closely connected with the topic of the *Letter*, for it arose from political circumstances in which the questions of religious toleration, exclusion, and persecution played a large part. In his lifetime (he was born in 1632) Locke had lived through the English civil wars that began in 1642 and led to the deposing and then the execution of a monarch (Charles I), a parliamentary regime that came to resemble a military dictatorship with theocratic overtones, the restoration (1660) of the executed king's son (Charles II) to the throne, and further acute difficulties about the distribution of powers between king and parliament. In all of these events, the question of the religious orientation of the state was at or very close to the forefront, and, as we shall see, entered into the very definition of what a state *is* – and also, correlatively, of what a church is. The question that the *Letter* addresses is central to the turmoil that had been the background to Locke's whole life: what is the relationship between political membership, political authority, and religious belief? What claims, if any, should states make on the religious lives and loyalties of citizens?

Since Locke was a student for much of the period, he took no active part in the civil war between king and parliament, although his father served briefly in the parliamentary army. Locke's early interests inclined towards medicine rather than politics, and our current view of him as an important political philosopher is based on work that he did not publish until his late fifties. But it was his medical skill that brought him, in 1666, into a life-changing relationship with a major political figure, Lord Ashley, later the Earl of Shaftesbury, who underwent timely and effective surgery under Locke's supervision. Thanks to that, and thanks too, of course, to his phenomenal intelligence and breadth of interest, Locke was drawn into Shaftesbury's political circle, which, as the years went by, became increasingly radical in its opposition to the political settlement that followed the civil war. As a prominent member of that circle, Locke was eventually exposed to real danger.

During the reign of Charles II (1660–85) the issue of toleration had become increasingly contested. In the early 1660s, several pieces of legislation known collectively as the Clarendon Code restored and extended the religious monopoly of the Anglican Church, imposing liturgical uniformity on worship, restricting the rights of association of non-Anglicans, and excluding them from holding public offices. Although Charles himself was sympathetic to a more tolerant policy, his sympathies extended (particularly) to Catholics as well as to nonconforming protestants, that is, to protestant sects that could not conscientiously fit within the doctrines and ceremonies of the Church of England. However, he was also inclined to resort to executive measures that bypassed the constitutional role of parliament. On both counts, moves towards toleration met with opposition in parliament, for the House of Commons was dominated by landed gentry who were not only immovably hostile to Catholicism but also fiercely protective of their constitutional role. In the 1680s an extra-parliamentary opposition emerged, driven in part by dislike of the king's Catholic leanings – and, even more, by a dislike for those of James, his son and eventual heir – and in part by a demand for toleration of the dissenting protestant sects. After the defeat of an attempted regicide in 1683 (the Rye House plot), conspirators and supporters were rounded up and executed or imprisoned. Locke, a prominent oppositional figure thanks to his membership in Shaftesbury's circle, fled to the Dutch Republic as a precautionary measure, and remained there until 1688.

While in exile Locke encountered a school of theology that was both congenial and influential, that of the Dutch Remonstrants. They rejected the stricter elements of Calvinism, taught that Christianity made minimal doctrinal demands, and that protestant sects who had opposing views of 'indifferent' matters of doctrine and liturgy should live in mutual tolerance and even respect. 'Indifferent things' included features of worship that were adopted by various churches but were not specifically prescribed by Scripture itself, and were thus in some sense non-essential to Christianity.[1] Such Remonstrant teachings were by no means new to Locke: Anglican divines such as William Chillingworth had advanced them in *The Religion of Protestants* (1637).

> [M]any of these controversies which are now disputed among Christians ... are either not decidable by that means which God hath provided, and so not necessary to be decided; or if they be, not so plainly and evidently as to oblige all men to hold one way; or lastly, if decidable, and evidently decided, yet you may hope that the erring part, by reason of some veil before his eyes ... does not see the question to be decided against him, and so opposes not that which he doth know to be the word of God.[2]

Locke himself had in fact already adopted these teachings in an earlier work, the *Essay on Toleration* (1667). But conversations with a leading Remonstrant theologian, Philip van Limborch, confirmed and reinforced this view of the Christian religion, and led him to address the topic of toleration again in the *Letter*.[3] It was Limborch who arranged to publish the work and, to Locke's great annoyance – for he published all of his political works anonymously – gave away the secret of its authorship to a mutual friend.

---

[1] For the earlier history of 'indifferent things' (*adiaphora*) see Bernard J. Verkamp, *The Indifferent Mean: Adiaphorism in the English Reformation to 1554* (Athens, OH: Ohio University Press, 1977). See also Jacqueline Rose, 'John Locke, "Matters Indifferent," and the Restoration of the Church of England', *Historical Journal* 48 (2005), 601–21.

[2] *Chillingworth's Religion of Protestants; A Safe Way to Salvation*, ed. John Patrick (London: Thomas Tegg, 1845), 77–8.

[3] When the *Epistola* was published, van Limborch wrote to Locke: 'People here believe that it was written by some Remonstrant, because the position it defends agrees with Remonstrant tenets.' *John Locke: Selected Correspondence*, ed. Mark Goldie (Oxford University Press, 2002), 142.

In addition to conversations with Limborch, however, wider European events provoked Locke to write the *Letter*. Its most immediate occasion was the official withdrawal (in October 1685) of the already fragile toleration that the French kingdom had extended to its protestant minority. Under the Edict of Nantes (1598), protestants in France, most of whom were Calvinists, were relieved of legal requirements for religious conformity to the majority Catholic faith. When this was revoked by Louis XIV, fierce repression and forced conversions followed, with cruelties that Locke recurrently invokes as the last and most vivid consequence of intolerance. Locke's translator, William Popple, chose to emphasize the French connection with special force – introducing references to the 'dragoons' whom Louis deployed against his protestant subjects – and Locke offered no objection to his doing so. This brings to light an important theme that comes to the forefront in Locke's later defences of toleration: his perspective is continental, even global. He broaches the question: is it a requirement of political theory that it should apply, successfully, beyond its immediate national context?[4] As we shall see, in defending toleration against his most persistent critic, Jonas Proast, Locke advances the view that a political theory's reach cannot be confined within assumptions that apply only within one nation's boundaries. It is, in part, this relative abstraction from local circumstances that gives Locke's *Letter* its enduring general appeal to political philosophers.

## From uniformity to toleration: belief and behaviour

Locke's early *Essay on Toleration* (1667) had been written with his patron Shaftesbury's encouragement, and perhaps at his instigation, at a time when, as a minister in Charles II's government, Shaftesbury still hoped to achieve reform through the use of the king's executive power. In distinguishing between the 'concernments' of this world and of the next, the *Essay* contains the same basic political message as the more famous *Letter*, and anticipates the later, richer, and more forceful statement. But there are even earlier texts on toleration, written by Locke in 1660 at the time of the restoration of the monarchy, that complicate our picture of

---

[4] See Tony Claydon, *Europe and the Making of England 1660–1750* (Cambridge University Press, 2007), for the importance of continent-wide issues to British politics in this period.

him as a prototype of liberalism. For in those texts, the so-called *Two Tracts on Government*, Locke defends the 'magistrate's' (ruler's) power to impose conformity in religion.[5] It is fruitful, in understanding what is significant in his defence of toleration, to consider briefly what steps he had to take in order to move from his early defence of conformity to his later advocacy of religious freedom.

The *First Tract* addressed the question: 'Whether the Civil Magistrate may lawfully impose and determine the use of indifferent things in reference to religious worship.' Arguing for an affirmative answer, Locke rejected the claim that conscience had inviolable rights as something inconsistent with organized society. Society is possible, he argued, only on the basis of an agreement that the sovereign has final judgement in relation to matters affecting the public good. Matters such as forms of worship, liturgy, rites, or clerical dress fall under the sovereign's authority to the extent that he judges them to contribute to good order. To believe otherwise is to adopt or imply a principle that overturns all order and guarantees religious and political turmoil of the kind that England had suffered for twenty years. To this the *Second Tract* (written in Latin) adds that, since the sovereign can command only external or behavioural obedience, those who object may make whatever mental reservations they wish about his commands, and so their conscience remains uncompromised.

We can see, then, the double-edged potential of the idea of 'indifferent things'. In the eyes of broad-church theorists such as Chillingworth, of religious libertarians such as Edward Bagshaw (against whose 1660 pamphlet, *The Great Question Concerning Things Indifferent*, Locke directed the *First Tract*), of the Dutch Remonstrants, and of Locke himself after 1667, the indifference of things was a reason not to impose them – part of a live-and-let-live view that called on people to accept divergence in matters of no consequence to the essentials of religious belief. As Bagshaw wrote, 'none can impose what our Saviour in his infinite wisdom did not think necessary, and therefore left free.'[6] But it could just as well be argued that the indifference of things provides a reason not to resist the sovereign's political judgement about them. We can see, too, the double-edged potential of the view – later to take on

---

[5] See Philip Abrams, ed., *Two Tracts on Government* (Cambridge University Press, 1967).
[6] Edward Bagshaw, *The Great Question Concerning Things Indifferent in Religious Worship, Briefly Stated* ([no place or publisher indicated] 1660), Preface.

much prominence in Locke's argument – that the sovereign can command action, but not belief: since one's beliefs remain intact, the Latin *Tract* argues, one should accept constraints on one's actions.

Although these two phases of Locke's thought, in the *Two Tracts* and the *Letter*, evidently result in different conclusions, they are linked by a consistent appeal to the requirements of political order. His earlier view is that conformity may, in the sovereign's judgement, promote order. His later view is that the demand for conformity promotes disorder, for if states try to impose religious belief, churches will struggle for control of it, so that their own beliefs are enforced and those of others persecuted.[7] In the later pages of the *Letter*, and in his subsequent defences of it, Locke makes the link between conformity and violence, a link, he says, of which 'history has surely given us enough evidence' (p. 42).[8] We can reach the latter view without reverting to anything like a doctrine of the absolute rights of conscience (despite what William Popple claims in the preface to his translation). And in fact Locke never adopted the doctrine about conscience that he had criticized in 1660. It is a striking feature of his mature view, in the *Letter*, that people's conscientious commitments are subordinate to the (valid) requirements of the public interest, so that while it would be tyrannical to strike at someone's religious practices for reasons of one's own religious preference, it is acceptable to do so if those practices turn out to be incompatible with some important public policy. Locke offers as his example a case in which disease depletes cattle stocks, and a government prohibits slaughter, with the unintended consequence that a religious cult devoted to animal sacrifice can no longer practise its religious beliefs. But the most famous (or notorious) example is the *Letter*'s exclusion of Catholics from toleration on the grounds that, having an external allegiance (to Rome), they are not trustworthy citizens. The other notable exclusion, that of atheists – also on the grounds of untrustworthiness, for according to Locke they have no reason to keep their word – falls into a slightly different category. Because they have no religion, he points out (p. 37), they fall outside the scope of *religious* toleration from the outset (i.e. they do not benefit from whatever the case is for tolerating religious beliefs).

---

[7] As William Walwyn, the Leveller, had tersely put it, conflict is produced 'not by, but for want of, a toleration'. *Toleration Justified and Persecution Condemned* (London, 1646), 10.

[8] Page references in parentheses are given for texts published in this volume.

At one level, then, we are dealing here with a simple difference in empirical political judgement about the likely consequences of different policies: will imposed conformity promote or destroy order? But connected with this are two interesting theoretical developments. The first is at the level of religious psychology. Locke comes to take much more seriously the attachment that people have to religious practices as things inseparable from the core of belief. That view had already been stated in several unpublished manuscript notes on the topic of toleration.[9] An under-appreciated feature of the *Letter* is its adoption of a sort of aesthetics of belief that connects forms of worship with deep tastes or temperaments. Why, he asks, should I be persecuted by others 'because I have come to feel that some people are not sufficiently serious while others are just too strait-laced for me to be happy to travel in their company?' (p. 18). His later description of such things as matters of 'temper' (p. 53) relates suggestively to his use of that term in *Thoughts on Education*, where, despite the well-known doctrine that the human mind is like a blank slate, he eventually acknowledges that children have tempers or dispositions that are perhaps innate or which at any rate escape the control of education.[10] All this goes on alongside his consistent view that religious forms are, considered rightly, indifferent or even (as he says immediately after the passage just quoted) matters that lack real significance.

This leads directly to the second interesting development, which is that Locke now drives a wedge between religious truth (*simpliciter*) and political theory. It is, he believes, a religious truth that forms are a matter of indifference. But it is a fact of basic importance to political theory that people act on the basis of what they take to be true, not on the basis of an enlightened judgement. That distinction, as we shall see, is one that Locke repeatedly defends in polemic, so that his argument often amounts, in effect, to advocacy of the distinct status of political theory, as an activity that requires attention to the plurality of agency. We shall return to this argument from order, as we may call it, for it plays much more than a supporting role in the structure of thinking in the *Letter*.

---

[9] See especially 'Toleration D' [1679], in Mark Goldie, ed., *Locke: Political Essays* (Cambridge University Press, 1997), 276–7: 'For even the circumstances of the worship of God cannot be indifferent to him that thinks them not so.'

[10] *The Works of John Locke* (London: Tegg, 1823), vol. IX, 204–5.

But it is not among the arguments that Locke formally lays out near the beginning of that work.

## The *Letter*'s arguments

The three arguments that Locke outlines at the beginning of the *Letter* may be termed the argument from the mandate of the state, the argument from belief, and the argument from error. How these three arguments relate to each other (and to the argument from order, mentioned above) is the leading interpretative question in considering Locke's case for toleration. Are they independent and alternative arguments? Or is one of them primary or basic, as is sometimes held, though those who hold such a view offer different candidates for the role?

The argument from mandate states that:

> [T]he civil ruler has no more mandate than others have for the care of souls. He has no mandate from God, for it nowhere appears that God has granted men authority over other men, to compel them to adopt their own religion. And no such power can be given to a ruler by men; for no one may abdicate responsibility for his own eternal salvation, by adopting a form of faith or worship prescribed to him by another person, whether prince or subject. (p. 7)

The first part of this claim evidently depends on a reading of Scripture: as the *Letter* goes on, Locke makes much of the fact that the New Testament, unlike the Old, neither confers power on anyone nor lays down rules for political order, so that, he says, there is no such thing as a 'Christian commonwealth' (p. 29), as opposed to a commonwealth whose members hold Christian beliefs. St Paul's pronouncement that all are 'subject unto the higher powers' comes to mind as the basis for objection: but, as Jeremy Waldron has argued, that edict presupposes (at least as Locke saw it) a prior view about which 'higher' (state) powers are *legitimate*, and so the Scriptural argument is (in this case) subordinate to such a view.[11] All citizens are therefore subject only to the legitimate powers of the commonwealth, and the power to decide the orthodoxy or otherwise of their religious beliefs is not one of them.

---

[11] Jeremy Waldron, *God, Locke, and Equality: Christian Foundations in Locke's Political Thought* (Cambridge University Press, 2002), 196–7.

The second part of the claim – that there is no commission from consent by 'the people' – implicitly invokes an argument of a contractualist kind. Locke cannot mean democratic consent, for two reasons. One is that he is not in any clear sense a democrat. Secondly, if he meant that lack of consent by the people was the only impediment to the commonwealth's authority to decide religious questions, he would thereby extend the powers of the state as far as popular consent warranted. However, Locke clearly wants to say that the imposition of religious conformity is beyond the state's scope, on the grounds that contracting parties would not consent to its being one of its powers. It seems proper, in examining this claim, to refer to the worked-out contractual argument in the *Second Treatise*. In that work, Locke argued that the powers of a state are limited to those that would emerge from a social contract in which, endowed with reason, we would reject absolute authority and agree only to a set of arrangements that would contribute to our common preservation.

The argument from belief states that:

> [The] care of souls cannot belong to the civil ruler, because his power consists wholly in compulsion. But true and saving religion consists in an inward conviction of the mind; without it, nothing has value in the eyes of God. Such is the nature of the human understanding, that it cannot be compelled by any external force. (p. 8)

We have already seen a version of this argument, put to a different (indeed, contrary) use in the *Two Tracts*. Locke was hardly original in exploiting its tolerant potential in the *Letter.* Earlier in the century, for example, it had been lucidly deployed for that purpose by the Leveller pamphleteer William Walwyn. '[Can] it in reason be judged the meetest way to draw a man out of his error, by imprisonment, bonds, or other punishment?' Nothing can remove error 'but the efficacy and convincing power of sound reason and argument'.[12] Going further back in time, we find it deployed by St Augustine, in arguing that the state's instruments – its power over merely earthly values – limited its role to that of constraining its subjects' behaviour.

Let us note, before moving on, that the argument from belief, as Locke develops it here, is an appeal to the rationality of the *ruler.* If a ruler sets

---

[12] *Toleration Justified*, 8.

out, as a holder of political power, to change people's minds by force, then he will fail, or so the argument says. The argument from mandate, on the other hand, is directed to the rationality of *subjects*. It is not in your interest to confer on a ruler a power to impose religious belief, because all that power could do is produce insincere or hypocritical conformity, which would be 'obstacles to [y]our salvation.'

The third argument, from error – or the 'needle-in-the-haystack' argument – is explicitly presented as an independent consideration. Locke writes: 'even granted that the authority of laws and the force of penalties *were* effective in changing people's minds' – i.e. even if it were rational for subjects to consent to have their minds changed for them, and rational for the ruler to undertake to do so – 'yet this would have no effect on the salvation of their souls' (p. 8) for there is but one true religion and many false ones, and so the chances are very much that the 'religion of the court' would be among the latter. Although Locke offers it as an argument that applies independently, it is still controlled by the mandate argument, for Locke writes, a little later: 'even if it *could* be finally determined' which of the competing churches were in the right, the right to impose would still not follow. How the rightness of one church or other could become manifest is mysterious, but we may read this as a purely hypothetical consideration that directs us not to rely fundamentally on the argument from error.

## Assessing the arguments

Locke claims that these three arguments 'seem to warrant the conclusion that the power of the commonwealth is concerned only with civil goods', that is, with the protection of life, liberty, and property, not reaching to religious imposition. Locke's critic, Jonas Proast, in his first reply to the *Letter*, claimed that the three arguments amounted essentially to one, that is, the argument from belief. Proast's interpretation has also been endorsed by Jeremy Waldron.[13] According to Waldron, Locke's 'main line' of argument depends on a view of the coercive nature of state power and hence of the limits of coercion. He quotes Locke's vividly concrete account of the state's resources ('fire and the sword', 'rods and axes') in

---

[13] Jeremy Waldron, 'Locke, Toleration, and the Rationality of Persecution', in Susan Mendus, ed., *Justifying Toleration: Conceptual and Historical Perspectives* (Cambridge University Press, 1988).

summarizing his view as one that depended fundamentally on the inefficacy of such things in terms of changing minds; but, like Proast, he seeks to show that such violent instruments are not the only (or the best) instruments available to the state if it pursues a goal of conformity in religious belief. Here Waldron draws upon some relevant considerations from Locke's *Essay Concerning Human Understanding*, where the basis of belief is examined.

There Locke says, indeed, that we have no choice in our perception of things – if I see something as yellow, I cannot choose to see it as black – but he also acknowledges the whole 'apparatus' that surrounds perception, such as decisions about what to attend to.[14] And that apparatus is responsive to choice – we can choose what to attend to. That dovetails very nicely with Proast's reply to Locke, and with Proast's proposals. Fire and sword, rods and axes, he says, have nothing to do with what the Church of England actually proposes. All that we propose are 'moderate' measures that are intended to induce dissenters to listen to what we say. He is (as Locke was to complain) unspecific about these penalties, but we may assume that he is referring to fines for refusing to attend the established church, and disabilities that limit the opportunities of dissenters in academic and public life. These are measures that are subject to state control and that could be justified, in support of Proast's argument, by reference to the 'apparatus' surrounding perception that Locke himself admits to be efficacious.

This objection is extremely damaging to Locke. While it is true that states cannot compel (sincere) conversion by fear, they certainly have the resources to control the information on the basis of which citizens make up their minds, by negative means (censorship, denial of broadcast licences) and positive means (state-controlled media, publication subsidy). Moreover, even if a state's control over an existing population by such means is limited, its potential control over what is available to future generations is surely greater – records can be destroyed, historical accounts rewritten, photographs airbrushed, and so on. To all this we may add the consideration that rulers may not actually be interested in changing people's minds at all; for political (or pathological) reasons of their own, they may just want people to fall into line. That topic does not

---

[14] *Essay Concerning Human Understanding*, Book IV, 13 and Book IV, 20 (both excerpted below). Cf. St Ignatius Loyola, *The Spiritual Exercises* [*c.* 1548], Eng. trans. (Chicago: Loyola University Press, 1992), 135: 'What seems to me to be white, I will believe to be black if the hierarchical Church thus determines it.' St Ignatius was the founder of the Jesuit order.

arise, however, in the debate between Locke and Proast, neither of whom adopts such a cynical view, although more than once Locke alleges that to be the secret motive behind persecuting policies.[15]

It is significant that, in his replies to Proast, Locke makes no attempt to defend the argument from belief in its original form. Instead, he notes that Proast simply accepts the *Letter*'s argument that sheer threats cannot change minds, and claims that what Proast advocates – the use of state compulsion to secure attention to the established church's doctrine – is 'new'; it is so new, in fact, that he could not be expected to have considered it in advance of Proast's reply. This is disingenuous on Locke's part. What Proast was proposing had a long and familiar pedigree. If Locke's view that the reach of coercion is essentially limited can be traced to Augustine's *City of God*, Proast's can be traced to Augustine's later decision that coercion can, after all, be used for educative purposes. He had drawn upon a verse in St Luke's gospel (Luke 14: 13) in which a rich man, disappointed that so few had come to a feast that he had prepared, tells his servants to go out into the streets and 'compel them to come in'. It was a commonplace that, in that parable, the rich man was a figure for God, the feast represented God's word, and the servants signified the church. Pierre Bayle, whom Locke had met in Holland, had written (in 1687) a whole book of commentary on St Luke's verse, attempting to show that it could not license persecution.[16] So Locke's 'all this is new to me' defence is unconvincing, as he eventually acknowledges, in effect, in the *Fourth Letter*, where he says that although the idea is not new, its application would be.

In his replies to Proast, Locke relies very little on the claim that states cannot induce belief, implicitly conceding the point in its original form. In fact, he shifts the focus of argument away from the issue of state *capacity* to the issue of state *authority*. A major point of contention concerns just that distinction. Proast, Locke complains, fails to distinguish between two different senses in which we may speak of a state's powers, conflating what a state has the power (capacity) to do with what it is empowered (authorized) to do, and reducing the latter to the former.

---

[15] There is a particularly nice formulation of his suspicion in a manuscript note, 'Toleration A' [*c.* 1675]: when churches employ coercion we are likely to feel that 'it is not the feeding of the sheep but the benefit of the fleece' that explains attempts to enlarge the fold, in Goldie, ed., *Locke: Political Essays*, 231.

[16] Pierre Bayle, *A Philosophical Commentary on the Words of the Gospel, Luke XIV. 23, 'Compel them to come in, that my house may be full'*, Eng. trans. (London: J. Darby. 1708).

> The natural force of all the members of any society, or of those who by the society can be procured to assist it, is in one sense called the power of that society. This power or force is generally put in some one or few persons' hands with direction and authority how to use it; and this in another sense is called also the power of the society. (p. 145)

Unless we take account of the authority by which a power-holder's role is defined, all institutional distinctions evaporate, for all institutions have capacities extending beyond their role: 'there will be no difference between church and state, a commonwealth and an army, or between a family and the East India Company, all of which have hitherto been thought distinct sorts of societies, instituted for different ends' (p. 103).

Here a very basic difference between Locke's and Proast's political assumptions comes into play. It is Proast's firm belief that if states have a capacity to do good then they are justified in doing it, or in fact are required to do it: or at least (he later clarifies) are required to do it when it is also necessary that the good be done by some agent. 'Doubtless commonwealths are instituted for the attaining of all the benefits which political government can yield' (p. 62). Otherwise, he says, the power is given in vain. Locke, however, holds that states are constrained by their mandate. An important passage in Locke's *Third Letter* encapsulates the central argument of the *Second Treatise*:

> The end of a commonwealth constituted can be supposed no other than what men in the constitution of, and entering into it, proposed; and that could be nothing but protection from such injuries from other men, which they desiring to avoid, nothing but force could prevent or remedy; all things but this being as well attainable by men living in neighbourhood without the bounds of a commonwealth, they could propose to themselves no other thing but this in quitting their natural liberty, and putting themselves under the umpirage of a civil sovereign, who therefore had the force of all the members of the commonwealth put into his hands to make his decrees to this end be obeyed. (p. 141)

At least provisionally, then, we may say that despite its prominence in the *Letter* and in the critical literature since the time of Proast, the argument based on the epistemic incapacity of states takes second place to an argument about what they have a mandate or commission to do. The difference between the two lines of argument becomes strikingly clear in the exchange, between Locke and Proast, on the legitimacy of state-imposed surgery. Locke insisted on the need for the patient's consent to give a mandate, while Proast claimed that the matter is settled by the medical capacity of the state-appointed surgeons (pp. 189, 129–31).

Considerations about the nature of coercion come into play in different ways in the first and second of Locke's arguments. In the second (the argument from belief) it is offered as an obstacle, as noted above, to a ruler's ambitions: it is irrational for rulers to attempt to do what is impossible, i.e. to coerce belief. But in the first argument (the argument from mandate) it is offered as a consideration that bears on *a citizen's* rationality. Let us suppose – reconstructing a possible line of thinking here – that, as a person contemplating a social contract, my options include subscribing to a political society that would lead me to the true faith. Suppose also that the proposed commonwealth would not try to do so by issuing futile threats; it would do so (as Proast proposes) by controlling the information available to me, placing 'briars and thorns' in my path if I strayed, and offering positive incentives when I behaved well. There are real-world parallels to this case, for example, in therapeutic programmes, which are effective in part at least because they secure their clients' advance commitment. As a client in such a programme, it would be in my prior interest to make my commitment secure if that would maximize the chances of subsequent success. So why would I not, correspondingly, secure my commitment to a state that promised the road to salvation, by signing on to a policy of religious imposition?

Exactly that question, we may note, was posed to Locke by Proast, who tried to take some account of the contractualist perspective and to turn it against his adversary. By signing on to a social contract, he said, you are seeking to secure your most important interests, so why would you not include among them your (supremely important) interests in salvation? Why seek protection only of a limited range of Lockean civil interests? That line of argument, which makes the state's power depend on specific consent, is not obviously consistent with Proast's other view that states already have that power under the law of nature, by virtue of sheer capacity (and necessity). However, since Locke is allowed more than one argument, Proast should be entitled to the same degree of privilege. The question, then, is: can this argument be used in support of Proast's position?

The prospect of subsequent success does not *generally* justify prior agreement. There certainly are cases in which people can promote their future welfare by voluntarily accepting present restrictions. In addition to therapeutic programmes, Ulysses comes to mind: he tied himself to the mast of his ship so that he could hear the Sirens' song without being able to steer his ship to destruction on the rocks. But such cases depend on a rarely available level of clarity in the means–end distinction. They depend on the agent knowing, with a level of foreknowledge that justifies the surrender of freedom, what it is that they want, such that they already understand in advance what will be provided subsequent to their agreement. The weight-loss client, the addict, and Ulysses all have a very clear prior understanding of what they want to achieve, and their surrender of freedom makes good sense. But to surrender one's freedom to a state offering salvation is more closely akin to a leap in the dark. It is to agree to evaluate a process by standards that the process itself will change. In part, then, the diverging views here reflect very different background exemplars of risk.

It is crucial to ask what *basically* underpins Locke's limited set of civil interests, because it helps to uncover other ways of grounding his argument. Proast alleges that Locke's position is circular and question-begging: the magistrate is limited to the protection of civil interests, and civil interests in turn are the things confided by citizens to the magistrate's protection. Unless Locke's case is purely circular, it must then be (on Proast's view) that in the last resort it depends on the (false) claim that states are incapable of controlling belief, and that only the citizen's conviction about this incapacity justifies the limits that contractors would place on a government's authority. So, despite all his protestations about having more than one argument – 'Who can stand against such a conqueror,' Locke writes facetiously, 'who by barely attacking of one, kills a hundred?'[17] – he has only one after all, and it is, Proast says, plainly false. But here there are several alternative possibilities that need exploring.

One view is that Locke's whole argument ultimately relies on a particular conception of religious belief. 'The force and effectiveness of true and saving religion lies in belief' (p. 7), Locke writes, and it is a short

[17] *Fourth Letter*, in *Works*, vol. VI, 551. Not included in the excerpt in this volume.

step from this to attributing to him a view, characteristic of some forms of protestant thinking, that faith is invalid unless it arises from personal enquiry and struggle. As Waldron rightly points out, that view puts a heavy emphasis on how we arrive at belief rather than what we believe, an emphasis that makes no sense outside a limited range of religious conceptions. However, although it is a short step from what Locke says to that conclusion, it is not one that should be taken, nor is it one that Locke took.

In an apparent paradox, it is in fact Proast who insists on the importance of 'consideration' in arriving at belief, and Locke who criticizes him for it (compelling a very damning retreat). Proast's argument for the use of compulsion rests entirely on its employment as an instructional tool that will induce people to consider carefully, and if necessary to reconsider repeatedly, the doctrine of the Church of England; I am not proposing to compel belief, he says, only to compel consideration. Against this, Locke adopts a notably relaxed attitude to the mode of acquisition of beliefs. We must, he says, allow people 'to rely on the learning, knowledge, and judgement of some persons whom they have in reverence or admiration' (p. 155). In part, this is because it is beyond human power, and an arrogant presumption of divine power, to fix the degree of consideration that is needed: how can we measure it, or decide if it is enough? In part it is because it must be the case that consideration sometimes leads to the wrong answer: in a rare light moment in the exchange, Locke cites the (apocryphal) story of the Reynolds brothers, both skilful theologians, one an Anglican and the other a Catholic, who succeeded in converting each other by argument. At least one of them, Locke points out, must have been mistaken, despite his exceptional skill. In part it is because salvation must be available to those who have limited leisure, education, and intellectual capacity, and who therefore cannot engage in profound consideration. Here again Locke's view is in line with Dutch Remonstrant beliefs. Would you have the poor ploughman sell his plough, Locke asks rhetorically, leaving his family to starve, so that he can buy learned books and explore fine points of controversy?[18] Finally, Locke's relaxed attitude to how religious beliefs are acquired

---

[18] The same view is found in Locke's *The Reasonableness of Christianity*, in *Works*, vol. VII, 157–8. See also *Chillingworth's Religion of Protestants*, 150: '[W]ho is there that is not capable of a sufficient understanding of the story, the precepts, the promises, and the threats of the gospel?'

rests on the fact that if we insist on consideration as a prerequisite to belief, we are at least as likely to find it among dissenters as among Anglicans – and in fact more likely to find lack of consideration among Anglicans, given the extraneous incentives to belong – so that to be consistent Proast should favour some kind of penalty to induce Anglicans to consider carefully, too. It is this that compels Proast's retreat: since they have the right view, they need not consider, he says,[19] thus badly damaging the credibility of his basic case.

Two things help to explain why Locke's case is taken to be one that rests on an unrealistic demand for earnest enquiry. The first is the stress given in the *Letter* to 'light' (or evidence) as the basis for belief. But the context in which Locke introduces this is specific to the case of *conversion*. It is only 'light,' he writes, that can 'change a belief in the mind'. So his argument is not about how people should get their beliefs in the first place – for which, as we have seen, he has no demanding conditions – but about how we should set about changing the beliefs of someone who already has them. On this question, he makes the reasonable point that we have to do so by presenting them with reasons to change their mind, not by giving extraneous inducements.

The second is that Locke's target is insincerely maintained belief, or hypocrisy. Relying on a much later distinction between 'sincerity' and 'authenticity', one can demand that people mean what they say without insisting that they have taken any particular steps to make the belief their own. It is insincerity that is the target of Locke's second argument in the *Letter*. In his subsequent defences, Locke emphasizes that inducements of any kind – not just violent threats, but 'moderate' Proastian inducements, too – are likely to produce opportunistic and insincere conversions for the sake of avoiding inconvenience or gaining some economic advantage (such as a licence to sell ale). But this, again, is a negative argument, not one that positively demands intense enquiry or struggle as a prerequisite to acquiring the kind of religious belief that is conducive to salvation.

A second general view depends on the argument from error, which we have not yet considered. In a hypothetical social contract, would our reason for rejecting religious imposition be that the true religion

---

[19] Jonas Proast, *A Third Letter to the Author of the Second Letter Concerning Toleration* (Oxford, 1691), 42. Not included in the excerpt in this volume.

cannot be known? If so, would Locke's position rest ultimately on some version of scepticism? Some commentators incline to this view and maintain that, as Locke's defence of toleration unfolded, he was compelled to rely progressively on its more sceptical elements. The incomplete *Fourth Letter* ends by rejecting Proast's claim that religious truth can be held with the same assurance as knowledge strictly understood. There can be no doubt that Locke distinguished clearly between knowledge and faith. But it is one thing to note what he believed, and something else to establish what his argument depends on: we should look carefully at the sceptical construction of it because – like the construction of it in terms of 'authenticity' – it would limit the appeal of the argument to those who shared its assumptions. For, while some persecutors are sceptics, most of them are probably not; therefore an argument based on the possible erroneousness of their beliefs would have no force for them.

The issue of 'true religion' plays a large role in Locke's defence because it relates to the view that Proast advances against him. Locke complains that if states were permitted to impose their favoured religions, that would not, in fact, work to the advantage of the true religion, since in many or perhaps all other countries it would lead to what Proast himself takes to be the imposition of false religions. In Locke's view, we must think about principles in a transnational context, and in that context the principle of toleration will allow the true religion to flourish wherever it is. Proast takes this to be a claim about prudence rather than political morality: how will toleration in England lead to toleration elsewhere, he asks. But, more importantly, he denies that his principle would license the imposition of false religions, for it states only that those magistrates who possess the *true* religion may impose it. That, of course, is how Proast understood his position. But Locke is surely right to retort that, whatever Proast intends, the principle will as a political matter empower all magistrates to impose what in their own view is the true religion, right or wrong. Proast replies that, in those circumstances, God will punish them if they impose false religions.

There is not much to say about this disagreement, except that Locke is thinking as a political theorist while Proast is not; that is, he is thinking about the consequences of the adoption of principles rather than the personal salvation of monarchs. His case, in so far as it involves scepticism at all, would best be described as one of political scepticism, as indeed the formulation of the argument from error shows – it is about whether we can suppose that those who govern us can reliably find the truth, not about whether the truth is available at all. As we have seen, it is Locke's view that religious convictions are in a different category from demonstrable truths, but scepticism (or, more simply, doubt) about the epistemic capacities of governments stands independently of that. Proast tries to revive the charge of scepticism by claiming that Locke's argument implies that he must think there are 'as clear and solid grounds' for false beliefs as for true ones. However, Locke can turn this aside easily enough by responding, in the *Fourth Letter*, that each person will determine in their own case what is sufficiently clear or solid, or what sufficiently meets whatever other qualifying adjectives Proast may care to add.

Perhaps an alternative to scepticism as an explanation is something akin to what John Rawls terms 'the burdens of judgment'.[20] Such is the internal complexity of worldviews, and the interpretative porosity of the elements that make them up, that our capacity to provide and communicate a full account of them is limited. But Locke goes further than Rawls, who introduces the idea in the context of the large and complex views of life that people form. For Locke, the burden of incommunicability is heavier, applying even to demonstrable truths. It is, after all, simply true that $9,467,172$ divided by $297$ equals $31,876$, 'and yet,' Locke writes,

> I challenge you to find one man of a thousand to whom you can tender this proposition with demonstrative or sufficient evidence to convince him of the truth of it in a dark room; or ever to make this evidence appear to a man that cannot write and read, so as to make him embrace it as a truth, if another, whom he hath more confidence in, tells him it is not so. (p. 154)

His example drives a wedge sharply between epistemic and communicative matters, and displays his conviction that in politics the limits of communicative possibility do not map onto the shape of truth. To the extent that Locke relies on considerations of this kind, then, considerations about the nature of truth recede into the background, for what is

[20] John Rawls, *Political Liberalism* (New York: Columbia University Press, 1993), 54–8.

at issue is not what can or cannot be known but what can or cannot be publicly conveyed.

The suspicion that sometimes arises here is that Locke has turned a principled argument into a pragmatic one, that he has no real answer to the claim that the true religion can be imposed, but only an objection based on the bad effects of supposing that it should be. This, however, misses the importance of the contractualist structure of the argument, which is about the authority of states; it employs the test of hypothetical consent, and hypothetical consent is guided by practical reasoning. In section six of the *Second Treatise*, Locke sets out the view that humans have the faculty of reason so that they can take steps to preserve themselves 'and the rest of mankind', and that the constitution of civil society and the authorization of political power must be examined in that light. Here the argument from order, mentioned above, takes its place within the general structure, for while Locke does not develop that argument as elaborately and convincingly as Bayle did in his book on St Luke, he clearly believes that it is an offence against the (divinely given) faculty of reason to adopt principles that are destructive of human society.

It is apparent that the principle of religious conformity will have destructive consequences, and Proast, as we have seen, does not even deny that. These consequences are not merely a practical problem for conformity, they provide a reason to abandon it as a principle within the practical reasoning that we have a natural duty to employ. It is a basic fact about political society that it involves the use of power and that its use is governed by rules that others will interpret, and which, therefore, must be robust enough to withstand interpretation without disaster. 'Obey the true God' is not such a rule. With a degree of detail that is sometimes tedious, Locke objects that Proast's talk of applying sufficient penalties to induce sufficient consideration is incapable of implementation: not merely a practical point, but an extension of the basic understanding that a political society involves co-operation among distinct agents, and hence requires intelligible rules. In contrast, Proast seems to hold a sort of telepathic view according to which his own private understanding can be directly transmitted to other minds, or else an authoritarian assumption that his own thoughts have mandatory force for those who hold power.

If we press this thought further, we are led to a very basic idea that, arguably, has a more convincing claim to be foundational for Locke's theory of toleration. This is the idea of equality that is set out in the

*Second Treatise*. It is not mentioned in the *Letter*, but it is implied in Locke's repeated view that those who propose to use power over others must be able, as discursive partners, to justify their use to them. We can see this revealed, for example, in the model of dialogue that surfaces from time to time in the exchange with Proast. Locke begins his first reply to his critic by pointing out that it would be inappropriate, as he is sure his interlocutor would agree, that either of them should use force against the other to advance their case. Proast's bewildered reply is that of course it would not be appropriate, since they are engaged in a 'private' argument, but it is clearly Locke's assumption that public life should be constrained in the same way as private debate, i.e. by the communication of reasons. The same point also emerges strikingly from a passage which, if not carefully read, seems to reinvite the charge of scepticism. Locke challenges Proast to justify his case for religious imposition to others 'without supposing all along [his] church [to be] the right' (p. 99). Proast offers the wounded reply that it seems very hard that he is not allowed to suppose himself to be in the right. But this misses the point. It is quite fundamental to Locke's own case, from the beginning, that people should believe themselves to be in the right: 'Everyone is orthodox in his own eyes' (p. 14). What he is denying is that one can properly use that belief as a supposition of dialogue, that is, as a starting point that one's interlocutor is bound to accept, for that amounts to a claim to justificatory privilege. 'If you come to arguments and proofs, which you must do before it can be determined whose is the true religion, it is plain your supposition is not allowed.'[21] Questions about toleration arise when a number of citizens hold different religious beliefs and each holds that their own beliefs are true. Without abandoning the latter conviction, such citizens must still find some way of living together in peace.

The egalitarian background comes out, too, in the language of contracting or bargaining that Locke employs. In the context of his contractualist model, he contends that the parties contemplating the terms of association could not include religious imposition among those terms,

---

[21] For a very similar use of the term, see Walwyn, *Toleration Justified*: those who persecute have the fallacious belief 'that they always suppose themselves to be competent examiners and judges of other men differing in judgment from them, and upon this weak supposition (by no means to be allowed) most of [their] reasons and arguments … are supported' (3).

because, as he puts it, that is not a matter about which they could 'stipulate' (p. 106). That word, in the English of the time, refers to a process of exchange by which parties provide undertakings to one another. They can plausibly undertake to exchange guarantees of security – not to harm one another, and to co-operate in maintaining a system of general rights-enforcement – but salvation is not something that one person can undertake to provide to another. The terms of association, then, are constrained by a process of negotiation in which each gives only what others can reciprocally provide. Like dialogue, the model of contracting or bargaining is emblematic of a conception of equality that demands that authority be justified in light of the interests of all those subjected to it.

Finally, the basic importance of equality for Locke is clear from his emphatic rejection of the essentially tutorial conception of the state that his adversary adopts. Proast deploys a simple analogy between the authority of a state and that of schoolmasters, tutors, and masters of guilds: 'That force does some service towards the making of scholars and artists [artisans]', he writes, is something that 'I suppose you will easily grant' (p. 109). Assuming this concession, he asks why we accept the use of force to bring young people to learning and skill, but we would not accept a parallel use of force to make citizens attend to the church's teaching. But Locke regards the parallel as defective. 'There is ... something else in the case' (p. 136), he writes, that is, the element of consent that Proast suppresses. Masters and tutors can legitimately discipline their charges because their charges' fathers have authorized them to do so. The authority of fathers over children, in turn, is not indeed based on consent, but on natural necessity. That, however, will not do as a political model, either, for it is a temporary necessity during the 'flexible and docile part of life' only; 'when the child is once come to the state of manhood, and to be the possessor and free disposer of his goods and estate, he is then discharged from this discipline of his parents' (p. 137). Here the profound anti-paternalism of Locke's view – expounded at length in his critique of Sir Robert Filmer's *Patriarcha* – comes into play (and points the way to a long liberal tradition). While the parallel is not explicitly drawn, the 'free disposition' of one's religious commitments is justified in the same way as the free disposition of 'goods and estate': it is a feature of adulthood itself.

## Toleration today

Locke's defence of toleration reflected some political circumstances specific to his time and, as the reader will see, was concerned in part with theological concerns that are no longer part of the conventions of public debate. Whether it is right, as one commentator famously claimed, to see Locke as an 'alien' figure is another matter altogether.[22] At several points, the discussion above has hinted at many aspects of Locke's argument that contemporary political theorists may find congenial: its cosmopolitanism, or its view that political theory must be more than national in its scope; its adoption of a political morality, that is, a view that what is politically legitimate cannot simply be read off from what can be ethically (or religiously, or epistemically) justified; the deep recognition of plurality as a feature of political association; the implicit adoption of a notion of public reason, and even fragments of a dialogical ethic; finally, the background belief in equality, what has been termed the 'egalitarian plateau' on which the disagreements among contemporary theorists take place. Of course there is always a real risk that, in coming to terms with an interesting text, one will read back into it the concerns and assumptions of one's own time. In this case, however, such has been the influence of Locke's work that it is highly probable that the political landscape has the above features because it was he who, in part, created them. To that extent, examining Locke's argument is a genealogical enterprise that leads to a better understanding of how we came to be where we are, so that aims and modes of political control that once seemed obviously appropriate (or 'decent') now seem tyrannical.

It is entirely another question, of course, whether, even so, Locke's argument or anything descended from it is adequate to contemporary political circumstances. The pluralism of modern society may have something in common with, but is clearly not identical to, the plurality of sects that concerned Locke in the late seventeenth century. In particular, it is sometimes claimed that the entire model of toleration has deservedly had its day. Toleration, it is complained, is a top-down notion according to which those who hold power forbearingly stay their hand, and it is thus inconsistent with stronger requirements of equality that demand the dismantling of hierarchy altogether. Freedom should not be a gift of the

---

[22] John Dunn, *Interpreting Political Responsibility* (Cambridge: Polity, 1990), 9.

strong to the weak. Moreover, what is called for is a different and more positive model of intergroup relations, one in which we do not merely overcome mutual dislike or disapproval but come to appreciate diversity and recognize the perspectives of the other.

Without discussing the merits of these claims in detail, I shall make two final points in Locke's favour. First, his model is about power-seeking rather than power-holding, and is not therefore directly a 'top-down' model, for throughout his writings on toleration he makes it clear that the starting point is the rivalry among churches themselves, whose zeal, as he repeatedly complains, leads them to seek power from states. Political domination is, in this context, a product of group competition, and the *Letter* begins with a plea for '*mutual* toleration' (emphasis added). Perhaps it is this that explains the otherwise curious difference in focus between the *Letter* and the *Second Treatise*, from which, as noted above, the topic of religious toleration is absent: this is less odd than it may at first seem, if we bear in mind that the *Second Treatise* is above all about the fear of domination that arises from the abuse of political power by those who hold it, while the *Letter* is preoccupied with the mutuality among groups whose exclusive beliefs incline them to seek power. Its main focus is, as it were, horizontal rather than vertical. How should citizens who belong to one church treat those who are equally citizens and belong with equal religious conviction to another church? How should their demands on the state be constrained?

Second, it is fundamental to Locke's whole discussion that, much as he regrets or even despises conflict over matters that to him are inessential, we cannot read off the features of political order from our personal conception of truth, but must constantly take account of the subjectivity of other agents. Diversity exists precisely because agents are (for the most part) not, themselves, broad-minded diversitarians, but hold mutually exclusive and rival views between which there is the permanent possibility of conflict. Diversitarian thought is different indeed from the Proastian demand for uniformity; but, oddly, it may be equally imperious if it demands the sacrifice of what agents themselves deem to be important.[23] What is above all admirable in Locke's defence of toleration is his recognition that others' conceptions of truth and importance cannot be

---

[23] See Peter Jones, 'Equality, Recognition and Difference', *Critical Review of International Social and Political Philosophy*, 9 (2006), 23–46, pp. 26–30.

assumed to match his own, and that the demand for uniformity over the true and the important is not just irrational, not just impracticable, but amounts to a sort of apolitical fantasy in which the real existence of other people is suppressed. In this sense, I think we may say that Locke's work on toleration is not just an important precursor of liberalism, but is also an important step in the recognition of political theory as an activity whose domain makes sense.

# Chronology

1632    John Locke born 29 August in Wrington, Somerset

1647    Enters Westminster School

1652    Elected to a Studentship at Christ Church, Oxford

1656    Receives Bachelor of Arts degree

1658    Receives Master of Arts degree

1660    Writes *Whether the Civil Magistrate Can Lawfully Determine the Use of Indifferent Things in Reference to Religious Worship*, in reply to Edward Bagshaw

1661    Elected lecturer in Greek at Christ Church; becomes a college tutor; writes a set of scholastic disputations entitled *Essays on the Law of Nature*; writes two tracts defending his position against Bagshaw and arguing against some Catholic doctrines; develops an interest in medicine

1663    Elected lecturer in Rhetoric at Christ Church

1664    Appointed censor of moral philosophy at Christ Church

1666    Meets Lord Anthony Ashley Cooper (later Earl of Shaftesbury)

1667    Becomes a member of the household of Lord Ashley as a tutor and physician; works with the physician Thomas Sydenham; writes but does not publish *An Essay Concerning Toleration*

1668    Elected a fellow of the Royal Society

1671    Begins work on early drafts of *An Essay Concerning Human Understanding*

1673    Serves as Secretary to the Council of Trade and Plantations

1675    Receives Bachelor of Medicine degree from Oxford; leaves England for France; continues work on *An Essay Concerning Human Understanding*

| | |
|---|---|
| 1679 | Returns to England |
| 1679 | Begins writing the *Two Treatises of Government* |
| 1681 | Shaftesbury arrested, charged with treason, released, and forced into hiding |
| 1683 | Shaftesbury dies; Locke forced into exile in the Netherlands |
| 1684 | Expelled from Studentship at Christ Church by the command of the king |
| 1685–6 | Writes *A Letter Concerning Toleration* |
| 1687 | Completes work on *An Essay Concerning Human Understanding* |
| 1688 | Abridgment of *An Essay Concerning Human Understanding* appears in the *Bibliothèque Universelle et historique* |
| 1689 | Returns to England; *Epistola de Tolerantia* published in the Netherlands, and Popple's English translation, *A Letter Concerning Toleration* (both anonymously); *Two Treatises on Government* (anonymous); *An Essay Concerning Human Understanding* |
| 1690 | Publishes *A Second Letter Concerning Toleration* in response to Jonas Proast |
| 1691 | Publishes *Some Considerations of the Consequences of the Lowering of Interest and Raising the Value of Money*; becomes a permanent guest at Oates, the home of Sir Francis Masham |
| 1692 | Publishes *A Third Letter for Toleration* |
| 1693 | Publishes *Some Thoughts Concerning Education* |
| 1694 | Publishes second edition of *An Essay Concerning Human Understanding* |
| 1695 | Publishes *The Reasonableness of Christianity* (anonymous); *A Vindication of the Reasonableness of Christianity*; *Short Observations on a Printed Paper, Intituled, For Encouraging the Coining Silver Money in England, and After for Keeping it Here;* third edition of *An Essay Concerning Human Understanding*; *Further Considerations concerning Raising the Value of Money* |
| 1696 | Begins serving as a Commissioner of Trade |
| 1697 | Publishes *A Second Vindication of the Reasonableness of Christianity*; begins controversy with the Bishop of Worcester, Edward Stillingfleet, through *A Letter to the Right Reverend Edward, Lord Bishop of Worcester*; *Mr Locke's Reply to the Right Reverend the Bishop of Worcester's Answer to his Letter*; |

| | |
|---|---|
| | *Mr Locke's Reply to the Right Reverend the Lord Bishop of Worcester's Answer to his Second Letter*; begins *The Conduct of the Understanding* |
| 1699 | Publishes fourth edition of *An Essay Concerning Human Understanding* |
| 1700 | Resigns as a Commissioner of Trade; begins work on *Paraphrase and Notes on the Epistles of St Paul* |
| 1702 | Writes *Discourse of Miracles* |
| 1704 | Begins work on a *Fourth Letter on Toleration*; dies in October at Oates, buried in the churchyard of High Laver, Essex; acknowledges authorship of his anonymous works in a codicil to his will |

# Further reading

There are two modern editions of Locke's *Epistola de Tolerantia*: Mario Montuori, *A Letter Concerning Toleration* (The Hague: Martinus Nijhoff, 1963), and Raymond Klibansky, ed., and J.W. Gough trans., *Epistola de Tolerantia: A Letter on Toleration* (Oxford: Clarendon Press, 1968). The former contains the Latin text and Popple's 1690 translation on facing pages; the latter contains the Latin text and a new translation on facing pages. Popple's translation is available in many editions. The edition published by Hackett (1983), edited by James H. Tully, is widely used. A volume edited by John Horton and Susan Mendus, *John Locke: A Letter Concerning Toleration in Focus* (London: Routledge, 1991), contains not only the text but also six valuable interpretative essays. The *Letter* is included in David Wootton's *Political Writings of John Locke* (New York: Mentor, 1993), and is discussed helpfully and at length in Wootton's introduction. As for Locke's later *Letters*, they are available in vol. VI of Locke's *Works* (several nineteenth-century editions). At the time of writing, a new edition of Locke's collected works is in preparation by Oxford University Press, and will include all four *Letters on Toleration*.

Proast's three critiques of Locke are available in microform in some university libraries, in a photoreprint, *Letters Concerning Toleration*, ed. Peter A. Schouls (New York: Garland, 1984), which is no longer in print, and in vol. V of *The Reception of Locke's Politics*, ed. Mark Goldie (London: Pickering and Chatto, 1999). The only other extant work by Proast is his *Articles of Visitation and Enquiry, Concerning Matters Ecclesiastical* ..., available at Early English Books Online. This work, which describes the minute supervision that Proast exercised as Archdeacon of Berkshire (after leaving Oxford), interestingly brings out how closely the 'decency' that he favoured in worship was connected with social as well as doctrinal control.

The literature on the Locke–Proast exchange is not extensive. Two essays by Mark Goldie are indispensable: 'The Theory of Religious Intolerance in Restoration England', in Ole Peter Grell, Jonathan I. Israel, and Nicholas Tyacke, eds., *From Persecution to Toleration: The Glorious Revolution and Religion in England* (Oxford: Clarendon Press, 1991), and 'John Locke, Jonas Proast and Religious Toleration 1688–92', in John Walsh, ed., *The Church of England c. 1688–c. 1833* (Cambridge University Press, 1993). Peter Nicholson discusses 'Locke's Later Letters on Toleration' in the volume edited by Horton and Mendus (see above). Adam Wolfson discusses Locke's defence in 'Toleration and Relativism: The Locke–Proast Exchange', *Review of Politics* 59 (1997), 213–31. The only book-length study is Richard Vernon, *The Career of Toleration: John Locke, Jonas Proast and After* (Montreal: McGill-Queen's University Press, 1997).

On Locke himself, of course, the literature is immense. Roger Woolhouse's *Locke: A Biography* (Cambridge University Press, 2007) is richly detailed. Readers wanting a briefer survey may consult J.R. Milton, 'Locke's Life and Times', in Vere Chappell, ed., *The Cambridge Companion to Locke* (Cambridge University Press, 1994), a volume that also contains valuable introductions to many aspects of Locke's philosophy. It may usefully be complemented by John W. Yolton, *A Locke Dictionary* (Oxford: Blackwell, 1993). For his view of toleration, see especially John Marshall, *John Locke, Toleration and Early Enlightenment Culture* (Cambridge University Press, 2006). Although there are many books on Locke's political thought, they tend to focus on the arguments of the *Second Treatise* (in which toleration is not mentioned) rather than the writings on toleration, but there are substantial treatments of toleration in Ian Harris, *The Mind of John Locke* (Cambridge University Press, 1994); John Marshall, *John Locke: Resistance, Religion, and Responsibility* (Cambridge University Press, 1994); James Tully, *An Approach to Political Philosophy: Locke in Contexts* (Cambridge University Press, 1993); and Jeremy Waldron, *God, Locke, and Equality: Christian Foundations in Locke's Political Thought* (Cambridge University Press, 2002). Richard Ashcraft's edition, *John Locke: Critical Assessments*, 4 vols. (London: Routledge, 1991) usefully assembles some of the best journal articles on Locke, but of course there has since been a large stream of publication in the major journals of political theory and intellectual history.

Several works examine the history of toleration in (mostly) European thought. John Christian Laursen and Cary J. Nederman, eds., *Beyond the Persecuting Society: Religious Toleration Before the Enlightenment* (Philadelphia: University of Pennsylvania Press, 1997) brings out the richness of the pre-modern discussion, while the chapters in Ole Peter Grell and Roy Porter, eds., *Toleration in Enlightenment Europe* (New York: Cambridge University Press, 2000) discuss Locke's successors. The Reformation context is explored by W.K. Jordan, *The Development of Religious Toleration in England*, 4 vols. (Gloucester, MA: Smith, 1965) and by Perez Zagorin, *How the Idea of Religious Toleration Came to the West* (Princeton University Press, 2003). Briefer studies include Philip Milton, 'Toleration', in Desmond Clarke and Catherine Wilson, eds., *The Oxford Handbook of Early Modern Philosophy* (Oxford University Press, forthcoming).

In contemporary political theory, some of the most stimulating work is contained in two edited collections: Susan Mendus, ed., *Justifying Toleration: Conceptual and Historical Perspectives* (Cambridge University Press, 1988) and David Heyd, ed., *Toleration: An Elusive Virtue* (Princeton University Press, 1996). Mendus's volume contains Jeremy Waldron's paper, 'Locke: Toleration and the Rationality of Persecution', which is central to understanding contemporary scholarly discussion. This essay is also included in the Horton and Mendus volume cited above, and in Waldron's *Liberal Rights: Collected Papers 1981–1991* (Cambridge University Press, 1993). Michael Walzer, *On Toleration* (New Haven, CT: Yale University Press, 1997), discusses different political forms taken by toleration. Wendy Brown, *Regulating Aversion: Tolerance in the Age of Identity and Empire* (Princeton University Press, 2006), is critical of the concept, while Anna Elisabetta Galeotti, *Toleration as Recognition* (Cambridge University Press, 2002), calls for its substantial revision in the context of modern pluralist societies.

# Note on the texts and translation

For Locke's *Second* and *Third Letters* I have used the first editions, 1690 and 1692 respectively (both printed in London for Awnsham and John Churchill), and for the posthumously published *Fourth Letter*, vol. VI of the 1801 *Works of John Locke* (London: printed for J. Johnson *et al.*). For the brief extracts from the *Second Treatise* and the *Essay Concerning Human Understanding*, I have used the last editions published in Locke's lifetime: the 1698 edition of *Two Treatises of Government* and the 1700 edition of the *Essay* (both printed in London for Awnsham and John Churchill). For Proast's three *Letters* I have used the first editions: 1690 (London: printed for George West and Henry Clements), 1691 (Oxford: printed for George West and Henry Clements), and 1704 (Oxford: printed for Henry Clements). This edition includes the full text of Proast's first response to Locke, the *Argument* (1690), and excerpts from his second and third letters to Locke.

In accordance with the 'modernizing' policy of this series, I have modified the use of upper-case characters, italics, and punctuation in order to minimize distractions for the modern reader, and in a few cases I have divided very long sentences. I have also introduced new paragraphs where the length of those written by Locke or Proast exceeds current practice. Obsolete verb forms ('hath', 'doth') have been replaced, but obsolete uses of existing verb forms ('be' for 'is' or 'are') have been retained. Occasionally, when an obsolete word has a close modern equivalent, I have replaced it ('chirurgeon' becomes 'surgeon', 'betwixt' becomes 'between'). Abbreviations have been expanded, and cross-references using the pagination of the original editions have been removed. I have added a few phrases in square brackets, in the text, to facilitate a smooth reading.

Locke and Proast frequently quote passages from each other's work and proceed to criticize them. Locke's quotations from Proast are often inexact or incomplete, and sometimes mix verbatim sentences or phrases with paraphrase. I have not corrected these passages. Although the quotations are often only approximate in terms of wording, the errors do not appear to me to change the substance of what was written by his interlocutor.

Commentators frequently complain, with some justice, about the repetitiveness of Locke's later *Letters*. It was evidently his view that replies to criticism had to be minute and exhaustive – the three later *Letters* take up over 500 pages of a volume of the 1801 *Works*. The selections minimize repetition, but I have sometimes allowed it in order to avoid breaking the text into fragments, or to provide transitions that set the context for Proast's replies. I believe that everything of substance has been included, with the exception of some more strictly theological issues (particularly, the role of miracles) that engaged Locke and his adversary. Readers may infer from the two forms of ellipsis used whether I have omitted a short phrase of the text – which is marked by an ellipsis within a sentence – or one or more whole paragraphs; the latter omissions are indicated by an ellipsis on a new line.

Editorial footnotes are provided to explain unusual terms or references that may not be familiar to some readers.

In the preparation of the translation of the *Letter* the editions of Montuori and Klibansky and Gough were used. The Gouda edition of 1689 and the edition of 1765 were also consulted.

The translator is grateful for the many helpful comments on his first draft by Richard Vernon and Desmond Clarke.

A brief rationale for our choice of translation of three of Locke's key terms, *res publica*, *magistratus*, and *coetus*, will be found in footnotes 6, 7 and 35 to the *Letter*.

*Locke on Toleration*

# A Letter concerning Toleration

My distinguished friend,

You ask me for my opinion of mutual toleration among Christians. I reply in a word that it seems to me to be the principal mark of the true church. Antiquity of titles and places of worship which some people boast of, the reformation of doctrine that others stress, the orthodoxy of one's faith that everyone claims (for everyone is orthodox in their own eyes) – these things are likely to be signs of competition for power and domination rather than marks of Christ's church. A person may have all of them and still not be a Christian, if he lacks charity, gentleness, and goodwill toward all human beings and toward those who profess the Christian faith in particular.

'The kings of the Gentiles exercise lordship over them,' says our Saviour to his disciples, 'but ye shall not be so' (Luke 22: [25], 26). True religion has a different object. It did not come into the world in order to establish outward pomp and ecclesiastical domination and violence, but to ground a life of goodness and piety. Anyone who wishes to enlist in Christ's church must, more than anything else, declare war on his own vices, on his own pride and lust. Without holiness of life, purity of morals, goodness of heart, and gentleness, any aspiration to the name of Christian is unjustified.

'When thou art converted, strengthen thy brethren', said Our Lord to Peter (Luke 22: 32). For one will hardly persuade other people that he is truly concerned for their salvation if he neglects his own. No one can sincerely strive with all his strength to make other people Christians if he has not yet truly embraced the religion of Christ in his own mind. For if we are to believe the Gospel and the Apostles, no one can be a

3

Christian without charity and without the faith that works by love[1] and not by violence.

Do those who beat and torture people on the pretext of religion, and rob them of their property and put them to death, do all this in a spirit of friendship and goodwill? I appeal to their conscience. I shall believe it myself when I see these fanatics inflicting the same chastisement on those of their friends and associates who openly sin against the precepts of the Gospel, and when I see them attacking with fire and sword those of their own partisans who are stained and corrupted by vice and who will certainly perish if they do not reform and bear better fruit, and when I see them expressing their love and longing for the salvation of *their* souls with every form of cruelty and torture. For if, as they claim, their only motive in seizing people's goods, mutilating their bodies, ruining their health in filthy prisons, and taking their lives, is charity and zeal for their souls, in order to ensure their faith and salvation, why do they allow their own followers to indulge, freely and with impunity, in fornication, fraud, malice, and all the other vices, which, as the Apostle declares (Romans 1: 28–32), are blatantly pagan? Such actions as these are more contrary to the glory of God, the purity of the church, and the salvation of souls than any mistaken conviction of conscience that falls foul of ecclesiastical decrees, or any failings in outward worship if they are combined with innocence of life. Why, I ask, does their zeal for God, the church, and the salvation of souls – which burns so fiercely it even burns people alive – why does it ignore, and not correct or punish, the vices and moral faults which everyone agrees are diametrically opposed to the profession of Christianity? Why does it insist on penalizing beliefs which are often too subtle for most people to understand or on imposing fine points of ritual? Why is this its driving ambition?

It will only finally become clear which of the parties to the conflict, the triumphant party or the vanquished party, has the sounder view on these matters, and which one is guilty of schism or heresy, when final judgement is given on the cause of their separation.[2] For no one is a heretic who follows Christ, and embraces his teaching and puts on his yoke, even if he does leave his mother and father and the usual ceremonies

---

[1] Galatians 5: 6: 'faith which worketh by love'.
[2] The Last Judgement. On 'separation' see 'Postscript: heresy and schism'.

and religious practices of his family and country and any other persons whatever.[3]

If sectarian divisions are so inimical to the salvation of souls, 'adultery, fornication, uncleanness, lasciviousness, idolatry' and so on are no less 'works of the flesh', on which the Apostle pronounces an explicit sentence that 'they which do such things shall not inherit the kingdom of God' (Galatians 5: [19]–21). Anyone who is sincerely concerned for the kingdom of God and seriously committed to working for its extension, needs to put as much care and effort into eliminating these vices as into eliminating sects. If he acts otherwise, if he is ruthless and implacable against people of different beliefs, but indulgent toward sins and immoralities unworthy of the name of Christian, he plainly shows that for all his talk about the church, it is some kingdom other than God's that he is building.

I marvel, as others also surely do, that anyone could accept that a person whose soul he ardently desires to save should die of torture in an unconverted state, but I simply cannot conceive that anyone would ever believe that such behaviour could be motivated by love, benevolence, or charity. If people are to be compelled by fire and sword to accept certain doctrines, or if they are forcibly driven to adopt some form of external worship without any concern for their morals, and if anyone converts heterodox persons to the faith in the sense of compelling them to profess what they do not believe, while permitting them to do what the Gospel forbids to Christians and the believer forbids to himself, I do not doubt that he wants a great many people to profess the same beliefs as himself, but who can believe that what he wants is a Christian church? No wonder, then, if such people use weapons inappropriate to the service of Christ, since, whatever their pretensions, they are not fighting for true religion and the Christian church. If they sincerely desired the salvation of souls, as he did who is the Captain of our salvation, they would walk in his footsteps and follow the excellent example of the Prince of Peace. He sent out his troops to subdue the nations and compel them to come into the church not with swords or spears or any other weapon of violence, but with the Gospel, with the message of peace and with the exemplary force of holiness.[4] If force of arms were the right way to convert unbelievers, if

---

[3] Cf. Matthew 11: 29–30; Luke 14: 26.
[4] Jesus sending out his disciples: Matthew 10: 1ff.; Mark 6: 6–13; Luke 9: 1–6. For 'compel', cf. Luke 14: 23.

armed soldiers were the best means of recalling blind or stubborn people from their errors, he had at hand a whole army of heavenly legions, in comparison with which the troops available to even the most powerful protector of the church are a mere squadron.

## Distinction of church and commonwealth fundamental[5]

Toleration of those who have different views on religious questions is so consistent with the Gospel and with reason that it seems incredible that people should be blind in so plain a matter. I do not want to blame either the arrogance and ambition of the one party or the bigotry and fanaticism of the other that knows nothing of charity and gentleness. These are vices that will probably never be eliminated from human affairs, though they are such that no one wants to be openly accused of them himself; anyone who has been led by them to act badly almost invariably seeks to preserve his reputation by giving them an honourable disguise. But I would not want anyone to use a concern for their country and obedience to its laws as a pretext for persecution and unchristian cruelty; I would not want anyone to seek moral licence and impunity for their crimes under the name of religion; I would not want anyone to deceive themselves or others that they are faithful subjects of the prince or sincere worshippers of God.

In order to avoid these things, I believe that we must above all distinguish between political and religious matters, and properly define the boundary between church and commonwealth.[6] Until this is done, no limit can be put to the disputes between those who have, or affect to have, a zeal for the salvation of souls and those who have a real or affected concern for the safety of the commonwealth.

## What is a commonwealth?

A commonwealth appears to me to be an association of people constituted solely for the purpose of preserving and promoting civil goods.

---

[5] The section headings within the text are supplied by the translator.
[6] The equivalent of *res publica* in Locke's English *Letters* is normally 'commonwealth', but sometimes 'state'. In this translation, for the sake of consistency with the other *Letters*, we have normally used the word 'commonwealth'.

By 'civil goods' I mean life, liberty, physical integrity, and freedom from pain, as well as external possessions, such as land, money, the necessities of everyday life, and so on.

It is the duty of the civil ruler[7] to guarantee and preserve the just possession of these things which relate to this life, for the people as a whole and for private subjects individually, by means of laws made equally for all. If anyone has a mind to violate the laws, contrary to right and justice, his reckless impulse has to be checked by fear of punishment. Punishment consists in the confiscation in whole or in part of those good things which he could and should otherwise have enjoyed. Since no one voluntarily gives up any of his goods, let alone his liberty or his life, the ruler is armed with force to inflict punishment on those who violate the rights of others, and this force consists in the united strength of his subjects.

The whole jurisdiction of rulers is concerned solely with these civil goods. All the right and authority of the civil power is confined and restricted to the protection and promotion of these civil goods and these alone. It should not, and cannot, be extended to the salvation of souls. I believe the following arguments demonstrate these points.

First, the civil ruler has no more mandate than others have for the care of souls. He has no mandate from God, for it nowhere appears that God has granted men authority over other men, to compel them to adopt their own religion. And no such power can be given to a ruler by men; for no one can abdicate responsibility for his own eternal salvation by adopting under compulsion a form of belief or worship prescribed to him by another person, whether prince or subject. For no one can believe at another's behest, however much they try to do so; and the force and effectiveness of true and saving religion lies in belief. No matter what you profess with your lips or what external worship you offer, if you are not inwardly and profoundly convinced in your own heart that it is both true and pleasing to God, it not only does not assist your salvation, it positively hinders it. For in addition to the other sins which your religion must expiate, you are adding a pretence of religion itself and a contempt of the Deity, for you are offering the great and good God a form of worship which you believe is displeasing to him.

---

[7] In the other *Letters* Locke normally uses 'magistrate' as the English equivalent to *magistratus*, but he also occasionally uses 'ruler'. We have preferred normally to translate this word as 'ruler'.

Secondly, care of souls cannot belong to the civil ruler, because his power consists wholly in compulsion. But true and saving religion consists in an inward conviction of the mind; without it, nothing has value in the eyes of God. Such is the nature of the human understanding that it cannot be compelled by any external force. You may take away people's goods, imprison them, even inflict physical torture on their bodies, but you will not achieve anything if what you are trying to do by this punishment is change the judgement of their minds about things.

But you will say:[8] a ruler can make use of arguments to bring heterodox persons to the truth and assure their salvation. True, but he shares this approach with others. In teaching, instructing, and using arguments to recall a person who has gone astray, he is certainly doing what a good man should; a ruler is not required to cease to be either a man or a Christian. However, it is one thing to persuade, another to command, one thing to use arguments in a dispute, another to issue decrees. The latter belong to the civil power, the former to human goodwill. It is open to anyone to advise, exhort, convict of error, and bring a person to their way of thinking by rational argument; but to command by edicts, to compel by the sword are exclusively the tools of the ruler. This then I say: the civil power should not use the civil law to prescribe articles of faith (or doctrines) or the manner in which one should worship God. For laws have no force if no penalties are attached; and if penalties are prescribed, they are completely inappropriate and unsuited to persuasion.

To accept a doctrine or a form of worship for the salvation of one's soul, one must believe sincerely that the doctrine is true, and that the form of worship will be acceptable and pleasing to God, but no penalty has any force to instil this kind of conviction in the mind. It is light that is needed to change a belief in the mind; punishment of the body does not lend light.

Thirdly, salvation of souls cannot be any business of the civil ruler. For even granted that the authority of laws and the force of penalties *were* effective in changing people's minds, yet this would have no effect on the salvation of their souls. For since there is only one true religion, one way which leads to the heavenly home, what hope would there be for the majority of mortals to get there, if they were obliged as a condition to

---

[8] Throughout the *First Letter* Locke makes use of the literary form of an academic *disputatio*, in which possible objections to Locke's thesis are attributed to an imaginary opponent.

discard the dictates of their reason and conscience and blindly accept the doctrines of their prince and worship God as the laws of their country required? Given the great variety of religious beliefs held by princes, it would follow that the narrow way and the strait gate that leads to heaven would be open only to a very few people who would all be living in one particular place; and the most absurd consequence, totally unworthy of God, would follow, that eternal happiness or torment would depend solely on the accident of birth.[9]

Many other arguments could be made on this question, but these seem to warrant the conclusion that the power of the commonwealth is concerned only with civil goods and is restricted to the things of this world and does not extend in any way to those things that look to the future life.

## What is a church?

Now let us see what a church[10] is. A church appears to me to be a free association of people coming together of their own accord to offer public worship to God in a manner which they believe will be acceptable to the Deity for the salvation of their souls.

It is, I stress, a free and voluntary association. No one is born a member of any church; otherwise the religion of one's father and forefathers would pass down by hereditary right along with their estates, and one would owe one's faith to one's birth. Nothing more absurd can be imagined. The truth is that no one is bound by nature to any church or tied to any sect. Of his own accord he joins the association in which he believes he has found true religion and a form of worship pleasing to God. The hope of salvation that he sees there is both the sole cause of his entering the church and the sole reason why he remains. And if he finds anything wrong with its doctrine or unseemly in its ritual, he must have the same liberty to leave as he had to enter; no bonds can be indissoluble but those attached to the certain expectation of eternal life. It is from members so united, of their own accord and for this purpose, that a church is formed.

[9] Cf. Gibbon, *Decline and Fall of the Roman Empire*, ed. J.B. Bury (London, 1909): 'Even the imperceptible sect of the Rogatians could affirm, without a blush, that when Christ should descend to judge the earth, he would find his true religion preserved only in a few nameless villages of the Caesarean Mauritania' (ch. 21, vol. II, p. 355).
[10] *ecclesia.*

9

It follows that we should ask what the power of a church is, and to what laws is it subject.

No association, however free, however insignificant its purpose and activities, can survive without the risk of speedy dissolution if it is completely without laws. This applies equally to an association of learned persons to pursue philosophy, of businessmen for commerce, or even of men of leisure seeking conversation and entertainment. Therefore a church too must have its laws. A schedule must be made of the time and place at which meetings will take place; conditions have to be published for admission to the association and exclusion from it; the various duties and the order of business have to be determined, and so on. But since people have come together to form this association of their own accord (as I have demonstrated), free of all compulsion, it necessarily follows that the right of making laws lies solely with the association, or at least – and this comes to the same thing – with those whom the association itself has approved by its own consent.

But you will say: it cannot be the true church if it does not have a bishop or presbytery endowed with an authority to govern that descends all the way from the Apostles themselves in continuous and uninterrupted succession.

First, I ask you to point to the edict in which Christ laid down this law for his church. And in a matter of such importance, it will not be asking too much to require an explicit statement. The saying 'where two or three are gathered together in my name, there am I in the midst of them' (Matthew 18: 20) appears to suggest otherwise. You can see for yourself whether a gathering which has Christ in its midst can fail to be a true church. Certainly, nothing essential to true salvation can be missing there, and that is enough for our purpose.

Secondly, I beg you to notice that those who claim that the governors of the church were instituted by Christ and must follow in unbroken succession disagree with each other right from the start. Their disagreement necessarily permits freedom of choice, with the consequence that everyone is at liberty to join whichever church they prefer.

Thirdly, you may have the governor you set over yourself, the one you believe to be inescapably designated in such a long succession, while I likewise commit myself to the association where I am convinced I will find what I need for the salvation of my soul. And thus ecclesiastical freedom (which you demand) is preserved for both of us, and neither has a legislator which he did not choose for himself.

But since you are so anxious about the true church, permit me, in passing, to ask this question: is it not more fitting for Christ's church to establish conditions for communion[11] which contain those things that the Holy Spirit has taught in clear and explicit words in Holy Scripture and those things alone, rather than to impose its own inventions or interpretations as divine law, and give them authority as absolutely essential to the profession of Christianity, though they are matters on which the divine oracles[12] have not pronounced, or at any rate not as a matter of law? Anyone who requires for communion in the church what Christ does not require for eternal life is perhaps cleverly contriving an association that suits his own views and his own interest, but how are we to call a church Christ's church if it is founded upon laws not his and excludes persons whom he will one day receive into the kingdom of heaven?

However, this is not the place to explore the marks of the true church. I would just like to give a word of warning to those who fight so fiercely for the doctrines of their own association and are always holding forth about the church and nothing else, making as much of a din as the silversmiths made long ago in Ephesus about their goddess Diana (Acts 19: 23–41) and perhaps from the same motive. I would remind them that the Gospel everywhere testifies that the true disciples of Christ must expect persecution and bear it, but I do not remember reading anywhere in the New Testament that the true church of Christ should persecute others or harass them, or compel them to adopt their own doctrines with violence, fire, and sword.

The purpose of a religious association, as I have said, is public worship of God and the attainment of eternal life by means of it. This is what the whole of the church's teaching should aim at; these are the only ends to which all of its laws should be directed. There is and can be no concern in this association with the possession of civil or earthly goods. No force is to be used here for any reason. All force belongs to the civil ruler; and the possession and use of external goods are subject to his power.

You will say: what sanctions will maintain the laws of a church in the absence of all coercion? I reply: the kind of sanction that is appropriate where outward profession and outward observance bring no benefit if they do not sink deep into the soul and there receive the full assent

11 *communio* also has the sense of 'participation'.
12 A periphrasis for the Holy Scriptures.

11

of conscience. And therefore the weapons of this association are exhortation, warning, and advice, and these are the means to keep its members to their duty. If these means fail to correct delinquents and put wanderers back on the right road, there is only one recourse, and that is to cut off from the association those who are rebellious and obstinate and give no hope of amendment, and throw them out. This is the supreme and ultimate sanction of ecclesiastical power, and its sole penalty is that, as the relation between the body and an amputated member ceases, so the convicted person ceases to be a part of that church.

## Duties of mutual toleration

### (i) Duties of individuals with regard to mutual toleration

On these premises, let us next ask what the duties of individual persons are with regard to toleration.

First, I say that a church is not obliged in the name of toleration to continue, after due warning, to keep in its midst anyone who persists in offending against the laws of the association. An association has no future, if there is no consequence to breaking its laws, since they are the conditions of participation in the association and its only bond. However, it must be careful not to embellish the decree of excommunication with verbal abuse or physical violence that would in any way harm the person or property of the ejected member. For as I have said, the use of force is restricted to rulers; private persons do not have the right to use force except in self-defence. Excommunication does not, and cannot, deprive the excommunicated person of any of the civil goods that he previously possessed; they belong to his civil status and are subject to the ruler's protection. The effect of excommunication is simply to dissolve the bond between the body and one of its members, once the association has declared its decision. When this relation ceases, participation in certain things which the association offers its members also ceases, necessarily, and no one has a civil right to them. An excommunicated person has suffered no civil wrong if the minister of a church, while celebrating the Lord's Supper, refuses to give him bread and wine which were not paid for with his own money but with someone else's.

Secondly, no private person has the right to attack or diminish another person's civil goods in any way because he professes a religion or ritual differing from his own; all of that person's human rights as well as his civil rights are to be scrupulously observed. They are not a matter of religion; whether he is a Christian or a pagan, all force and injury should be avoided. The standard of justice is to be supplemented by the duties of benevolence and charity. This is commanded by the Gospel, and recommended by reason and the common society of human beings with each other formed by nature. If anyone strays from the straight path, that is their problem, they are the losers by it; it does no harm to you. Just because you believe someone will perish in the life to come, that is no reason for you to mistreat them now and deprive them of the good things of this life.

### (ii) Duties of churches with regard to mutual toleration

What I have said about mutual toleration between private individuals who disagree with each other about religion, I would also apply to individual churches. In some ways they are private persons with regard to each other, and no one of them has jurisdiction over any other, not even if it so happens that the civil ruler belongs to one church rather than to another. For a commonwealth cannot grant any new right to a church, any more than vice versa a church can grant a new right to a commonwealth. A church remains what it always was, whether the ruler joins it or leaves it, a free and voluntary association. If the ruler joins it, it does not acquire the power of the sword; and if he leaves, it does not lose the discipline which it formerly had to teach and to excommunicate. It will always be the unalterable right of an association of people who have come together of their own accord,[13] to expel any of its own members it thinks fit, but it acquires no jurisdiction over outsiders, no matter who joins. This is the reason why different churches should, without discrimination, constantly maintain peace, friendship, and an even temper towards each other, as private persons do, without any one of them claiming superior rights.

To make things clear by an example, let us imagine two churches at Constantinople, one of Remonstrants, the other of Antiremonstrants.[14]

---

[13] Locke here uses the phrase *'spontanea societas'*. Normally he uses the phrase *'societas voluntaria'* or *'societas libera et voluntaria'*.

[14] Within the Calvinist church in the United Provinces, when Locke lived there, these two groups were sharply divided on a range of doctrines, especially about predestination.

Would anyone say that either church has the right to take away the liberty or property of those who disagree with them (as we see happens elsewhere), or to punish them with exile or death because they have different doctrines or rituals? The Turks meanwhile say nothing and laugh up their sleeves at the cruelty of Christians beating and killing each other. If, however, one of these churches does have authority to savage the other, which one is it, I ask, and by what right? The reply will undoubtedly be: the orthodox church has this right against the erroneous or heretical church. This is to use big, plausible words to say nothing. Every church is orthodox in its own eyes, and in the eyes of others it is erroneous or heretical, since it believes its own beliefs to be true and condemns other beliefs as wrong. For this reason the conflict between them about the truth of their doctrines and the correctness of their ritual is undecidable. No judicial sentence can settle it, for there is no judge of such things either at Constantinople or anywhere else on this earth. The verdict on this question rests solely with the supreme judge of all men, and he alone will correct the party in error. Meanwhile both parties should reflect how much more wrong they do in adding injustice to the sin of pride, if not of error, when they boldly and brazenly assault the servants of another master who are not answerable to them.

Even if it *could* be finally determined which of the conflicting parties held the correct views on religion, this would not authorize the orthodox church to plunder other churches, for churches have no jurisdiction in worldly matters, and fire and sword are not suitable instruments for disproving errors and forming or changing people's minds. Suppose, however, that the civil ruler supports one or other of the two parties, and is willing to put his sword in their hands, so that they may chastise the heterodox party in any way they wish, with his approval. Would anyone say that a Christian church could derive any right over its brethren from the Sultan of Turkey? An infidel cannot on his own authority punish Christians in matters of faith, and therefore he cannot in any way impart that authority to any Christian association; he cannot give a right which he does not have. Now apply this argument to a Christian kingdom. Civil power is the same everywhere, and it can bestow no more authority on a church if it is in the hands of a Christian prince than it can in the hands of a pagan prince; that is, it can bestow no authority at all.

But it is perhaps worth remarking that these bold partisans of truth, these warriors against error who will not tolerate schisms, rarely express that zeal for God which totally consumes them like a burning fire, unless they have the support of the civil ruler. As soon as they have his ear and the preponderance of power that goes with it, goodbye to peace and Christian charity; mutual tolerance is for other situations. When they are inferior in political strength, they can patiently and harmlessly tolerate around them the contagion of that idolatry, superstition, and heresy which at other times they fear will do so much harm to them and their religion. Nor do they willingly put any effort into refuting the errors in fashion with the court and the sovereign. Yet this is the only real way to spread the truth, to combine the weight of reason and argument with humanity and goodwill.

Neither persons, then, nor churches, nor even commonwealths can have any right to attack each other's civil goods and steal each other's worldly assets on the pretext of religion. I beg anyone who thinks otherwise to reflect what unlimited opportunities for conflicts and wars they are giving mankind, what an invitation to plunder and kill and nourish grievances for ever. It is impossible to build and maintain peace and security, let alone friendship, among men where there is a prevailing belief that dominion is founded in grace and that religion should be spread by force of arms.

### (iii) Duties of clergymen with regard to mutual toleration

Thirdly, let us see what the duty of toleration requires of those who are distinguished from the rest of society – from the 'laity' as they like to call it – by some ecclesiastical title or position, whether they are called bishops, priests, presbyters, ministers, or by some other name. This is not the place to investigate the origins of clerical authority or dignity. My point is this: whatever its origin, since it is an ecclesiastical authority, it should be confined within the bounds of the church; it cannot be extended to civil matters in any way, seeing that the church itself is utterly separate and distinct from the commonwealth and civil matters. On both sides the bounds are fixed and immoveable. You are confounding heaven and earth, things totally distinct from each other, if you try to run together these two associations, which are completely and utterly different from each other in origin, purpose, and substance. Hence no matter what ecclesiastical dignity a person may enjoy, he cannot deprive anyone who does not belong to his own church or faith, of life, liberty, or any part of his worldly goods for the sake of religion. For what is forbidden to the church as a whole cannot be permitted by ecclesiastical law to any member of it.

But it is not enough for clergymen to refrain from violence, plunder, and persecution in all its forms. One who professes to be a successor of the Apostles and has taken upon himself the task of teaching has a further obligation – to advise his people of their duties of peace and goodwill towards all men, towards those who are in error as well as to the orthodox, towards those who share their beliefs as well as those who differ in point of belief or ritual. He must encourage charity, gentleness, and tolerance in all of them, whether they are private citizens or political leaders, if there are any in his congregation, and he must restrain and mitigate their aversion towards those who are heterodox, whether it is inspired by their own fierce passion for their religion and sect or has been craftily instilled in their minds by others. I will not enumerate all the great advantages that would accrue to both church and commonwealth if the pulpits resounded with a message of peace and tolerance, because I do not want to appear to say anything to the discredit of men whose dignity I would not wish to see impaired by anyone, even by themselves. But I do say that this is what needs to be done, and anyone who claims to be a minister of the divine word and a preacher of the Gospel of peace and who teaches differently is either ignorant or careless of the task entrusted to him, and in either case he must one day answer for it to the Prince of Peace. If Christians are admonished not to seek vengeance even when they are repeatedly provoked by wrongs, 'even to seventy times seven',[15] how much more should they avoid all anger, hostility, and violence when they have suffered nothing from another person, and most of all should they be careful not to harm those who have done no harm to them, and particularly not to give trouble to people who are minding their own business and are anxious only to worship God in the way they believe is most acceptable to him without concern for the opinions of men, and to embrace the religion which offers them the greatest hope of salvation.

In matters of domestic economy and private property and in questions of health, it is up to each person to decide for himself what will be appropriate; he is allowed to follow his own judgement as to what is best. No one complains if his neighbour makes a poor job of looking after his domestic affairs; no one gets angry with someone who makes a poor job

---

[15] Cf. Matthew 18: 22.

of sowing his fields or marrying off his daughter; no one corrects a man who is squandering his money in taverns. A person may build or demolish, and spend as he pleases; no one says anything, he is allowed to get on with it. But if he does not regularly attend the public place of worship or if, when he does go, he does not make the approved ritual gestures, or if he does not bring his children to be initiated into the ceremonies of one or another church, the grumbling starts, there is a public outcry, and it ends in a prosecution. Everyone is keen to punish such a crime, and the fanatics can hardly restrain themselves from assaulting and robbing him until he is brought into court, and the judge's sentence delivers him to prison or execution or confiscates his property.

Clerical orators of every sect may, where they can, confute and confound by means of arguments other people's errors, but they must not touch their persons. Should they run out of effective arguments, they must not resort to the drastic instruments of a different court; these are not for men of the church to wield. They cannot borrow the rods and axes of the ruler to help out their eloquence and instruction, for fear that as they proclaim their love of truth, a burning passion for fire and sword will betray their secret appetite for domination. It will be difficult to persuade intelligent persons that you actively and sincerely desire to save your brother from the fires of hell in the world to come if in this world, with dry eyes and cordial assent, you hand him over to the executioner to be burned.

## (iv) Duties of rulers with regard to mutual toleration

Fourthly and finally, we must look at the role of the ruler, who certainly plays the most important role of all in the matter of toleration.

We showed above that a ruler has no care for souls, no care in his *official* capacity, I mean, if I can put it that way, because a ruler operates by means of legal commands and penal coercion; however, a charitable care for souls by way of teaching, advice, and persuasion can be denied to no one. Each person then has a care for his own soul and must be allowed to exercise this care. You will say: what if he neglects the care of his soul? I reply: what if he neglects his health; what if he neglects his property – things that are closer to the ruler's jurisdiction – will the ruler fashion a special edict to forbid a person to become poor or sick? The laws attempt, so far as they can, to protect the property and health of subjects from force or fraud on the part of others, not from neglect or waste on the part of the owner. No one can be compelled to be healthy or prosperous against his will. Even God cannot save people against their will. Nevertheless, suppose a prince does wish to make his subjects acquire wealth or look after their physical health. Will he make a law that they may consult only Roman doctors, and will everyone be required to live by their prescription? Will they not be allowed to take any medication or food unless it is prepared in the Vatican or cooked in the kitchens of Geneva? Or will all his subjects be obliged by law to practise commerce or music so that their homes may be prosperous and cultured? Or shall every individual be made an inn-keeper or a smith because some people keep their family in fair comfort and get to be well-off by these skills?

But you will say: there are a thousand ways to make money, but only one way to salvation. That is a very good thing to say, especially for those who want to try to force people to go one particular way; for if there were several ways, there could be no excuse for compulsion at all. But if I am pressing straight on to Jerusalem with all my strength, following the holy guidebook, why am I beaten because (it may be) I am not wearing the proper boots or have not washed or cut my hair in a particular fashion, or because I eat meat on the journey or take particular foods that are good for my stomach or my health? Or because I avoid byways on either side that seem to me to lead to cliffs and thorn bushes? Or because, among different tracks going the same way on the same road, I pick the one that appears least winding and muddy? Or because I have come to feel that some people are not sufficiently serious, while others are just too strait-laced for me to be happy to travel in their company? Or because I have, or do not have, a guide for my journey who wears a mitre or a white stole? Surely if we weigh it all up, most of the points that pit Christian brethren so bitterly against each other, even though they have identical correct beliefs about the essence of religion, are no more significant than these, and they may be observed or ignored without danger to religion or the salvation of souls, so long as there is no superstition or hypocrisy.

But suppose we grant to the fanatics and to those who condemn every way but their own that these incidental details imply different ways that lead in different directions, where will that get us? Grant that only one of these ways is the true way of salvation. Among the thousand paths that people take, it is not self-evident which is the right one, and the path that leads to heaven is not more surely revealed by the ruler's responsibility for the commonwealth or by his right to make laws than by an individual's own searching. Suppose I am sick and feeble in body, wasting away with a serious disease, and suppose there is only one cure and no one knows what it is. Is it the ruler's job to prescribe the remedy simply because there is only one, and it is not known which of the many possibilities it is? Will it be safe to follow the ruler's instructions simply because there is only one thing I can do to avoid death? We should not treat these questions as the privilege of any one set of people; they are for every individual to investigate by his own efforts, thinking, searching, judging, and reflecting for himself, in sincerity of heart. Princes are born superior in power to other mortals but equal by nature. Neither their right to rule nor their skill in ruling entails certain knowledge of other things, let alone of true religion. If it did, how does it come about that in matters of religion the lords of different countries differ so much from one another?

But let us grant the plausibility of the notion that the way to eternal life is better known to the prince than to his subjects, or at least that it is safer or more convenient to obey his instructions given the uncertainty of the question. In that case you will say: if he bade you make your living by trade, would you refuse because you doubt you would make money that way? I reply: I would become a merchant, if the prince told me to. For if the business failed, he has the resources to compensate me fully in some other way for the time and trouble I wasted in trade; and if he is willing to preserve me from hunger and poverty, as he claims to be, he can easily do that, even if I lost all my property when my unsuccessful business venture failed. But this is not the case with the future life. If my efforts are misdirected in that case; if my hopes are disappointed, no ruler can make good the damage, lessen the evil, or repair my loss in whole or in part. What guarantee can be given of the kingdom of heaven?

You will say perhaps: in sacred matters we credit the church, not the civil ruler, with the certain judgement which all must follow. The civil ruler orders us all to observe the rulings of the church, and uses his authority to ensure that no one behaves or believes otherwise than as the church teaches, and therefore the decision is in the hands of the church. The ruler himself obeys, and requires obedience from the rest of the people. I reply: anyone may see that the name 'church', so venerable in the time of the Apostles, has been frequently misappropriated in subsequent centuries in order to impose upon people. Anyway in the present case it gives us no help. I maintain that the one narrow path that leads to heaven is no better known to rulers than to private persons. Hence I cannot safely follow a leader who is as ignorant of the way as I am and is necessarily less concerned about my salvation than I am myself. Were there not numerous kings of the Jews of whom it may be said that any Israelite who followed them would have abandoned the true worship for idolatry and incurred certain destruction by his blind obedience?

Yet you tell me to have confidence, everything is fine, because in our day rulers do not pronounce their own decisions about religious questions for the people to follow but those of the church, and simply give them civil sanction. But then I ask: which church exactly? Obviously, the one that pleases the prince. As if in coercing me into one church or another by force of law and punishment, he is not imposing his own judgement about religion! What difference does it make whether he takes me there himself, or employs others to do it? In either case, I depend on his will, and in either case, he is making a decision about my salvation. Was a Jew much safer when he followed Baal by the king's edict, because he had been assured that the king made no decisions about religion on his own authority, and made no regulations for his subjects about divine worship, unless they had been approved and certified as divine by the council of priests and by the initiates of that religion? If then any church's religion is true and saving because the prelates, priests, and followers of that sect praise it, preach it, and give it all the support they can, what religion will be erroneous, false, or fatal? I have doubts about the faith of the Socinians,[16] I have reservations about the religion of the Papists or of the Lutherans – can I feel more secure about joining one of their churches at the behest of the ruler simply because he neither commands nor sanctions anything in the matter of religion except by the authority and advice of the doctors of that church?

But to tell the truth, a church – if we should use the word 'church' of a set of clergymen making decrees – usually adapts itself to the court rather than the court to the church. We know well enough what the church was like when the prince was orthodox and what it was like when he was Arian.[17] And if these instances are too remote, the recent history

---

[16] Socinians traced their unorthodox views on the nature of Christ back to Fausto Sozzini (1539–64). Locke is thought to have had some sympathy with their position.

[17] Locke alludes to the fourth-century controversy, initiated by Arius, over the relation of the Son to the Father within the Trinity. Whereas the Emperor Constantine had been orthodox, his successor, Constantius, was an Arian.

of England offers us some good examples from the reigns of Henry, Edward, Mary, and Elizabeth of how nimbly clergymen adapt decrees, articles of faith, forms of worship, and everything to the prince's will. These princes held such different religious beliefs and gave such different orders that only a madman – I almost said only an atheist – would assert that an honest person, a worshipper of the true God, could obey their decrees on religious matters without compromising his conscience and his respect for God. Need I say more? If a king presumes to make laws about another person's religion, it is all the same whether he does so by his own judgement or by the authority of a church, that is by the opinions of other men. The judgement of clergymen, whose conflicts and controversies are only too well known, is no more sensible and no more secure; and their support, fragmented as it is, adds no strength to the civil power. However, it is worth remarking that princes do not normally attach importance to the opinions and support of clergy who do not favour their own faith and form of worship.

But the heart of the matter is this, and it settles the question: even if the ruler's religious belief is better than mine, even if the way he directs me to go is truly that of the Gospel, it will not save me if I am not sincerely convinced of it. No way that I follow against the protests of my conscience will ever bring me to the mansions of the blest. I can grow rich by a profession I dislike, I can be cured by medicines I view with suspicion, but I cannot be saved by a religion I reject. It is useless for an unbeliever to adopt a certain mode of external behaviour, since pleasing God requires faith and inner sincerity. However attractive a remedy may be and recommended by others, it is useless to give it to a patient if his stomach will reject it as soon as it is taken, nor should you force a medicine into a person which by some quirk of his constitution will turn to poison inside him. One thing is certain about religion, whatever else may be called in question, that no religion which I do not believe to be true can be true for me or of any use to me. A ruler is wasting his time forcing his subjects to attend his own religious services on a pretext of saving their souls. If they believe, they will come of their own accord; if they do not believe, they will perish anyway, even if they come. You can say all you like about your goodwill for another person, you can strive as hard as you like for their salvation – a person cannot be forced to be saved. At the end of the day he must be left to himself and his own conscience.

## Duties of rulers with regard to toleration of ritual or external worship

So at last we have people liberated from the dominion of others in matters of religion. What now will they do? Everyone knows and agrees that God should be publicly worshipped – why else are we compelled to attend public services? That is why people living in this freedom must join an ecclesiastical association, so that they may attend services not only for their mutual spiritual development, but also to give public witness that they are worshippers of God and offer the divine Godhead a form of worship of which they are not ashamed and do not believe to be unworthy or displeasing to him. They also seek to attract others to a love of religion and truth by the purity of their doctrine, by the holiness of their lives, and by the decent grace of their ritual, and to provide for those other things that cannot be done by individuals privately.

It is these religious associations, which I call churches, that the ruler has a duty to tolerate. For a number of people meeting together for services in this way are engaged in an activity which is perfectly permissible for private individuals on their own, namely, the salvation of their souls; and there is no difference in this respect between the church favoured by the court and the others that are distinct from it.

In every church the two most important elements for us to consider are external worship or ritual, and doctrine. We must deal with each of them separately, in order to see more clearly the full scope of the argument for toleration.

First, a ruler cannot use the sanction of civil law to enforce the use of any ecclesiastical rites or ceremonies for the worship of God even in his own church, and still less in other people's churches. This is not simply because churches are free associations, but because there is only one reason to approve the offering of any particular thing to God, and that is the worshippers' confidence that it will be acceptable to him. Nothing done without this confidence is permissible or acceptable to God. Since the purpose of religion is to please God, it is contradictory to order a man who is permitted liberty in religion to displease him in the very act of worship.

You will say: do you then deny to the ruler the power that everyone would allow him over indifferent matters?[18] If you take this power away,

---

[18] Locke here uses the Greek term *adiaphoras*, which is equivalent to the Latin term, *indifferentes*, that he normally uses to describe indifferent acts.

will there be any subject on which he can legislate? In reply, I concede that indifferent matters, and these alone perhaps, are subject to legislative power.

(1) But it does not follow from this that it is permissible for a ruler to decree whatever he pleases on any indifferent matter. The end and measure of legislation is the public good. The sanction of law cannot simply be given to anything, however indifferent, if it is not in the interest of the commonwealth.

(2) Even things that are completely indifferent in their own nature are put beyond the jurisdiction of the ruler when they are introduced into a church and made an element of divine worship. For in this use they have no connection with civil matters at all. The only issue now is the salvation of souls, and it makes no difference to my neighbour or to my country whether one rite is adopted or another. The observation or omission of ceremonies in church services does not affect other people's lives, liberty, or property. For example, one may grant that washing a new-born baby with water is in its nature a matter of indifference. Grant too that a ruler may impose it by law, if he is aware that such washing helps to cure or prevent some disease to which infants are liable, and believes it to be so important that it needs to be prescribed by law. But will anyone therefore argue that by the same right a ruler may also prescribe by law that infants must be washed by a priest in a sacred font for the purification of their souls? Or that they have to be initiated into certain rituals? One sees at a glance that these things are totally different. Just suppose that the baby is the child of a Jew, and the thing speaks for itself; after all, a Christian ruler may well have Jewish subjects. Are you maintaining that one should inflict on a Christian an insult about a thing indifferent in itself which you acknowledge should not be inflicted on a Jew, namely, to force him to do something in the way of religious ritual which is against his beliefs?

(3) Things indifferent in themselves cannot be made an element of divine worship by human authority and at men's discretion. Since it is not a natural property of indifferent things to be peculiarly suited to propitiate the Deity, no human power or authority can lend them the dignity and excellence to win his favour. In social life any use of things indifferent in themselves which God has not prohibited is

free and permissible, and therefore in these cases there is room for human discretion or authority. But there is not the same freedom in religion and ritual. In divine worship the only ground of the legitimacy of indifferent things is their institution by God. By his certain command he has given them the dignity to be a part of the worship which the majesty of the supreme Deity will deign to approve and accept from poor sinful men. And it will not be enough to answer God's indignant question, 'Who required this?' by asserting that it was the ruler that ordered it. If civil jurisdiction extends that far, what will not be permitted in religion? What a mass of senseless rituals and superstitious novelties God's worshippers will have to accept, even against the protests and condemnation of their own conscience, just because rulers give them the support of their authority. For most worship consists of the use by a religion of things indifferent in their own nature, and the only way in which a ritual may be wrong is that God has not authorized it. Sprinkling with water and the use of bread and wine are things that are supremely indifferent in their own nature and in social life. Could they have been applied to sacred use and made part of divine worship without God's institution? If any human authority or civil power could do this, why could it not also prescribe as an item of divine worship a meal of fish and beer in the holy eucharist? Why not cut the throats of animals in a temple and sprinkle the blood, or purify by water or fire? Why not innumerable other such things that are indifferent outside religion but as hateful to God as the sacrifice of a dog if introduced into divine worship without his authorization? What is the difference between a puppy and a goat in comparison with the divine nature – which is equally and infinitely remote from all affinity with matter – except that God willed the use of the one species of animal in ritual and worship and rejected the other?

You see then that ordinary things, however much they may be subject to the civil power, cannot be introduced on that ground into a sacred liturgy and imposed upon religious groups; for as soon as they enter into religious ritual, they cease to be indifferent. The intention of any worshipper is to please God and win his favour. He cannot do this if, at another's behest, he offers something to God that he believes will offend him because God has not commanded it. This is not to placate God, but knowingly and deliberately to provoke him and show him open contempt, which is incompatible with the purpose of worship.

You will say: if human discretion has no place in divine worship, how is it that authority is given to churches to decide about times and places and so on? I reply: some things are *part* of a sacred rite and others are *incidentals*. A 'part' is what is believed to be required by God and to be pleasing to him, and is therefore necessary. 'Incidentals' are things which are essential in a general way to a ritual, but their specific form is not fixed, and therefore they are indifferent. Examples include the time and place of worship, the worshipper's clothing, and his physical posture. For the divine will has not given any specific ruling on these matters. Let me explain. Among the Jews, time and place and the dress of those who performed the rituals were not simply incidentals but a part of the cult: if they altered or omitted any item, they could not expect their worship to be pleasing and acceptable to God. But Christians have the liberty of the Gospel, and for them such things are merely incidentals of the rite, which the good sense of each church may handle as it believes this or that manner best serves the end of edification, with order and grace. However, for those who are persuaded under the Gospel that the sabbath day has been set apart by God for his worship, the sabbath is not an incidental but a part of divine worship which cannot be changed or neglected.

Secondly, rulers cannot prohibit the sacred liturgy and ritual adopted by any church in their religious assemblies. For in that way they would destroy the church itself, the end of a church being to worship God freely in its own fashion. You will say: so, if they want to sacrifice a child or – as was once said falsely of the Christians – engage in promiscuous conduct, should the ruler tolerate these things simply because they take place in a church service? I reply: these things are not permitted at home or in civil life, and therefore they are not permitted in a religious gathering or ritual, either. If, however, they should want to sacrifice a calf, that (I say) should not be forbidden by law. Meliboeus,[19] the owner of the beast, may kill his calf at home and burn in the fire any part of it he wishes. That does no harm to anyone, takes nothing from any other man's possessions. Hence cutting a calf's throat is likewise permitted in divine worship; it is for the worshippers to decide whether it pleases God. The ruler's only concern is

---

[19] Cf. Virgil, *Eclogues* 3.1: *Dic mihi, Damoeta, cuium pecus: an Meliboei?* 'Tell me, Damoetas, whose cattle are those? Do they belong to Meliboeus?'

to ensure that it does no harm to the commonwealth, and causes no loss to anyone else's life or property. Hence what could be used for a meal can be used for a sacrifice. But in a situation where it would be for the good of the country to avoid all slaughter of cattle in order to rebuild herds decimated by disease, it is clear that the ruler might forbid all his subjects to kill calves for any purpose. In this case, however, the law is made about a political matter rather than a religious matter. It is the killing of calves, not their sacrifice, that is forbidden.

You now see the difference between church and commonwealth. What the ruler allows in the commonwealth, he may not forbid in the church. What other subjects may do in their daily lives, the law cannot and should not forbid to be done in a church service or by members of this or that sect for sacred purposes. If at home one may legally take bread or wine sitting at table or kneeling, the civil law should not forbid one from doing the same in a sacred ritual, even though the use of the bread and wine in that case is very different, being adapted in the church for divine worship and acquiring a mystical meaning. Things that in themselves are harmful to the community in everyday life and are prohibited by legislation in the common interest cannot become legitimate when employed in a church for a sacred purpose or expect to go unpunished. But the ruler has to be particularly careful not to use the ground of public interest as a pretext for stifling any church's liberty. On the contrary, nothing that is lawful in everyday life and apart from God's worship may be forbidden by the civil law from being done in divine worship or in holy places.

You will say: what if some particular church is idolatrous? Has the ruler a duty to tolerate it too? I reply: is there a right that can be given to a ruler to suppress an idolatrous church which will not also, at the appropriate time and place, bring down an orthodox church? It is relevant to recall that civil power is the same everywhere, and every prince regards his own religion as orthodox. Hence, if on a religious question a civil ruler has been given an authorization which legitimates in Geneva[20] the extermination with violence and bloodshed of a religion which is held to be false and idolatrous, by the same right it will suppress the orthodox church in the neighbouring state and the Christian religion among the Indians. Civil power may either change everything to suit the beliefs of the prince, or it may change nothing. Once it is allowed to introduce

---

[20] Locke refers a number of times to Calvinism as the form of Christianity practised in Geneva.

anything in religion by means of law, force, and penalties, there will be no limit to it. It will be allowed to use the same weapons to bring everything into line with the rule of truth which the ruler has dreamed up for himself.

No one, and I mean no one, should be deprived of his worldly goods on account of religion, including Americans[21] who have been subjected to a Christian prince; they should not be stripped of their lives or property because they do not accept the Christian religion. If they believe they please God and attain salvation by their ancestral rites, they should be left to God and themselves. I will retrace the story from the beginning. A small, weak band of Christians, totally destitute, arrive at a territory inhabited by pagans; as foreigners they approach the indigenous people for material assistance, as one human being to another, which is normal. They are given the necessities of life; they are allowed places to settle, the two groups become one people. The Christian religion puts down roots and expands, but is not yet the stronger party. Peace, friendship, and good faith are still maintained, and equal rights are preserved. In the course of time their ruler converts to the Christian side, and the Christians become the stronger party. It is only then that it becomes a duty to trample upon agreements and violate rights to get rid of idolatry. From then on, innocent pagans, scrupulous observers of justice in that they have not offended against good morals and the civil law, are to be stripped of their lives, property, and ancestral lands, if they will not abandon their ancient worship and transfer their allegiance to new and foreign rites. At last it becomes quite evident what zeal for the church means, at least when it is combined with the passion to dominate, and it is clearly revealed how easily religion and the salvation of souls serve as a cover for robbery and lust for power.

If you believe that idolatry has to be exterminated in some place, change the name of the place, and the same principle will apply to you.[22] For it is no more right for pagans in America to lose their property than for Christians in a European kingdom who dissent from the court's church; and religion is no more reason to curtail civil rights in the one place than in the other.

---

[21] The native peoples of North America.
[22] Horace, *Satires* 1.1.69–70: *mutato nomine de te / fabula narratur*: 'with a change of name the story is about you'.

You will say: idolatry is a sin, and therefore not be tolerated. I reply: if you say, 'idolatry is a sin and therefore to be studiously avoided', your reasoning is absolutely correct. But if you say that it is a sin and therefore to be punished by the ruler, that is not correct. It is not the ruler's business to direct the law or draw the sword against everything that he believes to be a sin in the eyes of God. By general consent, greed is a sin, so is not helping others in need, so are idleness and many other things of that sort; but who has ever held that a ruler should punish them? Even in the places where they are regarded as sins, they are not condemned by law and legally suppressed, and the reason is that they do no damage to other people's possessions nor disturb the public peace. Laws everywhere are silent about liars and perjurers, except in certain cases in which the issue is not an oath before God or the immorality of the action but an attempt to do harm to the commonwealth or a neighbour. And what if a pagan or Muslim prince believes Christianity to be false and displeasing to God? Does he not, by the same right and in the same measure, have a duty to exterminate Christians?

You will say: extermination of idolaters is commanded by the law of Moses. I reply: the law of Moses is right to command this, but the law of Moses does not obligate Christians. You will surely not insist that we should follow every bit of legislation given to the Jews; nor will it help you to cite the trite old distinction (useless in this case) between moral, judicial, and ritual laws. For no positive law of any kind obligates anyone except those for whom it was made. 'Hear, O Israel' effectively restricts the obligation of the Mosaic law to the people of Israel.[23] This in itself is enough to refute those who want to prescribe capital punishment for idolaters on the basis of the law of Moses. But I would like to develop the argument a little further.

For the Jewish commonwealth there were two kinds of idolaters. First, there were those who had been initiated into the Mosaic rites and made members of that commonwealth but had fallen away from the worship of the God of Israel. These were treated as traitors and rebels, guilty of high treason. For the commonwealth of the Jews was very different from others, being based on theocracy. And there was not, and could not be, any such distinction as was made, after Christ's birth, between church and commonwealth. Among that people the laws about the worship of the one invisible Deity were civil laws and part of a regime in which God

---

[23] Deuteronomy 5: 1.

himself was the legislator. If you can show me anywhere a commonwealth based on that kind of juridical foundation, I will admit that in that commonwealth ecclesiastical laws should be accepted as civil laws, and that all the subjects can and should be barred from foreign worship and alien rites by the sword of the ruler. But under the Gospel there is absolutely no such thing as a Christian commonwealth. There are, I agree, many kingdoms and countries that have adopted Christianity, but they have retained and preserved the form of state and government which they formerly had, about which Christ in his law has said nothing. He has taught the faith and the morals by which individuals may gain eternal life. He did not, however, institute a commonwealth; he has introduced no new form of government peculiar to his own people; he has armed no ruler with a sword, to force people to adopt the faith or worship which he put before them or to bar them from the practices of a different religion.

Secondly, foreigners and those who were not members of the commonwealth of Israel were not forcibly compelled to accept Mosaic rituals, but in the same section (Exodus 22: 20–21) in which Israelite idolaters are threatened with death, the law warns that no one should trouble or oppress a stranger. Admittedly, the seven nations that possessed the land promised to Israel were to be utterly exterminated, but that was not because they were idolaters. If it were, why did the Israelites have to spare the Moabites and other tribes who were also idolatrous? But since God was king of the Hebrew people in a very particular sense, he could not permit veneration of another Deity (which was properly the crime of treason) in the country which was his own kingdom, namely, the land of Canaan. Such open revolt was not compatible with the political government of Jehovah in that territory. Hence they had to expel all idolatry from the borders of the kingdom, for idolatry was the acknowledgement, against the fundamental law of government, of another king, that is, of another God. The inhabitants too had to be driven out, so that vacant and unrestricted possession might be given to the Israelites. And that is clearly the reason why the descendants of Esau and Lot exterminated the peoples called Emmim and Horim when they invaded their territories which God had transferred to them by what is clearly the same right, as will be readily apparent to anyone who reads the second chapter of Deuteronomy.[24] This is also the reason why, though idolatry had been

---

[24] Deuteronomy 2: 1–12.

banished from the bounds of the land of Canaan, they still did not proceed against all idolaters. Joshua made an agreement to spare the family of Habab and the whole people of the Gideonites. Everywhere among the Hebrews were captives who were idolaters. Even beyond the limits of the promised land, territories were conquered by David and Solomon as far as the Euphrates, and reduced to provinces. Of so many captives, so many peoples subjected to the authority of the Hebrews, not one, so far as we can see, was ever punished for idolatry, of which they were certainly all guilty; no one was forced into the religion of Moses and the worship of the true God by punishment. Any proselyte who desired to have citizenship also accepted the law of the commonwealth of Israel, that is, its religion. But he did so willingly of his own accord, not forcibly because he was compelled to do so by the ruler; he sought it eagerly as a privilege, not submitting to it against his will as a token of obedience. As soon as he became a citizen, he was liable to the laws of the commonwealth, by which idolatry was forbidden within the bounds and limits of the land of Canaan. Nothing was laid down in that law about external territories and peoples beyond those limits.

## Duties of rulers with regard to the toleration of belief and doctrine

So much for outward worship. It remains to discuss belief.

Some of the doctrines of churches are practical, others are speculative. Though both consist in a knowledge of truth, speculative doctrines end in belief and understanding, whereas practical doctrines are directed towards the will and morals.

### (i) Speculative doctrines

Now with regard to speculative doctrines and what are called articles of faith, which require only to be believed, there is no way that civil law can introduce them into a church. What is the point of requiring by law what a person cannot do however hard he may try? It does not lie in our will that we should believe this thing or that thing to be true. But I have said enough about this above. 'Well, let him profess that he believes.' What? Lie before God and men for the salvation of his soul? A fine religion! If the ruler wants people to be saved in this way, he seems to have little understanding of the way to salvation; and if he is not acting for their salvation, why is he so very concerned about articles of faith that he commands them by law?

Again, no ruler should prohibit the holding or teaching of any speculative belief in any church; for speculative beliefs have nothing to do with the civil rights of his subjects. If a Catholic believes that what another man would call bread is truly the body of Christ, he does not hurt his neighbour. If a Jew does not believe that the New Testament is the word of God, he does not change any civil laws. If a pagan has doubts about both Testaments, he should not therefore be punished as a bad citizen. Whether anyone believes these things or not, the ruler's authority and the citizens' property may still be safe and secure. I am absolutely willing to admit that these are false and absurd beliefs, but laws have no business with the truth of beliefs, only with the protection and security of the individual's property and of the commonwealth. We need not regret this. For truth would certainly have done very well, if she were ever left to herself. She has received little help, and never will, from the dominion of the powerful, to whom the truth is rarely known and seldom pleasing. She does not require force to get entrance to people's minds, and takes no instruction from the voice of the law. The reign of error rests upon borrowed and imported forces. If truth does not strike the understanding with its own light, it cannot do it with outside help. But that is enough on this subject. We must move on to practical beliefs.

## (ii) Practical doctrines

Good morals, which are a major part of religion and sincere piety, also play a role in civil life; the safety of the commonwealth as well as the salvation of souls depends upon them. Hence moral actions belong to both the external and the internal court, and are subject to the jurisdiction of both the civil governor, which is the ruler and the individual governor, which is conscience. The problem here is that one governor may violate the right of the other, and a conflict may arise between the guardian of the peace and the guardian of the soul. But if we give due weight to the principles we laid out above about their respective limits, we shall easily settle this whole issue.

Every mortal has an immortal soul, capable of eternal happiness or eternal misery, whose salvation depends upon whether in this life each person has done the actions and held the beliefs that are necessary to win the Deity's favour and which God has prescribed. Hence it follows (1) that a person is obliged above all to observe these things and put all his care, zeal, and diligence into discovering them and putting them into practice. For this mortal state contains nothing that is in any way comparable with that eternal state.[25] It follows also (2) that each individual alone is responsible for their own salvation; for a person in no way violates the right of others by practising an erroneous ritual, nor does he do them an injury by not sharing their correct beliefs on divine matters, nor does his damnation diminish their happy state. I do not mean by this to exclude all friendly advice and willingness to refute errors; these are very much Christian duties. Anyone may devote as much reasoning and exhortation as he pleases to another's salvation, but there must be no violence and no compulsion, and nothing should be done in this context for the sake of control over others. No one is obliged to accept another person's advice or authority in this matter further than he himself believes it to be right; each person is the last and highest judge of his own salvation; it is his own business, and only his; nobody else stands to lose anything.

Besides his immortal soul, man also has a life in this world, a fragile life of uncertain duration which requires earthly goods to sustain it, and these he must get (or has already got) by labour and industry. For the things needful for a prosperous and happy life do not grow by themselves. Hence these things become a second concern for man. But such is human wickedness, that most people would prefer to enjoy things earned by other people's labour than to struggle to get them by their own. For the sake therefore of defending the wealth and resources he has already won or of protecting his means of winning them, such as his freedom and good health, a person must enter into association with others, the purpose of which is to secure each person in the private possession of things useful for life by mutual aid and united forces. Meantime the concern for his eternal soul is left to each individual, since salvation cannot be won by another person's industry, and one man's loss of salvation cannot hurt anyone else, nor can his hope of salvation be taken away by force. But though in coming together into a community[26] people have arranged for

---

[25] Cf. Romans 8: 18.

[26] Locke here uses the term *civitas* for the first stage of society which men enter by the first stage of the social contract; their appointment of a ruler establishes the fully formed commonwealth.

mutual assistance to protect their earthly goods, even so they can still be expelled from their properties by robbery and fraud on the part of their fellow citizens or by attack from foreign enemies. The remedy in the first case is found in laws, in the second case, in arms, wealth, and a large population, and in all these matters the association has mandated responsibility and authority to the ruler. This was the origin of legislative authority, which is the sovereign authority in any commonwealth, these are the purposes for which it was instituted, and these are the limits that restrict it. It is meant to protect the private possessions of individuals and thus the people as a whole and its common welfare, so that it may flourish and grow in peace and prosperity, and its own strength may keep it as safe as possible from attack by others.

On these premises, it is easy to see the end which governs the ruler's prerogative in making laws – it is the good of the people in this world, that is their earthly good, which is also the one and only argument for entering society and the unique and single end of a commonwealth once established. It is easy also to see, on the other side, the liberty that remains with private individuals in things concerning the future life – it is that every person should act as he believes is pleasing to God, on whose good pleasure[27] human salvation depends. For obedience is owed first to God, and then to the laws.

But you will say: what if a ruler has decreed something which seems to the private conscience to be wrong? I reply: this will rarely happen if the commonwealth is governed with good faith and the ruler's policies are truly directed to the common good of the citizens. But if it should happen, I insist that a private person must not do any action that his conscience tells him is wrong, and he must submit to any penalty which it is not wrong for him to bear. For an individual's private judgement concerning a law made for the public good on a political matter does not negate his obligation or merit toleration. If, on the other hand, a law deals with matters that are beyond the ruler's province – for example, a law that forces a people or part of it to adopt an alien religion and practise different forms of worship – those who disagree with it are not bound by such a law. For the purpose of entering into political association is solely to protect the individual's possession of the things of this life, and it has no other purpose. Care of one's soul and of heavenly matters (which have

---

[27] Cf. Ephesians 1: 9.

33

nothing to do with the commonwealth and cannot be subject to it) are the exclusive preserve of the private individual. Hence the business of the commonwealth is the protection of life and of the things related to this life, and the duty of the ruler is to assure them to those who have them. Therefore these worldly goods cannot be taken away from one party and given to another at the whim of the ruler, nor can private possession of them be transferred from one citizen to another, even by law, for a reason that has nothing to do with his fellow citizens, namely, his religion. For, whether it be true or false, a person's religion does not damage the worldly interests of other citizens, and only worldly interests are subject to the commonwealth.

But you will say: what if the ruler believes he is acting for the public good in this? I reply: a false private judgement on the part of an individual in no way exempts him from his legal obligation, and likewise what I may call the ruler's *private* judgement gives him no new right to legislate for his subjects, which he was not granted at the formation of the commonwealth and indeed could not have been given; much less if his motive is to reward his partisans, the members of his sect, and enrich them with spoils taken from others. You ask: what if the ruler believes that his commands are within his authority and in the best interests of the commonwealth, but his subjects take the opposite view? Who will be judge between them? I reply: God alone. For there is no judge on earth between a legislator and a people. In this case, I insist, God is the only arbiter. At the last judgement he will requite each person according to his desert, according to whether he has acted for the public good and peace and piety, sincerely and in accordance with right and justice. You will say: what will happen in the meantime? I reply: first care for your soul, and do all you can for peace, although there are few who believe it is peace when they see desolation wrought.[28] Men have two ways of working out conflicts: one is by law, the other by violence; and in the nature of the case the latter begins where the former ends. It is not my purpose to inquire how far the jurisdiction of the ruler extends in different nations; I know only what inevitably happens when a dispute arises in the absence of a judge. You will say:[29] in that case the ruler, having

---

[28] An allusion to Tacitus, *Agricola* 30, in which Calgacus is represented as exhorting his people in Scotland to resist the Romans who, he says, 'wreak devastation and call it peace' (*solitudinem faciunt, pacem appellant*).

[29] Translating the punctuation *Dices: Igitur magistratus*, as in the 1689 Gouda text.

the greater resources, will do what he believes is to his own advantage. I reply: undoubtedly he will, but we are not here discussing how hypothetical situations will work out, but seeking a rule of right conduct.

Let us now look at some particular questions:[30]

(1) I say, first, that a ruler should not tolerate any doctrines which are detrimental to human society and prejudicial to the good morals which are essential for the preservation of civil society. But examples of these are rare in any church. No sect normally reaches such a level of insanity that it feels entitled to put forward as religious dogmas any doctrines that plainly undermine the foundations of society and that are therefore condemned by the whole human race; for by such doctrines their own property, peace, and reputation will be put at risk.

(2) A more subtle but also more dangerous problem for a commonwealth arises from those who claim for themselves and their followers some special prerogative contrary to the civil laws, which is concealed in a form of words intended to deceive. Perhaps you will never find any party so outspoken as to teach openly that promises need not be kept, that a prince may be deposed by any sect that so wishes, or that dominion over all things belongs to themselves alone.[31] Open and naked avowal of these doctrines would immediately catch the eye of the ruler and focus the attention of the commonwealth on preventing the spread of this evil concealed in its midst. But there are those who say the same thing in other words. What else do people mean by teaching that promises to heretics need not be kept?[32] What they mean, of course, is that they themselves have the privilege of breaking promises, since all who are outside their own communion are declared to be heretics or may be so declared if the occasion arises. What do they mean by teaching that an excommunicated king forfeits his kingdom but that they assume for themselves the power to strip kings of their kingdoms, since they claim for their own hierarchy an exclusive right to excommunicate?[33] The doctrine that dominion is

---

[30] That is, particular questions with regard to practical beliefs.

[31] Locke is alluding here, as he makes clear later in the paragraph, to doctrines that had been held by various religious groups.

[32] The doctrine that promises to heretics need not to be kept (*fides non servanda haereticis*) was attributed to the Roman Catholic Church.

[33] Excommunication of a ruler by the pope was held to release subjects from their obligation to obey that ruler; Pope Pius V, for example, excommunicated Elizabeth I of England to this effect in 1570.

founded in grace, in the last analysis, gives possession of everything to those who hold this doctrine, since they will never fail to believe or to profess that they themselves are the truly pious, the true believers.[34] Such people can have no right to be tolerated by a ruler; for they give the faithful, the religious, the orthodox (i.e. themselves) some privilege or power in civil matters above the rest of mankind, or they claim for themselves, under the pretext of religion, some power over people who are outside the communion of their own church or in some way separate. Nor should the ruler extend toleration to those who refuse to teach that people who differ from them in religion must be tolerated. For what else are such people actually saying but that, given the opportunity, they will attack the laws of the commonwealth and the property and liberty of the citizens? And that the one thing they seek from the ruler is to be given immunity and liberty until they have sufficient strength and resources to make the attempt?

(3) A church can have no right to be tolerated by a ruler if those who join it transfer their loyalty and obedience to another prince simply by joining. Any ruler who granted such toleration would be giving a foothold in his own territories and cities to a foreign jurisdiction; he would be giving permission for soldiers to be conscripted from his own citizens against his own country. The empty and deceptive distinction between church and court affords no remedy for this disastrous situation. For both are equally subject to the absolute power of the same man, who can urge, or rather command, the members of his church to do whatever he pleases either as a spiritual matter or as a means to a spiritual end, under pain of eternal fire. It is useless for anyone to insist that they are Muslim only in religion and in all the rest faithful servants of a Christian ruler, if they admit that they owe blind obedience to the mufti in Constantinople, who in turn is completely submissive to the Ottoman emperor and formulates and publishes the fatwas of his religion at the emperor's pleasure. Still more obviously would such Turks living among Christians be rejecting a Christian commonwealth, if they recognized the same man as both head of their government and head of their church.

---

[34] The doctrine that dominion is founded in grace, deriving from John Wycliffe (*c.* 1320–84), was espoused by, among others, extremist groups during the English Civil War, such as the Fifth Monarchy men.

(4) Finally, those who deny that there is a Deity are not to be tolerated at all. Neither the faith of the atheist nor his agreement nor his oath can be firm and sacrosanct. These are the bonds of human society, and all these bonds are completely dissolved, once God or the belief in God is removed. In addition, an atheist cannot claim the privilege of toleration in the name of religion, since his atheism does away with all religion. As for other practical beliefs that may be partly errone-ous – provided they do not cover an attempt to acquire domination or civil immunity – there is no reason why the churches which teach them should not be tolerated.

## Assemblies

It remains to say a few words about assemblies,[35] which are thought to be a great stumbling-block for the doctrine of toleration, since they are com-monly suspected to be nurseries of sedition and centres of faction. They may have been so at times, but this was not because of some peculiar trait of their nature, but because of the tragedy that their freedom was either completely suppressed or precariously maintained. These accus-ations would immediately stop, if a condition of the toleration granted to those who deserve it was that all churches were obliged to teach, as the basis of their own liberty, that those who differ from them on sacred matters must be tolerated, and that no one should ever be coerced on a question of religion by any law or force whatsoever. If this one point could be established, every pretext for quarrels and disturbances in the name of religion would disappear. And if these causes of disorder and bad blood were removed, there is nothing about these assemblies that would make them less peaceable than others and more likely to create political disturbances. But let us go through the main points of accusation against them.

You will say: assemblies and gatherings of people are a danger to the commonwealth and threaten the peace. I reply: if this is so, why is there such a confluence of people every day in the marketplace? Why are there public sessions in the law courts, coteries in private clubs, and big crowds in the cities? You will say: these are civil assemblies, but we are talking

---

[35] Meetings or groups assembled for religious purposes or worship. The Conventicle Act of 1664 – part of the Clarendon Code that sought to impose religious uniformity – prohibited dissenters from holding religious 'assemblies' of more than five persons. The Latin word is *coetus*.

about ecclesiastical assemblies. I reply: how strange it would be if the assemblies which are the most remote of all from civil affairs should be the most likely to cause civil disturbances. You will say: civil assemblies are gatherings of people who have different beliefs from each other on matters of religion, but ecclesiastical assemblies are gatherings of people who all share the same belief. I reply: how strange it would be if sharing a belief on divine worship and the salvation of souls amounted to a conspiracy against the commonwealth. And the less freedom people have to meet, the more, not the less, fiercely they support their common belief. You will say: anyone is free to enter civil assemblies, but in the conventicles of co-religionists there is more opportunity for secret and clandestine intrigue. I reply: I deny that all public gatherings are open to everyone (e.g. private clubs, etc.). I also ask, if certain groups *do* hold their sacred gatherings in secret, who is to blame for that? Is it the people who would prefer to hold their meetings in public or those who forbid them? You will say: religious communion binds people's hearts together particularly closely, and is therefore particularly formidable. I reply: if that is the case, why is the ruler not afraid of his own church? Why does he not forbid their assemblies on the ground that they threaten him? You will say: because he is a part of them and their head. I reply: is he not part of the commonwealth itself and head of the whole people?

Let us make the situation clear: a ruler is afraid of other churches, but not of his own, because he favours his own and is kind to them, but he is rigorous and inflexible with the others. The condition of his own people is a condition of free men, and he indulges them to the point of permissiveness. The condition of the others is that of slaves, and the usual reward of their blameless lives is forced labour, prison, loss of rights, and the forcible auction of their property. His own people are indulged; the others are beaten on the slightest pretext. Change their positions, or apply the same law to them in civil matters as to the rest of the citizens, and you will see immediately that there is nothing to fear from religious assemblies. If people contemplate sedition, it is not because they meet for religious purposes, but because they are overwhelmed by misery. Just and moderate governments are everywhere quiet, always secure; unjust and tyrannical governments will always face a backlash from those they oppress. I know that seditions are common, and are very often started in the name of religion. But it is also very often because of religion that subjects are badly treated and suffer discrimination. Believe me, these reactions are not peculiar to certain churches or religious associations; they are common to all men everywhere who labour under an unfair burden and struggle to throw off the yoke that weighs so heavily upon their necks.

Suppose we forget religion, and imagine discrimination based upon a physical feature. Suppose black-haired or grey-eyed people had a different status from the rest of the citizens. Suppose they were not free to buy and sell, and were forbidden to practise a profession. Suppose that as parents they lost the right to raise and educate their own children. Suppose the courts were either closed to them or the judges unjust. What do you imagine would happen? Surely the ruler would have as much to fear from them as from people whose bond of union is religion, even though they have nothing in common but the colour of their hair or eyes and the persecution that goes with it. A common interest in buying and selling brings some people together to do business, leisure brings others together to enjoy themselves, a common city and a shared neighbourhood unites people in living together, and religion brings yet others together for the purpose of worship. But there is only one thing that unites people in sedition, and that is oppression.

You will say: what are you getting at? Do you want assemblies for religious worship to be held if the ruler forbids them? I reply: why forbid them? The activity is after all both legitimate and necessary. You say, 'but the ruler *does* forbid them'. That is precisely the point of my complaint, that is the source of the problem, that is the fundamental cause of our disastrous situation. Why is a gathering of human beings in a religious building more offensive than a gathering in a theatre or sports stadium? The people there are not more immoral nor more rowdy. In fact it all comes down to this in the end, that these people are badly treated and that is why they must not be tolerated. Take away the unjust legal discrimination, change the laws, and remove the threat of punishment, and all will be safe and secure. Those who dissent from the ruler's religion will feel particularly obliged to preserve the peace of the commonwealth, because they enjoy better conditions there than are commonly found elsewhere. And all the particular and mutually dissenting churches will act as guardians of the public peace by keeping a sharp eye on each other's behaviour, in order to check any tendency towards subversion. They will be keen to prevent any change in the form of government, since they cannot hope for a better situation than they already enjoy, namely, a relation of equality with the rest of the citizens under a just and moderate government. It is commonly held that the surest support of a civil government is a church which agrees with the prince in religion. And I have shown that this is the only reason why a ruler supports such a church and the laws favour it. But how much safer a commonwealth will be if it enlarges the number of those who support it by extending to all good citizens of *every* church the same courtesy from the prince and the same justice from the law without any discrimination on grounds of religion. Then the only people who will need to fear the severity of the laws will be genuine criminals and disturbers of the public peace.

## Conclusion

To bring this at last to a conclusion, we seek the rights that other citizens have been granted. Is worshipping God in the Roman manner permitted? Then permit the Genevan way also. Is speaking Latin allowed in the marketplace? Then allow those who so desire to speak it also in church. At home may we kneel, stand, sit, make various gestures, wear white or black clothes, and wear them short or ankle-length? It should not be wrong to eat bread in church or to drink wine or wash in water. And all the other things that are legally free in ordinary life should remain legally free for any church in its sacred worship. No one's life or health should be ruined for these things, no one's home or property destroyed. The church in your country is entrusted to the administration of presbyters; why should not administration by bishops likewise be allowed for those who prefer it? Ecclesiastical authority is the same everywhere, whether it is exercised by one person or several persons, and it has no competence in civil matters and no power to compel. Nor are wealth or annual revenues any business of the ruling body of a church.

Public acceptance shows that ecclesiastical assemblies and sermons are permitted. You allow them for citizens of one church or sect, why not for all citizens? If a plot is hatched against the public peace in a religious assembly, it has to be stopped in exactly the same way as if it happened at a bazaar. If anything seditious is said or done in a sermon in church, it should be punished in the same way as if the offence had happened in the marketplace. They should not be refuges for agitators and criminals. But a gathering of people in a dissenting chapel is no more illicit than a gathering in a church favoured by the court, and it is no more reprehensible for the one group than for the other. A person should be liable to suspicion and disrepute only for his own wrongdoing, not for other people's faults. Agitators, murderers, assassins, highwaymen, extortionists, adulterers, lawbreakers, slanderers, and so forth from any church, whether it be the court church or not, should be punished and deterred. But those whose doctrine is peaceful and whose morals are pure and blameless should be treated on the same terms as their fellow citizens. And if gatherings, solemn assemblies, celebration of feast days, sermons, and public worship are permitted at all, they should all be permitted on equal terms to Remonstrants, Antiremonstrants, Lutherans, Anabaptists,[36] and Socinians. Moreover if one may frankly say what is true and how it is fitting for human beings to treat each other, neither pagans, Muslims, nor Jews should be refused civil rights because of their religion. The Gospel has no such commandment, the church that 'judges not those that are without' (1 Corinthians 5: 12–13) does not desire it, and the commonwealth does not require it, but accepts and welcomes everyone provided they are honest, peaceful, and hard working. Will you allow a pagan to engage in trade in your country but forbid him to pray or worship God? The Jews are allowed to live among you and have private houses: why are they refused a synagogue? Is their doctrine more false, their worship more offensive, or their loyalty less assured in a public meeting-place than in their private homes?

And if these concessions are to be made to pagans and Jews, is the condition of Christians in a Christian commonwealth to be worse? You will say: yes indeed, because they will be more liable to faction, riot, and civil war. I reply: is there really this evil tendency in the Christian religion? If there is, Christianity is surely the worst of all religions; you should disown it and no commonwealth should tolerate it. For if it is the essential genius of the Christian religion and its natural bent, to be riotous and an enemy of public peace, then even the church favoured by the ruler will eventually turn out to be harmful.

But God forbid that this should be said about a religion that sets itself against avarice, ambition, dissensions, conflicts, and earthly passions, and is the most modest and peace-loving religion there has ever been. We must look for a different cause of the problems for which religion is held responsible. And if we look at it in the right way, it will be obvious that

---

[36] A variety of Protestant sects were known as Anabaptists because of their rejection of infant baptism. For Remonstrants and Antiremonstrants see n. 14, above. For Socinians, see n. 16, above.

the whole cause lies in the issue we are now discussing. It is not diversity of belief (which cannot be avoided) that has caused most of the quarrels and wars that have occurred in the Christian world, but refusal of tolerance to those who have different beliefs, while church leaders, motivated by greed and lust for power, have used every means to excite and inflame against them the frequently boundless ambition of the ruler and the universally fatuous superstition of the people. Contrary to the laws of the Gospel and the precepts of charity, they have always preached that schismatics and heretics should be fleeced and banished, thus mixing up two very different things, the church and the commonwealth. But people do not patiently allow themselves to be robbed of the property they have won by honest labour and, contrary to human and divine law, made victims of violence and theft, especially when they are otherwise completely blameless, over something that has nothing to do with the civil law but is concerned with the individual's own conscience and the salvation of his soul, for which he need render account only to God. This being so, what can really be expected but that people will grow tired of the sufferings to which they are subjected and come at last to the conviction that they may repel force with force, and defend, with whatever weapons they have, the rights which God and nature have given them, rights which may be forfeited only for crimes and not on account of religion?

History has surely given more than enough evidence that this has been the way of things in the past, and reason demonstrates that it will be so in the future, as long as this belief in persecution for religion's sake persists in the minds of the ruler and the people, and those who should be the heralds of peace and harmony sound the call to arms and blow the trumpet for war with all the power of their lungs. It would be hard to credit that rulers would tolerate such instigators of violence and disrupters of the public peace, if it were not notorious that they are offered a cut of the spoils and have often made use of the passion and pride of those agitators to augment their own power. For who does not see that *these good men* have not been ministers of the Gospel but agents of empire, sycophantically serving the ambition of princes and the domination of the powerful, and devoting their energy and passion to promoting in the commonwealth the tyranny that they would otherwise be unable to achieve in the church. This is what the concord between church and commonwealth has usually amounted to, whereas if they had both kept within their own limits, there could at least have been no discord, since one would have been devoted solely to the worldly interests of the community and the other to the salvation of souls.

But one is ashamed to make these reproaches. May the great and good God cause the Gospel of peace to be preached at last, and may civil rulers be punctilious in conforming their law to God's law, not in binding the consciences of others by human law. As fathers of their country, may they direct all their efforts and intelligence to increasing the civil happiness of all their children who are not violent, unjust to others, and disloyal. And may the clergy, who proclaim themselves the successors of the Apostles, walk in the Apostles' footsteps, and renouncing political ambition, devote all their energies solely to the salvation of souls, in all peace and moderation.

Farewell.

## Postscript: heresy and schism[37]

Perhaps it would not be irrelevant to add a few words here about heresy and schism. A Muslim is not, and cannot be, a heretic or a schismatic in relation to a Christian. And anyone who defects from Christianity to Islam does not thereby become a heretic or schismatic, but an apostate and unbeliever. No one doubts this. Therefore everyone agrees that one cannot be a heretic or schismatic in relation to people of a different religion.

We must therefore ask who it is that belongs to the same religion. The answer to this question is clear: those who have one and the same rule of faith and divine worship are of the same religion, and those who do not have the same rule of faith and worship are of different religions. For since all that belongs to a particular religion is contained in its rule, it follows that those who agree on the same rule, agree also on the same religion, and vice versa. Thus Turks and Christians are of different religions, because Christians acknowledge Holy Scripture and Turks acknowledge the Koran as the rule of their religion. By manifestly the same reasoning, there may be different religions under the name of Christian. Though both Papists and Lutherans are plainly Christians in that they profess faith in the name of Christ, they are not of the same religion. For the

---

[37] Popple heads this section of his translation *Postscriptum*. The 1689 Gouda text does not give it a separate title.

latter recognize Holy Scripture alone as the rule and foundation of their religion, while the former supplement Holy Scripture with tradition and the decrees of the pope in fashioning the rule of their religion. The so-called Christians of St John[38] and Genevan Christians are of different religions, though both are called Christians, because the latter have the Holy Scripture as the rule of their religion while the former have a variety of traditions. On these premises, it follows:

(1) That a heresy is a separation made within an ecclesiastical communion among people belonging to the same religion, on account of doctrines which are not contained in the actual rule.

(2) That among those who recognize Holy Scripture alone as the rule of faith, a heresy is a separation made within a Christian communion on account of doctrines not contained in the express words of Holy Scripture.

This separation may be made in two ways:

(i) When the larger part of a church, or the part which is stronger because of the ruler's patronage, separates itself from the rest by ejecting and excluding them from the communion because they refuse to profess that they believe certain doctrines which are not contained in the words of Scripture. For neither the minority status of those who are separated nor the authority of the ruler can make someone guilty of heresy. The heretic is simply the one who splits the church into parts because of such doctrines, and introduces names and notes to mark the distinctions and willingly causes a separation.

(ii) When someone separates himself from a church communion, because it does not make public profession of certain doctrines that Holy Scripture does not enunciate in explicit language.

Both of these persons are heretics. For they are in error on fundamental points, and deliberately and knowingly persist in error. Though they have taken Holy Scripture as the sole foundation of faith, they nevertheless accept another foundation, namely propositions found nowhere in Holy Scripture. And when others refuse to recognize these idiosyncratic and adventitious beliefs, which they have tacked on to Holy Scripture, as

---

[38] So named from St John the Baptist, they are also known as Mandaeans or Nasoreans, and a small community still survives in Iraq and Iran.

necessary and fundamental beliefs, and refuse to rely upon them, they either expel them or themselves withdraw, thus bringing about a secession. It is irrelevant to say that their confessions and articles of faith are consistent with Holy Scripture and the analogy of faith. For if they are formulated in the words of Holy Scripture, there can be no question about them, because these and all similar words are by universal consent fundamental, being inspired by God. But if you say that the articles which you require people to profess are *inferences* from Holy Scripture, you are right to believe and profess those which seem to you to be consistent with the rule of faith, which is Holy Scripture, but you are very wrong if you try to impose them on others to whom they do *not* seem to be indubitable doctrines of Holy Scripture. And you are a heretic if you cause a separation because of them, since they are not, and cannot be, fundamental. For I do not think that anyone is mad enough to dare to advertise his own inferences and interpretations of Holy Scripture as inspirations of God, and to endow articles of faith which he has fashioned to his own mind and measure with the authority of Holy Scripture.

I know that there are propositions which are so obviously consistent with Holy Scripture that no one can doubt that they follow from it, and there can be no quarrel about these. But you must not impose on others as a necessary article of faith anything that seems to you to follow by valid deduction from Holy Scripture, because you yourself believe it to be consistent with the rule of faith – unless you are willing to accept that other people's views be imposed by equal right upon you, and you be compelled to accept and profess different and mutually conflicting doctrines from Lutherans, Calvinists, Remonstrants, Anabaptists, and other sects, doctrines which the manufacturers of creeds and systems and confessions are apt to impose upon their followers and preach as necessary and genuine inferences from Holy Scripture. I cannot help but wonder at the unholy arrogance of those who think that they can teach what is necessary to salvation more clearly and plainly than the Holy Spirit, who is the infinite and eternal wisdom.

So much on heresy, a word which in common usage is applied only to doctrines. We must now look at schism, which is a fault related to heresy. To me both words seem to signify a separation rashly made within an ecclesiastical communion on inessential questions. But the prevailing usage applies 'heresy' to errors in faith and 'schism' to errors in the form of worship or discipline; and since usage is 'the arbiter, the authority and the norm of speech',[39] this is the distinction which we will have to use for our own discussion.

Schism then, for the reasons given above, is simply a separation in the communion of a church brought about over some inessential point of divine worship or church discipline. Nothing in divine worship and church discipline is essential to a Christian for communion except what is commanded by Christ the law-giver in explicit language or by the Apostles under the inspiration of the Holy Spirit.

I will put it in a word: a person who does not deny anything that the divine pronouncements[40] declare in explicit language and does not cause a separation over anything which is not overtly contained in the sacred text, cannot be a heretic or a schismatic, however much he may be slandered by any of the sects that go under the Christian name, and however much any or all of them may declare him to be destitute of true Christian religion.

These points might have been argued more fully and completely, but for a person of your sagacity these remarks will suffice.

---

[39] Locke is quoting from Horace, *The Art of Poetry* 71–2: *usus / quem penes arbitrium est et ius et norma loquendi.*

[40] Holy Scripture.

# From the *Second Treatise* (in *Two Treatises of Government*, 2nd edn, 1698)

## Chapter XI: *Of the extent of the legislative power*

§134. The great end of men's entering into society being the enjoyment of their properties in peace and safety, and the great instrument and means of that being the laws established in that society, the first and fundamental positive law of all commonwealths is the establishing of the legislative power, as the first and fundamental natural law which is to govern even the legislative itself is the preservation of the society and (as far as will consist with the public good) of every person in it. This legislative is not only the supreme power of the commonwealth, but sacred and unalterable in the hands where the community have once placed it; nor can any edict of anybody else, in what form soever conceived, or by what power soever backed, have the force and obligation of a law which has not its sanction from that legislative which the public has chosen and appointed; for without this the law could not have that which is absolutely necessary to its being a law, the consent of the society, over whom nobody can have a power to make laws but by their own consent and by authority received from them; and therefore all the obedience, which by the most solemn ties anyone can be obliged to pay, ultimately terminates in this supreme power, and is directed by those laws which it enacts. Nor can any oaths to any foreign power whatsoever, or any domestic subordinate power, discharge any member of the society from his obedience to the legislative, acting pursuant to their trust, nor oblige him to any obedience contrary to the laws so enacted or farther than they do allow; it being ridiculous to imagine one can be tied ultimately to obey any power in the society which is not the supreme.

§135. Though the legislative, whether placed in one or more, whether it be always in being or only by intervals, though it be the supreme power in every commonwealth, yet, first, it is not, nor can possibly be, absolutely arbitrary over the lives and fortunes of the people. For it being but the joint power of every member of the society given up to that person or assembly which is legislator, it can be no more than those persons had in a state of Nature before they entered into society, and gave it up to the community. For nobody can transfer to another more power than he has in himself, and nobody has an absolute arbitrary power over himself, or over any other, to destroy his own life, or take away the life or property of another. A man, as has been proved, cannot subject himself to the arbitrary power of another; and having, in the state of nature, no arbitrary power over the life, liberty, or possession of another, but only so much as the law of nature gave him for the preservation of himself and the rest of mankind, this is all he does or can give up to the commonwealth, and by it to the legislative power, so that the legislative can have no more than this. Their power in the utmost bounds of it is limited to the public good of the society. It is a power that hath no other end but preservation, and therefore can never have a right to destroy, enslave, or designedly to impoverish the subjects. The obligations of the law of nature cease not in society, but only in many cases are drawn closer, and have, by human laws, known penalties annexed to them to enforce their observation. Thus the law of nature stands as an eternal rule to all men, legislators as well as others. The rules that they make for other men's actions must, as well as their own and other men's actions, be conformable to the law of nature, i.e., to the will of God, of which that is a declaration, and the fundamental law of nature being the preservation of mankind, no human sanction can be good or valid against it.

...

§137. Absolute arbitrary power, or governing without settled standing laws, can neither of them consist with the ends of society and government, which men would not quit the freedom of the state of nature for, and tie themselves up under, were it not to preserve their lives, liberties, and fortunes, and by stated rules of right and property to secure their peace and quiet. It cannot be supposed that they should intend, had they a power so to do, to give any one or more an absolute arbitrary power over their persons and estates, and put a force into the magistrate's hand to execute his unlimited will arbitrarily upon them; this were to put themselves into a worse condition than the state of nature, wherein they had a liberty to defend their right against the injuries of others, and were upon equal terms of force to maintain it, whether invaded by a single man or many in combination …

# From *An Essay concerning Human Understanding* (4th edn, 1700)

## Book IV, Chapter 13: *Some farther considerations concerning our knowledge*

§1. Our knowledge, as in other things, so in this, has so great a conformity with our sight, that it is neither wholly necessary nor wholly voluntary. If our knowledge were altogether necessary, all men's knowledge would not only be alike, but every man would know all that is knowable: and if it were wholly voluntary, some men so little regard or value it, that they would have extreme little or none at all. Men that have senses cannot choose but receive some ideas by them; and if they have memory, they cannot but retain some of them; and if they have any distinguishing faculty, cannot but perceive the agreement or disagreement of some of them one with another: as he that has eyes, if he will open them by day, cannot but see some objects, and perceive a difference in them. But though a man with his eyes open in the light cannot but see, yet there be certain objects, which he may choose whether he will turn his eyes to; there may be in his reach a book containing pictures and discourses, capable to delight or instruct him, which yet he may never have the will to open, never take the pains to look into.

§2. There is also another thing in a man's power, and that is, though he turns his eyes sometimes towards an object, yet he may choose whether he will curiously survey it, and with an intent application endeavour to observe accurately all that is visible in it. But yet what he does see, he cannot see otherwise than he does. It depends not on his will to see that black which appears yellow, nor to persuade himself that what actually

50

scalds him feels cold. The earth will not appear painted with flowers, nor the fields covered with verdure, whenever he has a mind to it; in the cold winter he cannot help seeing it white and hoary, if he will look abroad. Just thus is it with our understanding: all that is voluntary in our knowledge is the employing or withholding any of our faculties, from this or that sort of objects, and a more or less accurate survey of them: but they being employed, our will hath no power to determine the knowledge of the mind one way or other; that is done only by the objects themselves, as far as they are clearly discovered. And therefore, as far as men's senses are conversant about external objects, the mind cannot but receive those ideas which are presented by them and be informed of the existence of things without: and so far as men's thoughts converse with their own determined ideas, they cannot but, in some measure, observe the agreement or disagreement that is to be found amongst some of them, which is so far knowledge: and if they have names for those ideas which they have thus considered, they must needs be assured of the truth of those propositions, which express that agreement or disagreement they perceive in them, and be undoubtedly convinced of those truths. For what a man sees, he cannot but see; and what he perceives, he cannot but know that he perceives.

## Book IV, Chapter 20: *Of wrong assent or error*

§12. ... Let never so much probability hang on one side of a covetous man's reasoning, and money on the other; it is easy to foresee which will outweigh. Earthly minds, like mud-walls, resist the strongest batteries; and though, perhaps, sometimes the force of a clear argument may make some impression, yet they nevertheless stand firm, and keep out the enemy truth that would captivate or disturb them. Tell a man, passionately in love, that he is jilted; bring a score of witnesses of the falsehood of his mistress, it is ten to one but three kind words of hers shall invalidate all their testimonies. '*Quod volumus, facile credimus*'; 'what suits our wishes, is forwardly believed' is, I suppose, what everyone has more than once experimented: and though men cannot always openly gainsay or resist the force of manifest probabilities that make against them, yet yield they not to the argument. Not but that it is the nature of the understanding constantly to close with the more probable side; but yet a man has a power to suspend and restrain its inquiries, and not permit a full and

51

satisfactory examination, as far as the matter in question is capable and will bear it to be made. Until that be done, there will be always these two ways left of evading the most apparent probabilities.

§13. First, that the arguments being (as for the most part they are) brought in words, there may be a fallacy latent in them, and the consequences being, perhaps, many in train, they may be some of them incoherent. There be very few discourses are so short, clear, and consistent, to which most men may not, with satisfaction enough to themselves raise this doubt, and from whose conviction they may not, without reproach of disingenuity or unreasonableness, set themselves free with the old reply, '*non persuadebis, etiamsi persuaseris*', 'though I cannot answer, I will not yield'.

§14. Secondly, manifest probabilities may be evaded, and the assent withheld upon this suggestion: that I know not yet all that may be said on the contrary side. And therefore though I be beaten, it is not necessary I should yield, not knowing what forces there are in reserve behind. This is a refuge against conviction so open and so wide that it is hard to determine when a man is quite out of the verge of it.

...

§16. As knowledge is no more arbitrary than perception, so, I think, assent is no more in our power than knowledge. When the agreement of any two ideas appears to our minds, whether immediately or by the assistance of reason, I can no more refuse to perceive, no more avoid knowing it, than I can avoid seeing those objects which I turn my eyes to, and look on in daylight; and what upon full examination I find the most probable, I cannot deny my assent to. But though we cannot hinder our knowledge, where the agreement is once perceived, nor our assent, where the probability manifestly appears upon due consideration of all the measures of it, yet we can hinder both knowledge and assent, by stopping our inquiry, and not employing our faculties in the search of any truth. If it were not so, ignorance, error, or infidelity could not in any case be a fault. Thus in some cases we can prevent or suspend our assent; but can a man, versed in modern or ancient history, doubt whether there is such a place as Rome, or whether there was such a man as Julius Cæsar? Indeed there are millions of truths that a man is not, or may not think himself concerned to know: as whether our king Richard the Third was crooked, or no; or whether Roger Bacon was a mathematician or a magician. In these and suchlike cases, where the assent one way or other is of no importance to the interest of anyone; no action, no concernment of his, following or depending thereon, there it is not strange that the mind should give itself up to the common opinion, or render itself to the first comer. These and the like opinions are of so little weight and moment that, like motes in the sun, their tendencies are very rarely taken notice of. They are there, as it were, by chance, and the mind lets them float at liberty. But where the mind judges that the proposition has concernment in it, where the assent or not assenting is thought to draw consequences of moment after it, and good and evil to depend on choosing or refusing the right side, and the mind sets itself seriously to inquire and examine the probability; there, I think, it is not in our choice to take which side we please, if manifest odds appear on either. The greater probability, I think, in that case will determine the assent: and a man can no more avoid assenting, or taking it to be true, where he perceives the greater probability, than he can avoid knowing it to be true, where he perceives the agreement or disagreement of any two ideas.

# The Argument of the Letter concerning Toleration, Briefly Considered and Answered (1690)

In the beginning of this letter, the author speaks of the 'mutual toleration of Christians in their different professions of religion'.[1] But toward the end of it he says: 'if we may openly speak the truth, and as becomes one man to another, neither pagan, nor Muslim, nor Jew ought to be excluded from the civil rights of the commonwealth, because of his religion'. And all that he requires of any, to qualify them for the benefit of the toleration he endeavours to promote, is only that they not be atheists; that they hold no opinions contrary to civil society; and that they own and teach the duty of tolerating all men in matters of mere religion.

So that the design of the author is evidently to show that all the religions and sects in the world that are but consistent with civil society, and ready to tolerate each other, ought everywhere to be equally tolerated and protected, or to enjoy an equal and impartial liberty, as the preface calls it.

I do not believe this author intends any prejudice, either to religion in general or to the Christian religion. But yet it seems hard to conceive how he should think to do any service to either, by recommending and persuading such a toleration as he here proposes. For how much soever it may tend to the advancement of trade and commerce (which some seem to place above all other considerations) I see no reason, from any experiment that has been made, to expect that true religion would be any way

---

[1] In the lengthy controversy that began with this 'Argument', both Proast and Locke cite the Popple translation of the original letter as if the author were anonymous. Occasionally, Locke comments on the accuracy of Popple's translation of the Latin text, as on p. 75 below.

a gainer by it; that it would be either the better preserved, or the more widely propagated, or rendered any whit the more fruitful in the lives of its professors by it. I am sure the fruits of a toleration not quite so large as our author's (some of which still remain with us) give no encouragement to hope for any such advantage from it.

But I do not design to argue against this toleration, but only to enquire what our author offers for the proof of his assertion, and to examine whether there is strength enough in it to bear the weight he lays upon it. And this I hope may be done in a very little compass. For, if I understand this letter, the whole strength of what it urges for the purposes of it lies in this argument:[2]

> There is but one way of salvation, or but one true religion. No man can be saved by this religion, who does not believe it to be the true religion. This belief is to be wrought in men by reason and argument, not by outward force and compulsion. Therefore all such force is utterly of no use for the promoting of true religion and the salvation of souls. And therefore nobody can have any right to use any force or compulsion for the bringing of men to true religion: neither any private person; nor any ecclesiastical officer (bishop, priest, or other); nor any church or religious society; nor the civil magistrate.

This, upon a careful perusal of this letter, I take to be the final argument by which the author endeavours in it to establish his position. And if every point of this were sufficiently proven, I must confess I think he would need no more for the accomplishing of his design. But whether he has sufficiently made out this argument, in all the parts of it, is that which I am now to examine.

As to the first two propositions, I have no difference with our author, but do fully agree with him in them.

And for the third, I readily grant that reason and arguments are the only proper means whereby to induce the mind to assent to any truth which is not evident by its own light, and that force is very improper to be used to that end instead of reason and arguments. For who knows not that 'the nature of the understanding is such, that it cannot be compelled to the belief of anything by outward force'?

---

[2] Proast presents this as if it were a quotation from Locke, when in fact it is Proast's summary reconstruction of Locke's argument.

But notwithstanding this, if force is used, not instead of reason and arguments, i.e. not to convince by its own proper efficacy (which it cannot do), but only to bring men to consider those reasons and arguments which are proper and sufficient to convince them, but which, without being forced, they would not consider: who can deny, but that indirectly and at a distance, it does some service toward the bringing of men to embrace that truth which otherwise, either through carelessness and negligence, they would never acquaint themselves with, or through prejudice they would reject and condemn unheard under the notion of error?

And by this we see how little of truth there is in the fourth proposition, which is this: 'that all outward force is utterly useless for the promoting of true religion and the salvation of souls'. For if force so applied as is above mentioned may, in such sort as has been said, be serviceable to the bringing of men to receive and embrace truth; there can be no reason assigned, why this should not hold with respect to the truths of religion, as well as with respect to any other truths whatsoever. For as the true religion, embraced upon such consideration as force drives a man to, is not the less true for being so embraced; so neither does it upon that account lose its acceptableness with God any more than that obedience does, which God himself drives men to by chastening and afflicting them.

All therefore that is here requisite to be considered for the clearing of this matter is, whether there be any need of outward force, for the bringing of men to the true religion, and so to salvation. For as I acknowledge such force to be no fit means to be used for this end (nor indeed for any other) where it is not needful or necessary; so if it shall appear to be ordinarily needful for this end, I suppose what has been already said, may be thought sufficient to show the usefulness of it in order to the same.

Now here I grant that if all men were but so faithful to their own souls, as to seek the way of saving them, with such care and diligence as the importance of the matter deserves, and with minds free from prejudice and passion, there could be no need of force to compel any man to do what in that case every man would be sure to do voluntarily, and of his own accord.

But then it must be granted withal that, if this were the case, as there is indeed but one true religion, so there could be no other religion but that in the world. Because (if we believe the Scriptures) no man can fail of finding the way of salvation, who seeks it as he ought; and in this case all men are supposed to seek it. And yet there is nothing more notorious than that men have sought out many inventions, and contrived a great variety of religions to themselves: so that there is nothing about which the world is more divided than it is about the way that leads to eternal blessedness, which is an evident demonstration that all men have not sought the truth in this matter, with that application of mind, and that freedom of judgement, which was requisite to assure their finding it.

And as all the false religions now on foot in the world may reasonably be thought to have taken their rise from the slight and partial consideration, which the inventors of them contented themselves with in searching after the true, whilst they suffered their lusts and passions to sit in judgement and to manage the enquiry: so it is obvious to observe, that notwithstanding that there are so many religions in the world, and that only one of them can be true; yet there is nothing in which men are more generally wanting to themselves, than they are in the consideration on which they ought to use in making their choice among them. It's strange indeed: but yet whoever looks abroad into the world must see that, in this affair, the impressions of education, the reverence and admiration of persons, worldly respects, and the like incompetent motives determine far greater numbers than reason, or such considerations as are apt and proper to manifest the truth of things.

Nor is it less easy to observe that whatever religion men take up without reason, they usually adhere to it likewise without reason. That which hinders a due consideration of things at first, and prevails with men to choose without reason, has commonly the same power afterwards to keep them from considering, and to hold them to what they so choose, without reason. Besides, men have generally an overweening conceit of their own judgements, and are prone to value what themselves have chosen, even because they thought fit to choose it; and this prejudices their minds against all that can be said to the disparagement of their choice, and possesses them with an opinion that nothing of that nature can deserve their consideration. To which I may add, that when once men have espoused a religion, it is then become their own, and that alone (such is the power of self-love) is enough to endear it to them, and to make them grow fond of it: as men are apt to dote upon their children, because they are theirs, even when they have little or nothing besides to recommend them. And this also renders them averse to the consideration of anything that may be offered against their religion, or on behalf of any other.

But though it be so ordinary a thing for men both to choose and to persist in their religion without reason, yet it must be confessed that those who do so are not willing to think they do so, nor that others should think so of them. But then this only puts them upon enquiring how their leaders and the champions of their cause are wont to defend it, and to attack their adversaries: and so, studying only their own side of the controversy, they come to be the more confirmed in the way they have chosen, and to think they can show that they have reason on their side. And when it is come to this; when such an appearance of reason strikes in with their affections and prejudices, they are so much the further from thinking it possible that they may be in the wrong; and then they have no patience any longer to hear of descending to a severe and impartial examination of both sides of the questions in debate, but reject the motion with scorn, and grow angry with him that troubles them with it.

Now if this is the case (as I think it cannot be denied to be, being a matter of common observation), if men are generally so averse to a due consideration of things, where they are most concerned to use it; if they usually take up their religion without examining it as they ought, and then grow so opinionated and so stiff in their prejudices, that neither the gentlest admonitions nor the most earnest entreaties shall ever prevail with them afterwards to do it: what means is there left (besides the grace of God) to reduce those of them that are got into a wrong way, but to lay thorns and briars in it? Since they are deaf to all persuasions, the uneasiness they meet with may at least put them to a stand, and incline them to lend an ear to those who tell them they have mistaken their way and offer to show them the right. When men fly from the means of a right information, and will not so much as consider how reasonable it is thoroughly and impartially to examine a religion, which they embraced upon such inducements as ought to have no sway at all in the matter, and therefore with little or no examination of the proper grounds of it: what human method can be used to bring them to act like men, in an affair of such consequence, and to make a wiser and more rational choice, but that of laying such penalties upon them, as may balance the weight of those prejudices which inclined them to prefer a false way before the true, and recover them to so much sobriety and reflection, as seriously to put the question to themselves, whether it be really worth the while to undergo such inconveniences, for adhering to a religion, which, for anything they know, may be false, or for rejecting another (if that be the case) which, for anything they know, may be true, until they have brought it to the bar of reason and given it a fair trial there? Where instruction is simply refused, and all admonitions and persuasions prove vain and ineffectual, there is no room for any other method but this: and then I am sure there is need enough of it, and it is well if that will produce the desired effect. But there is no reason to question the success of this method (if it be rightly used) upon such as are not altogether incurable; and those that are so must be left to God.

I say, if it be rightly used, i.e. if the force applied be duly proportioned to the design of it. For, though upon the considerations here offered, I take it to be clear in the general, that outward force is neither useless nor needless for the bringing of men to do what the saving of their souls may require of them: yet I do not say, that all manner of force, or all degrees of it, are fit to be used for this purpose. But then to determine precisely the just measures of it, and to say upon good grounds, thus much may fitly and reasonably be applied for the purpose we speak of and no more; this may perhaps require some consideration. And to me, I confess, this seems to be the only point concerning which there is any ground for controversy in this whole matter.

Now here I must profess myself perfectly agreed with this author, that to 'prosecute men with fire and sword', or to 'deprive them of their estates, to main them with corporal punishments, to starve and torment them in noisome prisons, and in the end even to take away their lives to make them Christians', is but an ill way of expressing men's desire of the salvation of those whom they treat in this manner. And that 'it will be very difficult to persuade men of sense that he, who with dry eyes, and satisfaction of mind, can deliver his brother to the executioner to be burnt alive, does sincerely and heartily concern himself to save that brother from the flames of hell in the world to come'.

And (besides the manifest absurdity of taking away men's lives to make them Christians, etc.) I cannot but remark, that these methods are so very improper in respect to the design of them, that they usually produce the quite contrary effect. For whereas all the use which force can have for the advancing of true religion and the salvation of souls, is (as has already been shown) by disposing men to submit to instruction, and to give a fair hearing to the reasons which are offered for the enlightening of their minds and the discovering of the truth to them: these cruelties have the misfortune to be commonly looked upon as so just a prejudice against any religion that uses them, as makes it needless to look any further into it; and to tempt men to reject it, as both false and detestable, without ever vouchsafing to consider the rational grounds and motives of it. This effect they seldom fail to work upon the sufferers of them. And as to the spectators, if they are not beforehand well instructed in those grounds and motives, they will be much tempted likewise, not only to entertain the same opinion of such a religion, but withal to judge much more favourably of that of the sufferers; who, they will be apt to think, would not expose themselves to such extremities, which they might avoid by compliance, if they were not thoroughly satisfied of the justice of their cause.

These severities therefore I take to be utterly unapt and improper for the bringing of men to embrace that truth which must save them. But how far, within these bounds, that force extends itself, which is really serviceable to this end, I shall not take upon me to determine. It may suffice to say, that so much force, or such penalties as are ordinarily sufficient to prevail with men of common discretion, and not desperately severe and obstinate, to weigh matters of religion carefully and impartially, and without which ordinarily they will not do this; so much force, or such penalties may fitly and reasonably be used for the promoting of true religion in the world and the salvation of souls.

If then this fourth proposition is not true (as perhaps by this time it appears it is not), then the last proposition, which is built upon it, must fall with it. Which last proposition is this, that nobody can have any right to use any outward force or compulsion to bring men to the true religion, and so to salvation: neither any private person, nor any ecclesiastical officer, nor any church, or religious society, nor the civil magistrate.

And certainly, if there be so great a use and necessity of outward force (duly tempered and applied) for the promoting of true religion and the salvation of souls, as I have endeavoured to show there is; this is as good an argument to prove that there is somewhere a right to use such force for that purpose, as the utter uselessness of force (if that could be made out) would be to prove that nobody has any such right. For this is indeed the point upon which this controversy turns: if all force and compulsion be utterly useless and unserviceable to the promoting of these ends; then to use it for that purpose, will be only to abuse it, which no man can have a right to do: but if, on the contrary, such a degree of outward force as has been mentioned, be really of great and even necessary use for the advancing of these ends (as, taking the world as we find it, I think it appears to be), then it must be acknowledged that there is a right somewhere to use it for the advancing of those ends; unless we will say (what without impiety cannot be said) that the wise and benign disposer and governor of all things has not furnished mankind with competent means for the promoting of his own honour in the world, and the good of souls.

And if there be such a right somewhere, where should it be but where the power of compelling resides? That is principally, and in reference to the public, in the civil sovereign (whom this author calls the civil magistrate) and in those who derive authority from him: but also, in a lower degree, in parents, masters of families, tutors, etc. For I agree with this author (1) that no private person (if by private persons he means such as have no coactive power over others) 'has any right, in any manner, to prejudice another person in his civil employments', because he is of another church or religion. For how should he that has no coactive power have any right to use such power, either upon that or upon any other account whatsoever? (2) That no ecclesiastical officer, as such, nor yet (3) any church or religious society, as such, has any externally coactive power: and that therefore neither the one, nor the other, can, as such, have any right to use or exercise any such power upon any pretence whatsoever. (Though I confess I do not yet understand why ecclesiastics, or clergymen, are not as capable of such power as other men.)

But in reference to the civil magistrate, our author tells us that 'the commonwealth seems to him to be a society of men constituted only for the procuring, preserving, and advancing of their own civil interests'. By which interests he tell us he means 'life, liberty, health and indolence of body; and the possession of outward things, such as money, lands, houses, furniture, and the like'. And agreeably to this hypothesis, he would persuade us that 'the whole jurisdiction of the magistrate reaches only to these civil concerns; and that all civil power, right, and dominion is bounded and confined to the only care of promoting these things: and that it neither can nor ought in any manner to be extended to the salvation of souls'.

But in answer to this (1) I acknowledge (as this author here seems to do) that the extent of the magistrate's jurisdiction is to be measured by the end for which the commonwealth is instituted. For in vain are men combined in such societies as we call commonwealths, if the governors of them are not invested with sufficient power to procure the end for which such societies are intended. But then, (2) I must say that our author does but beg the question, when he affirms that the commonwealth is constituted only for the procuring, preserving, and advancing of the civil interests of the members of it. That commonwealths are instituted for these ends, no man will deny. But if there be any other ends besides these, attainable by civil society and government; there is no reason to affirm that these are the only ends for which they are designed. Doubtless commonwealths are instituted for the attaining of all the benefits which political government can yield. And therefore, if the spiritual and eternal interests of men may in any way be procured or advanced by political government, the procuring and advancing of those interests must in all reason be reckoned among the ends of civil societies, and so, consequently, fall within the compass of the magistrate's jurisdiction.

But our author offers three considerations, which seem to him 'abundantly to demonstrate that the civil power neither can nor ought in any manner to be extended to the salvation of souls'. And the first of them is, 'because the care of souls is not committed to the civil magistrate any more than to other men'. But this seems to be no consideration at all, but only the proving of the thing by itself in other words. For to extend the civil power to the salvation of souls, is nothing else but to say, that the care of souls is committed to the magistrate, more than to other men. And therefore to say, that 'the civil power neither can nor ought to be extended to the salvation of souls, because the care of souls is not committed to the magistrate, any more than to other men', is in effect no more than to say, that the civil power neither can nor ought to be extended to the salvation of souls, because it neither can nor ought to be extended to the salvation of souls.

But (to let this pass) if what I said but now be true, it appears from thence, that besides that care which charity obliges all men, especially Christians, to take of each others' souls; and besides that care of souls also which is committed to the proper ministers of religion, who by special designation are appointed, not only to exhort, admonish, reprove, and correct by spiritual censures those who, having embraced the truth, do find themselves obliged by it to submit to their spiritual authority; but likewise to seek that which was lost, and to endeavour by wholesome instruction and due information, to bring to the right way those who never knew it, and to reduce such as have gone astray from it: I say, besides that fraternal care of souls, which is common to all, and this pastoral care, which is purely spiritual and operates immediately upon the consciences of men, there is an external and more remote care of souls; which is exercised, not only by obliging under temporal sanctions both the spiritual pastors to perform their duties, and those who own their authority, to pay them reverence and due submission; but also by laying such penalties upon those who refuse to embrace their doctrine, and to submit to their spiritual government, as may make them rethink themselves, and put it out of the power of any foolish humour, or unreasonable prejudice, to alienate them from the truth and their own happiness. Which care of souls, as it can only belong to the civil magistrate, so I think it appears from what has been said, that it is indeed committed to him.

But our author attempts to prove the contrary. 'It is not,' he says, 'committed to him by God; because it appears not that God has ever given any such authority to one man over another, as to compel anyone to his religion.' But this is quite beside the business. For the authority of the magistrate is not an authority to compel anyone to his religion, but only an authority to procure all his subjects the means of discovering the way of salvation, and to procure withal, as much as in him lies, that none remain ignorant of it or refuse to embrace it, either for want of using those means, or by reason of any such prejudices as may render them ineffectual. And certainly this authority may be committed to the magistrate by God, though he has given no man authority to compel another to his religion.

Our author adds: 'Nor can any such power be vested in the magistrate by the consent of the people; because no man can so far abandon his own salvation, as blindly as to leave it to the choice of any other, whether prince or subject, to prescribe to him what faith or worship he shall embrace.' To which I answer: as the power of the magistrate in reference to religion is ordained for the bringing of men to take such care as they ought of their salvation, that they may not blindly leave it to the choice, neither of any other person nor yet of their own lusts and passions, to prescribe to them what faith or worship they shall embrace; so if we suppose this power to be vested in the magistrate by the consent of the people; this will not import their abandoning the care of their salvation, but rather the contrary. For if men, in choosing their religion, are so generally subject, as has been shown, when left wholly to themselves, to be so much swayed by prejudice and passion, as either not at all, or not sufficiently to regard the reasons and motives which ought alone to determine their choice; then it is in every man's true interest, not to be left wholly to himself in this matter, but that care should be taken, that in an affair of so vast a concern to himself, he may be brought even against his own inclination, if it cannot be done otherwise (which is ordinarily the case) to act according to reason and sound judgement. And then what better course can men take to provide for this, than by vesting the power I have described in him who bears the sword? Not that I think the sword is to be used in this business (as I have sufficiently declared already), but because all coactive power resolves at last into the sword; since all (I do not say, that will not be reformed in this matter by lesser penalties, but) that refuse to submit to lesser penalties, must at last fall under the stroke of it.

In the second place, our author says 'the care of souls cannot belong to the civil magistrate, because his power consists only in outward force; but true and saving religion consists in the inward persuasion of the mind, without which nothing can be acceptable to God. And such is the nature of the understanding, that it cannot be compelled to the belief of anything by outward force.' But that care of souls, which I affirm to belong to the magistrate, does therefore belong to him because his power consists in outward force. For it consists altogether in applying outward force, in such a manner as has been said, for the procuring of the salvation of souls. And that outward force may be so applied as to procure the salvation of souls, notwithstanding that true and saving religion consists in the inward persuasion of the mind, and that the understanding cannot be compelled to the belief of anything by outward force, appears, I hope, sufficiently from the foregoing discourse.

The third consideration is this: 'the care of the salvation of souls cannot belong to the magistrate because, though the rigour of laws and the force of penalties were capable to convince and change men's minds, yet would not that help at all to the salvation of their souls'. I believe no more than this author does, that the rigour of laws and the force of penalties are capable to convince and change men's minds. (Though I hope I have shown that moderate penalties may do good service toward the procuring of the conviction and change of men's minds.) But if they were capable of working these effects, I confess I do not see why it should be said that that would not help at all to the salvation of their souls. But our author's meaning appears by what follows:

For there being but one truth, one way to heaven, what hope is there that more men would be led into it, if they had no rule but the religion of the court, and were put under a necessity to quit the light of their own reason, and oppose the dictates of their own consciences, and blindly to resign themselves to the will of their governors, and to the religion, which either ignorance, ambition, or superstition has chanced to establish in the countries where they were born? In the variety and contradiction of the opinions in religion, wherein the princes of the world are as much divided as in their secular interest, the narrow way would be much straightened; one country alone would be in the right, and all the rest of the world put under an obligation of following their princes in the ways that lead to destruction, and that which heightens the absurdity, and very ill suits the notion of a Deity, men would owe their eternal happiness or misery to the places of their nativity.

Now all this I acknowledge to be very true. But to what purpose it is here alleged, I do not understand. For who requires that men should have no rule but the religion of the court? Or that they should be put under a necessity to quit the light of their own reason, and oppose the dictates of their own consciences, and blindly resign themselves to the will of their governors, etc.? No man certainly, who thinks religion worthy of his serious thoughts. The power I ascribe to the magistrate is given him to bring men, not to his own, but to the true religion; and though (as our author puts us in mind) 'the religion of every prince is orthodox to himself'; yet if this power keep within its bounds, it can serve the interests of no other religion but the true, among such as have any concern for their eternal salvation (and those that have none deserve not to be considered); because the penalties it enables him that has it to inflict, are not such as may tempt such persons either to renounce a religion which they believe to be true, or to profess one which they do not believe to be so; but only such as are apt to put them upon a serious and impartial examination of the controversy between the magistrate and them: which is the way for them to come to the knowledge of the truth. And if, upon such examination of the matter, they chance to find that the truth does not lie on the magistrate's side, they have gained thus much however, even by the magistrate's misapplying his power, that they know better than they did before, where the truth does lie. And all the hurt that comes to them by it, is only the suffering of some tolerable inconveniences for their following the light of their own reason, and the dictates of their own

65

consciences: which certainly is no such mischief to mankind, as to make it more eligible that there should be no such power vested in the magistrate, but the care of every man's soul should be left to himself alone (as this author demands it should be). That is, that every man should be suffered, quietly and without the least molestation, either to take no care at all of his soul, if he be so pleased; or in doing it, to follow his own groundless prejudices or unaccountable humour, or any crafty seducer whom he may think fit to take for his guide.

By what has been said to these considerations, I hope it sufficiently appears, that as they afford us no new argument, so they are far enough from demonstrating what they are brought to prove.

Thus I have, as briefly as I could, examined the argument which this author makes use of, to prove what he so much desires to make the world believe: not omitting any part of his *Letter*, wherein he seems to place any part of his strength. And I hope by this time an ordinary reader may discern, that whereas his design obliged him to show that all manner of outward force is utterly useless to the purpose of bringing men to seek the truth with that care and diligence, and that freedom of judgement which they ought to use, that so they may find and embrace it, and attain salvation by it, which would have been a good foundation for his conclusion; instead of attempting that, he has contented himself with making a good declamation upon the impossibility of doing that by outward force, which can only be done by reason and argument; and upon the inhumanity, as well as absurdity, of using fire and sword and capital punishments, to convince men's minds of error, and inform them of the truth. Which was much more easy to be done, and might serve as well among weak and unwary people, though it was not really to his purpose.

# From *A Second Letter concerning Toleration* (1690)

You will pardon me if I take the same liberty with you that you have done with the author of the *Letter Concerning Toleration*:[1] to consider your arguments, and endeavour to show you the mistakes of them. For since you have so plainly yielded up the question to him, and do own that 'the severities he would dissuade Christians from, are utterly unapt and improper to bring men to embrace that truth which must save them', I am not without some hopes to prevail with you to do that yourself, which you say is the only justifiable aim of men differing about religion, even in the use of the severest methods, viz. carefully and impartially to weigh the whole matter, and thereby to remove that prejudice which makes you yet favour some remains of persecution; promising myself that so ingenious a person will either be convinced by the truth which appears so very clear and evident to me, or else confess that, were either you or I in authority, we should very unreasonably and very unjustly use any force upon the other, which differed from him, upon any pretence of want of examination. And if force be not to be used in your case or mine, because unreasonable or unjust, you will, I hope, think fit that it should be forborne in all others where it will be equally unjust and unreasonable, as I doubt not but to make it appear it will unavoidably be, wherever you will go about to punish men for want of consideration; for the true way to try such speculations as these is to see how they will prove when they are reduced into practice.

The first thing you seem startled at in the author's letter, is the largeness of the toleration he proposes; and you think it strange that he would

---

[1] Throughout the exchange, Locke attempts to hide his identity by referring to the *Letter*'s author in the third person.

not have so much as a 'pagan, Mahometan, or Jew, excluded from the civil rights of the commonwealth because of his religion'. We pray every day for their conversion, and I think it our duty so to do; but it will, I fear, hardly be believed that we pray in earnest, if we exclude them from the other ordinary and probable means of conversion, either by driving them from us or persecuting them when they are amongst us. Force, you allow, is improper to convert men to any religion. Toleration is but the removing that force; so that why those should not be tolerated as well as others, if you wish their conversion, I do not see. But you say, 'it seems hard to conceive how the author of that letter should think to do any service to religion in general, or to the Christian religion, by recommending and persuading such a toleration. For how much soever it may tend to the advancement of trade and commerce (which some seem to place above all other considerations), I see no reason, from any experiment that has been made, to expect that true religion would be a gainer by it; that it would be either the better preserved, the more widely propagated, or rendered any whit the more fruitful in the lives of its professors by it.' Before I come to your doubt itself, 'Whether true religion would be a gainer by such a toleration', give me leave to take notice that if, by other considerations, you mean anything but religion, your parenthesis is wholly beside the matter; and that if you do not know that the author of the letter places the advancement of trade above religion, your insinuation is very uncharitable. But I go on.

'You see no reason,' you say, 'from any experiment that has been made, to expect that true religion would be a gainer by it.' True religion and Christian religion are, I suppose, to you and me, the same thing. But of this you have an experiment in its first appearance in the world, and several hundreds of years after. It was then 'better preserved, more widely propagated (in proportion), and rendered more fruitful in the lives of its professors', than ever since; though then Jews and pagans were tolerated, and more than tolerated by the governments of those places where it grew up. I hope you do not imagine the Christian religion has lost any of its first beauty, force, or reasonableness, by having been almost two thousand years in the world; that you should fear it should be less able now to shift for itself without the help of force. I doubt not but you look upon it still to be 'the power and wisdom of God for our salvation'; and therefore cannot suspect it less capable to prevail now, by its own truth and light, than it did in the first ages of the church, when poor contemptible men, without authority or the countenance of authority, had alone the care of it.

This, as I take it, has been made use of by Christians generally, and by some of our church in particular, as an argument for the truth of the Christian religion; that it grew, and spread, and prevailed, without any aid from force or the assistance of the powers in being; and if it be a mark of the true religion that it will prevail by its own light and strength, but that false religions will not, but have need of force and foreign helps to support them, nothing certainly can be more for the advantage of true religion, than to take away compulsion everywhere; and therefore it is no more 'hard to conceive how the author of the letter should think to do service to religion in general, or to the Christian religion', than it is hard to conceive that he should think there is a true religion, and that the Christian religion is it; which its professors have always owned not to need force, and have urged that as a good argument to prove the truth of it. The inventions of men in religion need the force and helps of men to support them. A religion that is of God wants not the assistance of human authority to make it prevail. I guess, when this dropped from you, you had narrowed your thoughts to your own age and country. But if you will enlarge them a little beyond the confines of England, I do not doubt but you will easily imagine that if in Italy, Spain, Portugal, etc., the Inquisition, and in France their dragooning, and in other parts those severities that are used to keep or force men to the national religion, were taken away, and instead thereof the toleration proposed by the author were set up, the true religion would be a gainer by it.

The author of the letter says:

> Truth would do well enough, if she were once left to shift for herself. She seldom has received, and ... never will receive, much assistance from the power of great men, to whom she is but rarely known and more rarely welcome. Errors indeed prevail, by the assistance of foreign and borrowed succours. Truth makes way into our understanding by her own light, and is but the weaker for any borrowed force that violence can add to her.

These words of his, how hard soever they may seem to you, may help you to conceive how he should think to do service to true religion, by recommending and persuading such a toleration as he proposed. And now pray tell me yourself, whether you do not think true religion would be a gainer by it, if such a toleration, established there, would permit the doctrine of the Church of England to be freely preached, and its worship set up, in any popish, Mahometan, or pagan country? If you do not, you have a very ill opinion of the religion of the Church of England, and must own that it can only be propagated and supported by force. If you think it would gain in those countries, by such a toleration, you are then of the author's mind, and do not find it so hard to conceive how the recommending such a toleration might do service to that which you think true religion. But if you allow such a toleration useful to truth in other countries, you must find something very peculiar in the air that must make it less useful to truth in England; and it will savour of much partiality, and be too absurd, I fear, for you to own that toleration will be advantageous to true religion all the world over, except only in this island. Though, I much suspect, this, as absurd as it is, lies at the bottom, and you build all you say upon this lurking supposition: that the national religion now in England, backed by the public authority of the law, is the only true religion, and therefore no other is to be tolerated; which being a supposition equally unavoidable, and equally just in other countries (unless we can imagine that everywhere but in England men believe what at the same time they think to be a lie), will in other places exclude toleration, and thereby hinder truth from the means of propagating itself.

What the fruits of toleration are, which in the next words you complain do 'remain still among us', and which you say 'give no encouragement to hope for any advantages from it', what fruits, I say, these are, or whether they are owing to the want or wideness of toleration among us, we shall then be able to judge when you tell us what they are. In the meantime I will boldly say that if the magistrates will severely and impartially set themselves against vice, in whomsoever it is found, and leave men to their own consciences in their articles of faith and ways of worship, 'true religion will be spread wider, and be more fruitful in the lives of its professors', than ever hitherto it has been by the imposition of creeds and ceremonies.

You tell us 'that no man can fail of finding the way of salvation, who seeks it as he ought'. I wonder you had not taken notice, in the places you quote for this, how we are directed there to the right way of seeking. The words (John 7: 17) are: 'If any man will do his will, he shall know of the doctrine whether it be of God.' And Psalm 25: 9, 12, 14, which are also quoted by you, tell us: 'The meek will he guide in judgement, and the meek will he teach his way. What man is he that feareth the Lord, him shall he teach in the way that he shall choose. The secret of the Lord is with them that fear him, and he will show them his covenant.' So that these places, if they prove what you cite them for, 'that no man can fail of finding the way of salvation, who seeks it as he ought', do also prove that a good life is the only way to seek as we ought; and that therefore the magistrates, if they would put men upon seeking the way of salvation as they ought, should, by their laws and penalties, force them to a good life: a good conversation being the readiest and surest way to a right understanding. Punishments and severities thus applied, we are sure, are practicable, just, and useful. How punishments will prove in the way you contend for, we shall see when we come to consider it.

Having given us these broad marks of your goodwill to toleration, you tell us 'It is not [your] design to argue against it, but only to enquire what our author offers for the proof of his assertion.' And then you give us this scheme of his argument.

(1) 'There is but one way of salvation, or but one true religion.'
(2) 'No man can be saved by this religion, who does not believe it to be the true religion.'
(3) 'This belief is to be wrought in men by reason and argument, not by outward force and compulsion.'
(4) 'Therefore all such force is utterly of no use for the promoting true religion and the salvation of souls.'
(5) 'And therefore nobody can have any right to use any force or compulsion, for the bringing men to the true religion.'

And you tell us, 'the whole strength of what that letter urged for the purpose of it, lies in this argument', which I think you have no more reason to say, than if you should tell us that only one beam of a house had any strength in it, when there are several others that would support the building were that gone.

The purpose of the letter is plainly to defend toleration, exempt from all force, especially civil force or the force of the magistrate. Now, if it be a true consequence 'that men must be tolerated, if magistrates have no commission or authority to punish them for matters of religion', then the only strength of that letter lies not in the unfitness of force to convince men's understanding.

Again, if it be true that 'magistrates being as liable to error as the rest of mankind, their using of force in matters of religion would not at all advance the salvation of mankind' (allowing that even force could work upon them, and magistrates had authority to use it in religion), then the argument you mention is not 'the only one in that letter of strength to prove the necessity of toleration'. For the argument of the unfitness of force to convince men's minds being quite taken away, either of the other would be a strong proof for toleration. But let us consider the argument as you have put it.

The two first propositions, you say, you agree to. As to the third, you grant 'that force is very improper to be used to induce the mind to assent to any truth'. But yet you deny 'that force is utterly useless for the promoting true religion, and the salvation of men's souls', which you call the author's fourth proposition. But indeed that is not the author's fourth proposition, or any proposition of his to be found in the pages you quote, or anywhere else in the whole letter, either in those terms or in the sense you take it. In [the page that you quote], the author is showing that the magistrate has no power, that is, no right, to make use of force in matters of religion, for the salvation of men's souls. And the reason he gives for it there is, because force has no efficacy to convince men's minds; and that without a full persuasion of the mind, the profession of the true religion itself is not acceptable to God. 'Upon this ground,' says he, 'I affirm that the magistrate's power extends not to the establishing any articles of faith, or forms of worship, by the force of his laws. For laws are of no force at all without penalties; and penalties in this case are absolutely impertinent, because they are not proper to convince the mind.' And so again ... [in] the other place you quote, the author says: 'Whatsoever may be doubted in religion, yet this at least is certain, that no religion which I believe not to be true, can be either true, or profitable unto me. In vain therefore do princes compel their subjects to come into their church-communion, under the pretence of saving their souls.' And more to this purpose.

But in neither of those passages, nor anywhere else that I remember, does the author say that it is impossible that force should any way, at any time, upon any person, by any accident, be useful towards the promoting of true religion and the salvation of souls; for that is it which you mean by 'utterly of no use'. He does not deny that there is anything which God in his goodness does not, or may not, sometimes graciously make use of towards the salvation of men's souls (as our Saviour did of clay and spittle to cure blindness); and that so force also may be sometimes useful. But that which he denies, and you grant, is that force has any proper efficacy to enlighten the understanding or produce belief. And from thence he infers that therefore the magistrate cannot lawfully compel men in matters of religion. This is what the author says, and what I imagine will always hold true, whatever you or anyone can say or think to the contrary.

That which you say is: 'Force, indirectly and at a distance, may do some service.' What you mean by doing service at a distance, towards the bringing men to salvation or to embrace the truth, I confess I do not understand, unless perhaps it be what others, in propriety of speech, call by accident. But be it what it will, it is such a service as cannot be ascribed to the direct and proper efficacy of force. And so, say you, 'Force, indirectly and at a distance, may do some service.' I grant it: make your best of it. What do you conclude from thence to your purpose? That therefore the magistrate may make use of it? That I deny. That such an indirect and at-a-distance usefulness will authorize the civil power in the use of it, that will never be proved. Loss of estate and dignities may make a proud man humble; sufferings and imprisonment may make a wild and debauched man sober; and so these things may 'indirectly, and at a distance, be serviceable towards the salvation of men's souls'. I doubt not but God has made some or all of these the occasions of good to many men. But will you therefore infer that the magistrate may take away a man's honour, or estate, or liberty for the salvation of his soul, or torment him in this, that he may be happy in the other world?

What is otherwise unlawful in itself (as it certainly is to punish a man without a fault), can never be made lawful by some good that, indirectly and at a distance, or if you please, indirectly and by accident, may follow from it. Running a man through may save his life, as it has done by chance, opening a lurking imposthume.[2] But will you say, therefore, that this is lawful, justifiable surgery? The galleys, it is like, might reduce many a vain, loose protestant to repentance, sobriety of thought, and a true sense of religion: and the torments they suffered in the late persecution might make several consider the pains of Hell, and put a due estimate of vanity and contempt on all things of this world. But will you say, because those punishments might, indirectly and at a distance, serve to the salvation of men's souls, that therefore the King of France had right authority to make use of them? If your indirect and at-a-distance serviceableness may authorize the magistrate to use force in religion, all

---

[2] Abscess.

the cruelties used by the heathens against Christians, by papists against protestants, and all the persecuting of Christians one among another are all justifiable.

But what if I should tell you now of other effects, contrary effects, that punishments in matters of religion may produce, and so may serve to keep men from the truth and from salvation? What then will become of your indirect and at-a-distance usefulness? For in all pleas for anything because of its usefulness, it is not enough to say as you do, and is the utmost that can be said for it, that it may be serviceable: but it must be considered not only what it may, but what it is likely to produce, and the greater good or harm like to come from it ought to determine of the use of it. To show you what effects one may expect from force, of what usefulness it is to bring men to embrace the truth, be pleased to read what you yourself have writ: 'I cannot but remark,' say you,

> that these methods (viz. depriving men of estates, corporal punishment, starving and tormenting them in prisons, and in the end even taking away their lives, to make them Christians) are so very improper in respect to the design of them, that they usually produce the quite contrary effect. For whereas all the use which force can have for the advancing true religion and the salvation of souls, is (as has already been shown) by disposing men to submit to instruction, and to give a fair hearing to the reasons which are offered for the enlightening their minds, and discovering the truth to them; these cruelties have the misfortune to be commonly looked upon as so just a prejudice against any religion that uses them, as makes it needless to look any farther into it: and to tempt men to reject it, as both false and detestable, without ever vouchsafing to consider the rational grounds and motives of it.

Here then you allow that taking away men's estates, or liberty, and corporal punishments, are apt to drive away both sufferers and spectators from the religion that makes use of them, rather than to it. And so these you renounce. Now if you give up punishments of a man, in his person, liberty, and estate, I think we need not stand with you for any other punishments that may be made use of.

But, by what follows, it seems you shelter yourself under the name of severities. For moderate punishments, as you call them in another place, you think may be serviceable indirectly, and at a distance serviceable, to bring men to the truth. And I say, any sort of punishments disproportioned to the offence, or where there is no fault at all, will always be severity, unjustifiable severity, and will be thought so by the sufferers and bystanders, and so will usually produce the effects you have mentioned, contrary to the design they are used for. Not to profess the national faith, whilst one believes it not to be true; not to enter into church-communion with the magistrate as long as one judges the doctrine there professed to be erroneous, or the worship not such as God has either prescribed or will accept; this you allow, and all the world with you must allow, not to be a fault. But yet you would have men punished for not being of the national religion; that is, as you yourself confess, for no fault at all. Whether this be not severity, nay so open and avowed injustice, that it will give men a just prejudice against the religion that uses it and produce all those ill effects you there mention, I leave you to consider. So that the name of severities, in opposition to the moderate punishments you speak for, can do you no service at all. For where there is no fault, there can be no moderate punishment. All punishment is immoderate, where there is no fault to be punished. But of your 'moderate punishment' we shall have occasion to speak more in another place. It suffices here to have shown that, whatever punishments you use, they are as likely to drive men from the religion that uses them as to bring them to the truth; and much more likely, as we shall see before we have done, and so by your own confession they are not to be used.

One thing in this passage of the author, it seems, appears absurd to you: that he should say, 'That to take away men's lives, to make them Christians, was but an ill way of expressing a design of their salvation.' I grant there is great absurdity somewhere in the case. But it is in the practice of those who, persecuting men under a pretence of bringing them to salvation, suffer the temper of their goodwill to betray itself in taking away their lives. And whatever absurdities there be in this way of proceeding, there is none in the author's way of expressing it, as you would more plainly have seen if you had looked into the Latin original, where the words are: '*Vita denique ipsa privant, ut fideles, ut salvi fiant*'; which, though more literally, might be thus rendered: 'to bring them to the faith and to salvation'. Yet the translator is not to be blamed, if he chose to express the sense of the author in words that very livelily represented the extreme absurdity they are guilty of, who, under pretence of zeal for the salvation of souls, proceed to the taking away their lives. An example whereof we have in a neighbouring country, where the prince declares he will have all his dissenting subjects saved, and pursuant thereunto has taken away the lives of many of them. For thither at last persecution must come; as I fear, notwithstanding your talk of moderate punishments, you yourself intimate in these words: 'Not that I think the sword is to be used in this business (as I have sufficiently declared already), but because all coactive power resolves at last into the sword; since all (I do not say that will not be reformed in this matter by lesser penalties, but) that refuse to submit to lesser penalties must at last fall under the stroke of it.' In which words, if you mean anything to the business in hand, you seem to have a reserve for greater punishments, when lesser are not sufficient to bring men to be convinced. But let that pass.

You say, 'if force be used, not instead of reason and arguments, that is, not to convince by its own proper efficacy, which it cannot do', etc. I think those who make laws, and use force, to bring men to church-conformity in religion seek only the compliance, but concern themselves not for the conviction of those they punish, and so never use force to convince. For, pray tell me, when any dissenter conforms and enters into the church-communion, is he ever examined to see whether he does it upon reason and conviction, and such grounds as would become a Christian concerned for religion? If persecution, as is pretended, were for the salvation of men's souls, this would be done; and men not driven to take the sacrament to keep their places, or to obtain licences to sell ale (for so low have these holy things been prostituted); who perhaps knew nothing of its institution, and considered no other use of it but the securing some poor secular advantage, which without taking of it they should have lost. So that this exception of yours, of the 'use of force, instead of arguments, to convince men', I think is needless, those who use it not being (that ever I heard) concerned that men should be convinced.

But you go on in telling us your way of using force, 'only to bring men to consider those reasons and arguments which are proper and sufficient to convince them, but which, without being forced, they would not consider'. And, say you, 'who can deny but that, indirectly and at a distance, it does some service towards bringing men to embrace that truth which either through negligence they would never acquaint themselves with, or through prejudice they would reject and condemn unheard?'. Whether this way of punishment is like to increase or remove prejudice, we have already seen. And what that truth is, which you can positively say any man, 'without being forced by punishment, would through carelessness never acquaint himself with', I desire you to name. Some are called at the third, some at the ninth, and some at the eleventh hour. And whenever they are called, they embrace all the truth necessary to salvation.

But these slips may be forgiven, amongst so many gross and palpable mistakes, as appear to me all through your discourse. For example: you tell us that 'force used to bring men to consider, does, indirectly, and at a distance, some service'. Here now you walk in the dark, and endeavour to cover yourself with obscurity, by omitting two necessary parts. As first, who must use this force: which, though you tell us not here, yet by other parts of your treatise it is plain you mean the magistrate. And, secondly, you omit to say upon whom it must be used, who it is must be punished: and those, if you say anything to your purpose, must be dissenters from the national religion, those who come not into church-communion with the magistrate. And then your proposition, in fair plain terms, will stand thus: 'If the magistrate punish dissenters, only to bring them to consider those reasons and arguments which are proper to convince them; who can deny but that, indirectly and at a distance, it may do service, etc. towards bringing men to embrace that truth which otherwise they would never be acquainted with?' etc. In which proposition, (1) there is something impracticable, (2) something unjust, and (3) whatever efficacy there is in force, your way applied, to bring men to consider and be convinced, it makes against you.

(1)  It is impracticable to punish dissenters, as dissenters, only to make them consider. For if you punish them as dissenters (as certainly you do if you punish them alone, and them all without exception), you punish them for not being of the national religion. And to punish a man for not being of the national religion, is not to punish him only to make him consider; unless not to be of the national religion, and not to consider, be the same thing. But you will say, the design is only to make dissenters consider; and therefore they may be punished only to make them consider. To this I reply: it is impossible you should punish one with a design only to make him consider, whom you punish for something else besides want of consideration, or if you punish him whether he consider or no; as you do, if you lay penalties on dissenters in general. If you should make a law to punish all stammerers, could anyone believe you if you said it was designed only to make them leave swearing? Would not everyone see it was impossible that

punishment should be only against swearing, when all stammerers were under the penalty? Such a proposal as this is, in itself, at first sight monstrously absurd. But you must thank yourself for it. For to lay penalties upon stammerers, only to make them not swear, is not more absurd and impossible than it is to lay penalties upon dissenters only to make them consider.

(2) To punish men out of the communion of the national church, to make them consider, is unjust. They are punished, because [they are] out of the national church: and they are out of the national church, because they are not yet convinced. Their standing out therefore in this state, whilst they are not convinced, not satisfied in their minds, is no fault, and therefore cannot justly be punished. But your method is: 'Punish them, to make them consider such reasons and arguments as are proper to convince them.' Which is just such justice, as it would be for the magistrate to punish you for not being a Cartesian, 'only to bring you to consider such reasons and arguments as are proper and sufficient to convince you', when it is possible: (i) That you being satisfied of the truth of your own opinion in philosophy, did not judge it worthwhile to consider that of Descartes; (ii) It is possible you are not able to consider and examine all the proofs and grounds upon which he endeavours to establish his philosophy; (iii) Possibly you have examined, and can find no reasons and arguments proper and sufficient to convince you.

(3) Whatever indirect efficacy there be in force, applied by the magistrate your way, it makes against you. 'Force used by the magistrate to bring men to consider those reasons and arguments, which are proper and sufficient to convince them, but which without being forced they would not consider, may,' say you, 'be serviceable, indirectly and at a distance, to make men embrace the truth which must save them.' And thus, say I, it must be serviceable to bring men to receive and embrace falsehood, which will destroy them. So that force and punishment, by your own confession, not being able directly, by its proper efficacy, to do men any good in reference to their future estate; though it be sure directly to do them harm, in reference to their present condition here; and indirectly, and in your way of applying it, being proper to do at least as much harm as good; I desire to know what the usefulness is which so much recommends it, even to a degree that you pretend it needful and necessary. Had you some new untried chemical preparation that

was as proper to kill as to save an infirm man (of whose life I hope you would not be more tender than of a weak brother's soul), would you give it your child, or try it upon your friend, or recommend it to the world for its rare usefulness? I deal very favourably with you, when I say as proper to kill as to save. For force, in your indirect way, of the magistrate's 'applying to make men consider those arguments that otherwise they would not; to make them lend an ear to those who tell them they have mistaken their way, and offer to show them the right', I say, in this way, force is much more proper, and likely, to make men receive and embrace error than the truth.

(i) Because men out of the right way are as apt, I think I may say, apter to use force than others. For truth, I mean the truth of the Gospel, which is that of the true religion, is mild, and gentle, and meek, and apter to use prayers and entreaties than force, to gain a hearing.

(ii) Because the magistrates of the world (or the civil sovereigns, as you think it more proper to call them) being few of them in the right way, not one of ten, take which side you will, perhaps you will grant not one of a hundred, being of the true religion, it is likely your indirect way of using of force would do a hundred, or at least ten times as much harm as good; especially if you consider that as the magistrate will certainly use it to force men to hearken to the proper ministers of his religion, let it be what it will, so you having set no time nor bounds to this consideration of arguments and reasons, short of being convinced, you, under another pretence, put into the magistrate's hands as much power to force men to his religion as any the openest persecutors can pretend to. For what difference, I beseech you, between punishing you to bring you to Mass, and punishing you to consider those reasons and arguments which are proper and sufficient to convince you that you ought to go to Mass? For till you are brought to consider reasons and arguments proper and sufficient to convince you, that is, till you are convinced, you are punished on. If you reply, you meant reasons and arguments proper and sufficient to convince them of the truth, I answer, if you meant so, why did you not say so? But if you had, it would in this case do you little service. For the Mass in France is as much supposed the truth as the liturgy here. And your way of applying force will as much promote popery in France as protestantism in England. And so you see how serviceable it is to make men 'receive and embrace the truth that must save them'.

However you tell us, in the same page, that 'if force so applied, as is above-mentioned, may in such sort as has been said, i.e. indirectly and at a distance, be serviceable to bring men to receive and embrace truth', you think it sufficient to show the usefulness of it in religion: where I shall observe (I) that this usefulness amounts to no more but this, that it is not impossible but that it may be useful. And such a usefulness one cannot deny to auricular confession, doing of penance, going of a pilgrimage to some saint, and what not. Yet our church does not think fit to use them: though it cannot be denied, but they may have some of your indirect and at a distance usefulness; that is, perhaps may do some service indirectly and by accident. (II) Force, your way applied, as it may be useful, so also it may be useless. For (i) where the law punishes dissenters, without telling them it is to make them consider, they may through ignorance and oversight neglect to do it, and so your force proves useless. (ii) Some dissenters may have considered already, and then force employed upon them must needs be useless, unless you can think it useful to punish a man to make him do that which he has done already. (iii) God has not directed it: and therefore we have no reason to expect he should make it successful.

(3) It may be hurtful: nay, it is likely to prove more hurtful than useful. (i) Because to punish men for that which it is visible cannot be known whether they have performed or no, is so palpable an injustice, that it is likelier to give them an aversion to the persons and religion that use it, than to bring them to it. (ii) Because the greatest part of mankind, being not able to discern between truth and falsehood, that depend upon long and many proofs and remote consequences, nor have ability enough to discover the false grounds, and resist the captious and fallacious arguments of learned men versed in controversies, are so much more exposed to it by the force which is used to make them hearken to the information and instruction of men appointed to it by the magistrate, or those of his religion, to be led into falsehood and error, than they are likely this way to be brought to embrace the truth that must save them; by how much the national religions of the world are, beyond comparison, more of

them false or erroneous, than such as have God for their author and truth for their standard.

And that seeking and examining, without the special grace of God, will not secure even knowing and learned men from error, we have a famous instance in the two Reynolds (both scholars and brothers, but one a protestant, the other a papist), who, upon the exchange of papers between them, were both turned, but so that neither of them, with all the arguments he could use, could bring his brother back to the religion which he himself had found reason to embrace.[3] Here was ability to examine and judge beyond the ordinary rate of most men. Yet one of these brothers was so caught by the sophistry and skill of the other, that he was brought into error, from which he could never again be extricated. This we must unavoidably conclude, unless we can think that wherein they differed they were both in the right; or that truth can be an argument to support a falsehood; both which are impossible. And now, I pray, which of these two brothers would you have punished, to make him bethink himself and bring him back to the truth? For it is certain some ill-grounded cause of assent alienated one of them from it. If you will examine your principles, you will find that, according to your rule, the papist must be punished in England, and the protestant in Italy. So that, in effect, by your rule passion, humour, prejudice, lust, impressions of education, admiration of persons, worldly respect, and the like incompetent motives, must always be supposed on that side on which the magistrate is not.

I have taken the pains here, in a short recapitulation, to give you the view of the usefulness of force, your way applied, which you make such a noise with and lay so much stress on. Whereby I doubt not but it is visible that, its usefulness and uselessness laid in the balance against each other, the pretended usefulness is so far from outweighing that it can neither encourage nor excuse the using of punishments, which are not lawful to be used in our case without strong probability of success. But when to its uselessness mischief is added, and it is evident that more, much more, harm may be expected from it than good, your own argument returns upon you. For if it be reasonable to use it, because it may be serviceable to promote true religion and the salvation of souls, it is much more

---

[3] An apocryphal story about two seventeenth-century clergymen who were such persuasive preachers that it was fancifully supposed that each would convert the other.

reasonable to let it alone, if it may be more serviceable to the promoting falsehood and the perdition of souls. And therefore you will do well hereafter not to build so much on the usefulness of force, applied your way, your indirect and at-a-distance usefulness, which amounts but to the shadow and possibility of usefulness, but with an overbalancing weight of mischief and harm annexed to it. For upon a just estimate, this indirect and at-a-distance usefulness, can directly go for nothing, or rather less than nothing.

But suppose force, applied your way, were as useful for the promoting true religion, as I suppose I have showed it to be the contrary; it does not from hence follow that it is lawful and may be used. It may be very useful in a parish that has no teacher, or as bad as none, that a layman who wanted not abilities for it (for such we may suppose to be) should sometimes preach to them the doctrine of the Gospel, and stir them up to the duties of a good life. And yet this (which cannot be denied, may be at least 'indirectly, and at a distance, serviceable towards the promoting true religion and the salvation of souls') you will not (I imagine) allow for this usefulness to be lawful: and that because he has not commission and authority to do it. The same might be said of the administration of the sacraments, and any other function of the priestly office. This is just our case. Granting force, as you say, indirectly and at a distance, useful to the salvation of men's souls; yet it does not therefore follow that it is lawful for the magistrate to use it: because as the author says, the magistrate has no commission or authority to do so. For however you have put it thus, as you have framed the author's argument, 'force is utterly of no use for the promoting of true religion, and the salvation of souls; and therefore nobody can have any right to use any force or compulsion for the bringing men to the true religion'; yet the author does not, in those pages you quote, make the latter of these propositions an inference barely from the former, but makes use of it as a truth proved by several arguments he had before brought to that purpose. For though it be a good argument: it is not useful, therefore not fit to be used, yet this will not be good logic: it is useful, therefore anyone has a right to use it. For if the usefulness makes it lawful, it makes it lawful in any hands that can so apply it, and so private men may use it.

'Who can deny,' say you, 'but that force, indirectly and at a distance, may do some service towards the bringing men to embrace that truth, which otherwise they would never acquaint themselves with?' If this be good arguing in you, for the usefulness of force towards the saving of men's souls, give me leave to argue after the same fashion. (1) I will suppose, which you will not deny me, that as there are many who take up their religion upon wrong grounds, to the endangering of their souls, so there are many that abandon themselves to the heat of their lusts, to the endangering of their souls. (2) I will suppose, that as force applied your way is apt to make the inconsiderate consider, so force applied another way is apt to make the lascivious chaste. The argument then, in your form, will stand thus: 'Who can deny but that force, indirectly and at a distance, may, by castration, do some service towards bringing men to embrace that chastity, which otherwise they would never acquit themselves with?' Thus, you see, 'castration may, indirectly and at a distance, be serviceable towards the salvation of men's souls'. But will you say, from such a usefulness as this, because it may, indirectly and at a distance, conduce to the saving of any of his subjects' souls, that therefore the magistrate has a right to do it, and may by force make his subjects eunuchs for the kingdom of Heaven? It is not for the magistrate or anybody else, upon an imagination of its usefulness, to make use of any other means for the salvation of men's souls, than what the author and finisher of our faith has directed.

You may be mistaken in what you think useful. Dives[4] thought, and so perhaps should you and I too, if not better informed by the Scriptures, that it would be useful to rouse and awaken men if one should come to them from the dead. But he was mistaken. And we are told that if men will not hearken to Moses and the prophets' means appointed, neither will the strangeness nor terror of one coming from the dead persuade them. If what we are apt to think useful were thence to be concluded so, we should, I fear, be obliged to believe the miracles pretended to by the Church of Rome. For miracles, we know, were once useful for the promoting true religion and the salvation of souls, which is more than you say for your political punishments. But yet we must conclude that God thinks them not useful now, unless we will say (that which without impiety cannot be said), that the wise and benign disposer and governor of all things does not now use all useful means for promoting his own honour

---

[4] See Luke 16: 19–31: Dives, a rich man, in Hell, asks that Lazarus, a beggar, be resurrected in order to warn his brothers of the duty to aid the poor, but is told that sufficient instruction had been given already.

in the world and the good of souls. I think this consequence will hold as well as what you draw in near the same words.

Let us not therefore be more wise than our Maker, in that stupendous and supernatural work of our salvation. The Scripture that reveals it to us contains all that we can know, or do, in order to it; and where that is silent, it is in us presumption to direct. When you can show any commission in Scripture for the use of force to compel men to hear, any more than to embrace the doctrine of others that differ from them, we shall have reason to submit to it, and the magistrate have some ground to set up this new way of persecution. But till then, it will be fit for us to obey that precept of the Gospel, which bids us 'take heed what we hear' (Mark 4: 24). So that hearing is not always so useful as you suppose. If it [were], we should never have had so direct a caution against it. It is not any imaginary usefulness, you can suppose, which can make that a punishable crime, which the magistrate was never authorized to meddle with. 'Go and teach all nations', was a commission of our Saviour's; but there was not added to it, 'punish those that will nor hear and consider what you say'. No, but 'if they will not receive you, shake off the dust of your feet', leave them, and apply yourselves to some others. And St Paul knew no other means to make men hear but the preaching of the Gospel; as will appear to anyone who will read Romans 10: 14, etc.: 'Faith cometh by hearing, and hearing by the word of God.'

You go on, and in favour of your beloved force you tell us that it is not only useful but needful. And here after having at large, in the four following pages, set out the negligence or aversion, or other hindrances that keep men from examining, with that application and freedom of judgement they should, the grounds upon which they take up and persist in their religion, you come to conclude force necessary. Your words are:

> If men are generally averse to a due consideration of things, where they are most concerned to use it; if they usually take up their religion without examining it as they ought, and then grow so opinionative and so stiff in their prejudice, that neither the gentlest admonitions nor the most earnest entreaties shall ever prevail with them afterwards to do it; what means is there left (besides the grace of God) to reduce those of them that are gone into a wrong way, but to lay thorns and briars in it? That since they are deaf to all persuasions, the uneasiness they meet with may at least put them to

a stand, and incline them to lend an ear to those who tell them they have mistaken their way and offer to show them the right.

'What means is there left,' say you, 'but force?' What to do? 'To reduce men, who are out of it, into the right way.' So you tell us here. And to that, I say there is other means besides force: that which was appointed and made use of from the beginning, the preaching of the Gospel.

'But,' say you, 'to make them hear, to make them consider, to make them examine, there is no other means but punishment; and therefore it is necessary.'

I answer:

(1) What if God, for reasons best known to himself, would not have men compelled to hear; but thought the good tidings of salvation, and the proposals of life and death, means and inducements enough to make them hear and consider, now as well as heretofore? Then your means, your punishments, are not necessary. What if God would have men left to their freedom in this point, if they will hear, or if they will forbear, will you constrain them? Thus we are sure he did with his own people, and this when they were in captivity (Ezekiel 11: 5, 7), and it is very like were ill-treated for being of a different religion from the national, and so were punished as dissenters. Yet then God expected not that those punishments should force them to hearken more than at other times, as appears by Ezekiel 3: 11. And this also is the method of the Gospel. 'We are ambassadors for Christ; as if God did beseech you in Christ's stead', says St Paul (2 Corinthians 5: 20). If God thought it necessary to have men punished to make them give ear, he could have called magistrates to be spreaders and ministers of the Gospel, as well as poor fishermen, or Paul a persecutor; who yet wanted not power to punish where punishment was necessary, as is evident in Ananias and Sapphira, and the incestuous Corinthian.[5]

(2) What if God, foreseeing this force would be in the hands of men as passionate, humoursome, as liable to prejudice and error as the rest of their brethren, did not think it a proper means to bring men into the right way?

(3) What if there be other means? Then yours ceases to be necessary, upon the account that there is no means left. For you yourself allow

---

[5] For Ananias and Sapphira, see Acts 5; for the incestuous Corinthian, see 2 Corinthians 5 (St Paul pardons him in the name of Christ).

'that the grace of God is another means'. And I suppose you will not deny it to be both a proper and sufficient means and, which is more, the only means; such means as can work by itself, and without which all the force in the world can do nothing. God alone can open the ear that it may hear, and open the heart that it may understand; and this he does in his own good time, and to whom he is graciously pleased, but not according to the will and fancy of man, when he thinks fit, by punishments, to compel his brethren. If God has pronounced against any person or people, what he did against the Jews (Isaiah 6: 10), 'Make the heart of this people fat, and make their ears heavy and shut their eyes; lest they see with their eyes, and hear with their ears, and understand with their heart, and convert, and be healed'; will all the force you can use be a means to make them hear and understand, and be converted?

But, Sir, to return to your argument; you see 'no other means left (taking the world as we now find it) to make men thoroughly and impartially examine a religion, which they embraced upon such inducements as ought to have no sway at all in the matter, and with little or no examination of the proper grounds of it'. And thence you conclude the use of force, by the magistrates upon dissenters, necessary. And, I say, I see no other means left (taking the world as we now find it, wherein the magistrates never lay penalties, for matters of religion, upon those of their own church, nor is it to be expected they ever should) to make men of the national church, anywhere, thoroughly and impartially examine a religion, which they embrace upon such inducements, as ought to have no sway at all in the matter, and therefore with little or no examination of the proper grounds of it. And therefore I conclude the use of force by dissenters upon conformists necessary. I appeal to the world, whether this be not as just and natural a conclusion as yours.

Though if you will have my opinion, I think the more genuine consequence is that force, to make men examine matters of religion, is not necessary at all. But you may take which of these consequences you please. Both of them, I am sure, you cannot avoid. It is not for you and me, out of an imagination that they may be useful or are necessary, to prescribe means in the great and mysterious work of salvation, other than what God himself has directed. 'God has appointed force as useful or necessary, and therefore it is to be used', is a way of arguing, becoming the ignorance and humility of poor creatures. But 'I think force useful or necessary, and therefore it is to be used', has, methinks, a little too much presumption in it. You ask, 'What means else is there left?' None, say I, to be used by man, but what God himself has directed in the Scriptures, wherein are contained all the means and methods of salvation. 'Faith is the gift of God.' And we are not to use any other means to procure this gift to anyone, but what God himself has prescribed. If he has there appointed that any should be forced 'to hear those who tell them they have mistaken their way, and offer to show them the right'; and that they should be punished by the magistrate if they did not; it will be past doubt, it is to be made use of. But till that can be done, it will be in vain to say what other means is there left. If all the means God has appointed, to make men hear and consider, be 'exhortation in season and out of season', etc. together with prayer for them, and the example of meekness and a good life, this is all ought to be done, 'Whether they will hear or whether they will forbear.'

By these means the Gospel at first made itself to be heard through a great part of the world, and in a crooked and perverse generation, led away by lusts, humours, and prejudice, as well as this you complain of, prevailed with men to hear and embrace the truth, and take care of their own souls, without the assistance of any such force of the magistrate, which you now think needful. But whatever neglect or aversion there is in some men, impartially and thoroughly to be instructed, there will upon a due examination, I fear, be found no less a neglect and aversion in others, impartially and thoroughly to instruct them. It is not the talking even general truths in plain and clear language, much less a man's own fancies in scholastic or uncommon ways of speaking, an hour or two, once a week in public, that is enough to instruct even willing hearers in the way of salvation, and the grounds of their religion. They are not politic discourses which are the means of right information in the foundations of religion. For with such (sometimes venting antimonarchical principles, sometimes again preaching up nothing but absolute monarchy and passive obedience, as the one or other have been in vogue, and the way to preferment) have our churches rung in their turns, so loudly, that reasons and arguments proper and sufficient to convince men of the truth in the controverted points of religion, and to direct them in the right way to salvation, were scarce anywhere to be heard. But how many, do you think, by friendly and Christian debates with them at their houses, and by the gentle methods of the Gospel made use of in private conversation, might have been brought into the church; who, by railing from the pulpit, ill and unfriendly treatment out of it, and other neglects and miscarriages of those who claimed to be their teachers, have been driven from hearing them? Paint the defects and miscarriages frequent on this side, as well as you have done those on the other, and then do you, with all the world, consider whether those whom you so handsomely declaim against, for being misled by 'education, passion, humour, prejudice, obstinacy', etc. do deserve all the punishment. Perhaps it will be answered: if there be so much toil in it, that particular persons must be applied to, who then will be a minister? And what if a layman should reply: if there be so much toil in it, that doubts must be cleared, prejudices removed, foundations examined, etc. who then will be a protestant? The excuse will be as good hereafter for the one as for the other.

This new method of yours, which you say 'nobody can deny but that indirectly, and at a distance, it does some service towards bringing men to embrace the truth', was never yet thought on by the most refined persecutors. Though indeed it is not altogether unlike the plea made use of to excuse the late barbarous usage of the protestants in France (designed to extirpate the reformed religion there) from being a persecution for religion. The French king requires all his subjects to come to Mass; those who do not, are punished with a witness. For what? Not for their religion, say the pleaders for that discipline, but for disobeying the king's laws. So by your rule, the dissenters (for thither you would, and thither you must come, if you mean anything) must be punished. For what? Not for their religion, say you; not for 'following the light of their own reason; nor for obeying the dictates of their own consciences'. That you think not fit. For what then are they to be punished? 'To make them,' say you, 'examine the religion they have embraced, and the religion they have rejected.' So that they are punished, not for having offended against a law, for there is no law of the land that requires them to examine. And which now is the fairer plea, pray judge. You ought, indeed, to have the credit of this new invention. All other law-makers have constantly taken this method, that where anything was to be amended, the fault was first declared, and then penalties denounced against all those who, after a set time, should be found guilty of it. This the common sense of mankind, and the very reason of laws, which are intended not for punishment but correction, has made so plain that the subtlest and most refined law-makers have not got out of this course; nor have the most ignorant and barbarous nations missed it.

But you have outdone Solon and Lycurgus, Moses, and our Saviour, and are resolved to be a law-maker of a way by yourself. It is an old and obsolete way, and will not serve your turn, to begin with warnings and threats of penalties to be inflicted on those who do not reform, but continue to do that which you think they fail in. To allow of impunity to the innocent, or the opportunity of amendment to those who would avoid the penalties, are formalities not worth your notice. You are for a shorter and surer way. Take a whole tribe, and punish them at all adventures, whether guilty or no of the miscarriage which you would have amended, or without so much as telling them what it is you would have them do, but leaving them to find it out if they can. All these absurdities are contained in your way of proceeding, and are impossible to be avoided by anyone who will punish dissenters, and only dissenters, to make them 'consider and weigh the grounds of their religion, and impartially examine whether it be true or no; and upon what grounds they took it up, that so they may find and embrace the truth that must save them'.

But that this new sort of discipline may have all fair play, let us inquire, first, who it is you would have be punished. In the place above cited, they are 'those who are got into a wrong way, and are deaf to all persuasions'. If these are the men to be punished, let a law be made against them; you have my consent; and that is the proper course to have offenders punished. For you do not, I hope, intend to punish any fault by a law, which you do not name in the law; nor make a law against any fault you would not have punished. And now, if you are sincere and in earnest, and are (as a fair man should be) for what your words plainly signify, and nothing else: what will such a law serve for? Men in the wrong way are to be punished, but who are in the wrong way is the question. You have no more reason to determine it against one who differs from you, than he has to conclude against you, who differ from him. No, not though you have the magistrate and the national church on your side. For if to differ from them be to be in the wrong way, you, who are in the right way in England, will be in the wrong way in France. Everyone here must be judge for himself: and your law will reach nobody, till you have convinced him he is in the wrong way. And then there will be no need of punishment to make him consider, unless you will affirm again, what you have denied, and have men punished for embracing the religion they believe to be true, when it differs from yours or the public.

Besides being in the wrong way, those whom you would have punished must be such as are 'deaf to all persuasions'. But any such, I suppose, you will hardly find who hearken to nobody, not to those of their own way. If you mean by deaf to all persuasions, all persuasions of a contrary party or of a different church; such, I suppose, you may abundantly find in your own church, as well as elsewhere; and I presume to them you are so charitable, that you would not have them punished for not lending an ear to seducers. For constancy in the truth, and perseverance in the faith, is (I hope) rather to be encouraged, than by any penalties checked in the orthodox. And your church, doubtless, as well as all others, is orthodox to itself, in all its tenets. If you mean by all persuasion, all your persuasion, or all persuasion of those of your communion, you do but beg the question, and suppose you have a right to punish those who differ from and will not comply with you.

Your next words are:

> When men fly from the means of a right information, and will not so much as consider how reasonable it is thoroughly and impartially to examine a religion, which they embraced upon such inducements as ought to have no sway at all in the matter, and therefore with little or no examination of the proper grounds of it: what human method can be used to bring them to act like men, in an affair of such consequence, and to make a wiser and more rational choice, but that of laying such penalties upon them, as may balance the weight of those prejudices which inclined them to prefer a false way before the true, and recover them to so much sobriety and reflection, as seriously to put the question to themselves, whether it be really worth the while to undergo such inconveniencies, for adhering to a religion, which, for anything they know, may be false, or for rejecting another (if that be the case) which, for anything they know may be true, till they have brought it to the bar of reason, and given it a fair trial there?

Here you again bring in such as prefer a false way before a true: to which having answered already, I shall here say no more, but that, since our church will not allow those to be in a false way who are out of the Church of Rome, because the Church of Rome, which pretends infallibility, declares hers to be the only true way, certainly no one of our church, nor any other, which claims not infallibility, can require anyone to take the testimony of any church as a sufficient proof of the truth of her own doctrine. So that true and false, as it commonly happens, when we suppose them for ourselves or our party, in effect signify just nothing, or nothing to the purpose: unless we can think that true or false in England, which will not be so at Rome or Geneva, and vice versa.

As for the rest of the description of those on whom you are here laying penalties, I beseech you consider whether it will not belong to any of your church, let it be what it will. Consider, I say, if there be none in your church

> who have embraced her religion, upon such inducements as ought to have no sway at all in the matter, and therefore with little or no examination of the proper grounds of it; who have not been inclined by prejudices; who do not adhere to a religion, which for anything they know may be false, and who have rejected another which for anything they know may be true.

If you have any such in your communion (and it will be an admirable, though I fear but a little, flock that has none such in it), consider well what you have done. You have prepared rods for them, for which I imagine they will con you no thanks. For to make any tolerable sense of what you here propose, it must be understood that you would have men of all religions punished, to make them consider 'whether it be really worth the while to undergo such inconveniencies for adhering to a religion which for anything they know may be false'. If you hope to avoid that, by what you have said of true and false, and pretend that the supposed preference of the true way in your church ought to preserve its members from your punishment, you manifestly trifle. For every church's testimony, that it has chosen the true way, must be taken for itself; and then none will be liable, and your new invention of punishment is come to nothing: or else the differing churches' testimonies must be taken one for another; and then they will be all out of the true way, and your church need penalties as well as the rest. So that, upon your principles, they must all or none be punished. Choose which you please: one of them, I think, you cannot escape.

What you say in the next words, 'Where instruction is stiffly refused, and all admonitions and persuasions prove vain and ineffectual', differs nothing but in the way of expressing from 'deaf to all persuasions', and so that is answered already.

In another place, you give us another description of those you think ought to be punished, in these words: 'Those who refuse to embrace the doctrine, and submit to the spiritual government of the proper ministers of religion, who by special designation are appointed to exhort, admonish, reprove', etc. Here then, those to be punished 'are such who refuse to embrace the doctrine, and submit to the government of the proper ministers of religion'. Whereby we are as much still at uncertainty as we were before, who those are who (by your scheme and laws suitable to it) are to be punished, since every church has, as it thinks, its proper ministers of religion. And if you mean those that refuse to embrace the doctrine, and submit to the government of the ministers of another church, then all men will be guilty, and must be punished; even those of your church, as well as others. If you mean those who refuse, etc. the ministers of their own church, very few will incur your penalties. But if, by these proper ministers of religion, the ministers of some particular church are intended, why do you not name it? Why are you so reserved in a matter wherein, if you speak not out, all the rest that you say will be to no purpose? Are men to be punished for refusing to embrace the doctrine, and submit to the government, of the proper ministers of the Church of Geneva?

For this time (since you have declared nothing to the contrary), let me suppose you of that church; and then, I am sure that is it that you would name. For of whatever church you are, if you think the ministers of any one church ought to be hearkened to and obeyed, it must be those of your own. There are persons to be punished, you say. This you contend for all through your book, and lay so much stress on it that you make the preservation and propagation of religion and the salvation of souls to depend on it; and yet you describe them by so general and equivocal marks that, unless it be upon suppositions which nobody will grant you, I dare say neither you nor anybody else will be able to find one guilty. Pray find me, if you can, a man whom you can judicially prove (for he that is to be punished by law must be fairly tried) is in a wrong way, in respect of his faith; I mean 'who is deaf to all persuasions, who flies from all means of a right information, who refuses to embrace the doctrine, and submit to the government of the spiritual pastors'. And when you have done that, I think, I may allow you what power you please to punish him, without any prejudice to the toleration the author of the letter proposes.

But why, I pray, all this boggling, all this loose talking as if you knew not what you meant, or durst not speak it out? Would you be for punishing somebody, you know not whom? I do not think so ill of you. Let me then speak out for you. The evidence of the argument has convinced you that men ought not to be persecuted for their religion; that the severities in use amongst Christians cannot be defended; that the magistrate has not authority to compel anyone to his religion. This you are forced to yield.

But you would fain retain some power in the magistrate's hands to punish dissenters, upon a new pretence, viz. not for having embraced the doctrine and worship they believe to be true and right, but for not having well considered their own and the magistrate's religion. To show you that I do not speak wholly without book, give me leave to mind you of one passage of yours. The words are: 'Penalties to put them upon a serious and impartial examination of the controversy between the magistrates and them.' Though these words be not intended to tell us who you would have punished, yet it may be plainly inferred from them. And they more clearly point out whom you aim at, than all the foregoing places, where you seem to (and should) describe them. For they are such as between whom and the magistrate there is a controversy; that is, in short, who differ from the magistrate in religion. And now indeed you have given us a note by which these you would have punished may be made known. We have, with much ado, found out at last whom it is we may presume you would have punished. Which in other cases is usually not very difficult, because there the faults to be mended easily design the persons to be corrected. But yours is a new method, and unlike all that ever went before it.

In the next place, let us see for what you would have them punished. You tell us, and it will easily be granted you, that not to examine and weigh impartially, and without prejudice or passion (all which, for shortness' sake, we will express by this one word 'consider'), the religion one embraces or refuses, is a fault very common and very prejudicial to true religion, and the salvation of men's souls. But penalties and punishments are very necessary, say you, to remedy this evil.

Let us see now how you apply this remedy. Therefore, say you, let all dissenters be punished. Why? Have no dissenters considered of religion? Or have all conformists considered? That you yourself will not say. Your project therefore is just as reasonable, as if a lethargy growing epidemical in England, you should propose to have a law made to blister and scarify[6] and shave the heads of all who wear gowns: though it be certain

---

[6] To cut lightly, or score.

that neither all who wear gowns are lethargic, nor all who are lethargic wear gowns:

> – *Dii te Damasippe deæque*
> *Verum ob consilium donent tonsore.*[7]

For there could not be certainly a more learned advice, than that one man should be pulled by the ears because another is asleep. This, when you have considered of it again, for I find, according to your principle, all men have now and then need to be jogged, you will, I guess, be convinced it is not like a fair physician to apply a remedy to a disease but, like an enraged enemy, to vent one's spleen upon a party. Common sense, as well as common justice, requires that the remedies of laws and penalties should be directed against the evil that is to be removed, wherever it be found. And if the punishment you think so necessary be, as you pretend, to cure the mischief you complain of, you must let it pursue and fall on the guilty, and those only, in what company soever they are; and not, as you here propose, and is the highest injustice, punish the innocent considering dissenter with the guilty; and, on the other side, let the inconsiderate guilty conformist escape with the innocent. For one may rationally presume that the national church has some, nay more in proportion, of those who little consider or concern themselves about religion, than any congregation of dissenters. For conscience, or the care of their souls, being once laid aside, interest, of course, leads men into that society, where the protection and countenance of the government, and hopes of preferment, bid fairest to their remaining desires. So that if careless, negligent, inconsiderate men in matters of religion, who 'without being forced would not consider', are to be roused into a care of their souls and a search after truth by punishments, the national religion, in all countries, will certainly have a right to the greatest share of those punishments; at least not to be wholly exempt from them.

This is that which the author of the letter, as I remember, complains of; and that justly, viz. 'That the pretended care of men's souls always expresses itself, in those who would have force any way made use of to that end, in very unequal methods; some persons being to be treated with severity, whilst others guilty of the same faults, are not to be so much

---

[7] 'May the gods and goddesses send you a barber for your good advice, Damasippus.' Horace, *Satires* II. 3, 16–17. Horace ironically suggests to an interlocutor that a shave will change his mind for the better.

as touched.' Though you are got pretty well out of the deep mud, and renounce punishments directly for religion, yet you stick still in this part of the mire; whilst you would have dissenters punished to make them consider, but would not have anything done to conformists, though ever so negligent in this point of considering. The author's letter pleased me, because it is equal to all mankind, is direct, and will, I think, hold everywhere, which I take to be a good mark of truth. For I shall always suspect that neither to comport with the truth of religion, or the design of the Gospel, which is suited to only some one country or party. What is true and good in England, will be true and good at Rome too, in China, or Geneva. But whether your great and only method for the propagating of truth, by bringing the inconsiderate by punishments to consider, would (according to your way of applying your punishments only to dissenters from the national religion) be of use in those countries, or anywhere but where you suppose the magistrate to be in the right, judge you. Pray, Sir, consider a little, whether prejudice has not some share in your way of arguing. For this is your position: 'Men are generally negligent in examining the grounds of their religion.' This I grant. But could there be a more wild and incoherent consequence drawn from it, than this: 'therefore dissenters must be punished'?

...

To conclude, your system is, in short, this: You would have all men (laying aside prejudice, humour, passion, etc.) examine the grounds of their religion, and search for the truth. This, I confess, is heartily to be wished. The means that you propose to make men do this, is that dissenters should be punished to make them do so. It is as if you had said: men generally are guilty of a fault, therefore let one sect, who have the ill luck to be of an opinion different from the magistrate, be punished. This at first sight shocks any who has the least spark of sense, reason, or justice. But having spoken of this already, and concluding that upon second thoughts you yourself will be ashamed of it, let us consider it put so as to be consistent with common sense, and with all the advantage it can bear; and then let us see what you can make of it: 'Men are negligent in examining the religions they embrace, refuse, or persist in; therefore it is fit they should be punished to make them do it.' This is a consequence, indeed, which may, without defiance to common sense, be drawn from it. This is the use, the only use, which you think punishment can indirectly, and at a distance, have in matters of religion. You would have men by punishments driven to examine. What? Religion. To what end? To bring them to the knowledge of the truth. But I answer, first, everyone has not the ability to do this; secondly, everyone has not the opportunity to do it.

Would you have every poor protestant, for example, in the Palatinate, examine thoroughly whether the pope be infallible, or head of the church; whether there be a purgatory; whether saints are to be prayed to, or the dead prayed for; whether the Scripture be the only rule of faith; whether there be no salvation out of the church; and whether there be no church without bishops; and a hundred other questions in controversy between the papists and those protestants; and when he had mastered these, go on to fortify himself against the opinions and objections of other churches he differs from? This, which is no small task, must be done before a man can have brought his religion to the bar of reason, and give it a fair trial there. And if you will punish men till this be done, the countryman must leave off ploughing and sowing, and betake himself to the study of Greek and Latin; and the artisan must sell his tools, to buy fathers[8] and schoolmen, and leave his family to starve.

If something less than this will satisfy you, pray tell me what is enough. Have they considered and examined enough, if they are satisfied themselves where the truth lies? If this be the limits of their examination, you will find few to punish, unless you will punish them to make them do what they have done already; for, however he came by his religion, there is scarce anyone to be found who does not own himself satisfied that he is in the right. Or else, must they be punished to make them consider and examine till they embrace that which you choose for truth? If this be so, what do you but in effect choose for them, when yet you would have men punished, 'to bring them to such a care of their souls, that no other person might choose for them'? If it be truth in general you would have them by punishments driven to seek; that is to offer matter of dispute, and not a rule of discipline; for to punish anyone to make him seek till he find truth, without a judge of truth, is to punish for you know not what; and is all one as if you should whip a scholar to make him find out the square root of a number you do not know. I wonder not therefore that you could not resolve with yourself what degree of severity you would have used, nor how long continued, when you dare not speak out directly

[8] Works by Fathers of the Church, i.e. prominent theologians of the first centuries of Christianity.

whom you would have punished, and are far from being clear to what end they should be under penalties.

Consonant to this uncertainty, of whom or what to be punished, you tell us, 'that there is no question of the success of this method. Force will certainly do, if duly proportioned to the design of it.' What, I pray, is the design of it? I challenge you, or any man living, out of what you have said in your book, to tell me directly what it is. In all other punishments that ever I heard of yet, till now that you have taught the world a new method, the design of them has been to cure the crime they are denounced against, and so I think it ought to be here. What I beseech you is the crime here? Dissenting? That you say not anywhere is a fault. Besides you tell us, 'that the magistrate has not authority to compel anyone to his religion': and that you do 'not require that men should have no rule but the religion of the country'. And the power you ascribe to the magistrate is given him to bring men, 'not to his own, but to the true religion'. If dissenting be not the fault, is it that a man does not examine his own religion, and the grounds of it? Is that the crime your punishments are designed to cure? Neither that dare you say; lest you displease more than you satisfy with your new discipline. And then again (as I said before), you must tell us how far you would have them examine, before you punish them for not doing it. And I imagine, if that were all we required of you, it would be long enough before you would trouble us with a law, that should prescribe to everyone how far he was to examine matters of religion; wherein if he failed and came short, he was to be punished; if he performed, and went in his examination to the bounds set by the law, he was acquitted and free. Sir, when you consider it again, you will perhaps think this a case reserved to the great day when the secrets of all hearts shall be laid open; for I imagine it is beyond the power or judgement of man, in that variety of circumstances, in respect of parts, tempers, opportunities, helps, etc. men are in, in this world, to determine what is everyone's duty in this great business of search, inquiry, examination, or to know when anyone has done it. That which makes me believe you will be of this mind is, that where you undertake for the success of this method, if rightly used, it is with a limitation, upon such as are not altogether incurable.

So that when your remedy is prepared according to art, which art is yet unknown; and rightly applied, and given in a due dose, all which are secrets; it will then infallibly cure. Whom? All that are not incurable by it. And so will a pippin posset,[9] eating fish in Lent, or a Presbyterian lecture, certainly cure all that are not incurable by them; for I am sure you do not mean it will cure all, but those who are absolutely incurable, because you yourself allow one means left of cure, when yours will not do, viz. the grace of God. Your words are: 'what means is there left (except the grace of God) to reduce them, but lay thorns and briars in their way'. And here also, in the place we were considering, you tell us, 'the incurable are to be left to God'. Whereby, if you mean they are to be left to those means he has ordained for men's conversion and salvation, yours must never be made use of: for he indeed has prescribed preaching and hearing of his word; but as for those who will not hear, I do not find anywhere that he has commanded they should be compelled or beaten to it.

There is a third thing that you are as tender and reserved in, as either naming the criminals to be punished, or positively telling us the end for which they should be punished: and that is with what sort of penalties, what degree of punishment they should be forced. You are indeed so gracious to them, that you renounce the severities and penalties hitherto made use of. You tell us, they should be but moderate penalties. But if we ask you what are moderate penalties, you confess you cannot tell us. So that by moderate here you yet mean nothing. You tell us 'the outward force to be applied should be duly tempered'. But what that due temper is, you do not, or cannot say: and so in effect it signifies just nothing. Yet if in this you are not plain and direct, all the rest of your design will signify nothing; for it being to have some men, and to some end, punished, yet if it cannot be found what punishment is to be used, it is, notwithstanding all you have said, utterly useless. You tell us, modestly, 'that to determine precisely the just measure of the punishment, will require some consideration'. If the faults were precisely determined, and could be proved, it would require no more consideration to determine the measure of the punishment in this than it would in any other case where those were known. But where the fault is undefined, and the guilt not to be proved (as I suppose it will be found in this present business of examining), it will without doubt require consideration to proportion the force to the design. Just so much consideration as it will require to fit a coat to the moon, or proportion a shoe to the foot of those who inhabit her; for to proportion a punishment to a fault that you do not name, and so we in

[9] A therapeutic drink made from pips of fruit and curdled milk.

charity ought to think you do not yet know; and a fault that, when you have named it, will be impossible to be proved who are or are not guilty of it; will I suppose require as much consideration as to fit a shoe to feet whose size and shape are not known.

...

... I think the author, and whosoever else are most for liberty of conscience, might be content with the toleration you allow, by condemning the laws about religion, now in force, and rest satisfied till you had made your new method consistent and practicable, by telling the world plainly and directly,

(1) Who are to be punished.
(2) For what.
(3) With what punishments.
(4) How long.
(5) What advantage to true religion it would be, if magistrates everywhere did so punish.
(6) And lastly, whence the magistrate had commission to do so.

When you have done this plainly and intelligibly, without keeping in the uncertainty of general expressions, and without supposing all along your church in the right and your religion the true (which can no more be allowed to you in this case, whatever your church or religion be, than it can be to a papist or a Lutheran, a Presbyterian or an Anabaptist; nay no more to you, than it can be allowed to a Jew or a Mahometan) when, I say, you have by settling these points framed the parts of your new engine, set it together, and shown that it will work, without doing more harm than good in the world; I think then men may be content to submit to it. But imagining this, and an engine to show the perpetual motion, will be found out together, I think toleration in a very good state, notwithstanding your answer; wherein you have said so much for it, and for aught I see nothing against it: unless an impracticable chimera be, in your opinion, something mightily to be apprehended.

We have now seen and examined the main of your treatise; and therefore I think I might here end, without going any farther. But, that you may not think yourself or any of your arguments neglected, I will go over the remainder, and give you my thoughts on everything I shall meet with in it that seems to need any answer.

In one place you argue against the author thus: if then the author's fourth proposition, as you call it, viz., that force is of no use for promoting true religion and the salvation of souls 'be not true (as perhaps by this time it appears it is not) then the last proposition, which is built upon it, must fall with it'; which last proposition is this, viz. 'that nobody can have any right to use any outward force or compulsion to bring men to the true religion, and so to salvation'. If this proposition were built, as you allege, upon that which you call his fourth, then indeed if the fourth fell, this built upon it would fall with it. But that not being the author's proposition (as I have showed), nor this built wholly on it, but on other reasons (as I have already proved, and anyone may see in several parts of his letter …) what you allege falls of itself.

The business of the next paragraph is to prove that if 'force be useful, then somebody must certainly have a right to use it'. The first argument you go about to prove it by is this: 'That usefulness is as good an argument to prove there is somewhere a right to use it, as uselessness is to prove nobody has such a right.' If you consider the things of whose usefulness or uselessness we are speaking, you will perhaps be of another mind. It is punishment, or force used in punishing. Now all punishment is some evil, some inconvenience, some suffering: by taking away or abridging some good thing, which he who is punished has otherwise a right to. Now to justify the bringing any such evil upon any man, two things are requisite. First, that he who does it has commission and power so to do. Secondly, that it be directly useful for the procuring some greater good. Whatever punishment one man uses to another, without these two conditions, whatever he may pretend, proves an injury and injustice, and so of right ought to have been let alone. And therefore, though usefulness (which is one of the conditions that makes punishments just) when it is away, may hinder punishments from being lawful in anybody's hands; yet usefulness, when present (being but one of those conditions), cannot give the other, which is a commission to punish; without which also punishment is unlawful.

From whence it follows, that though useless punishment be unlawful from any hand, yet useful punishment from every hand is not lawful. A man may have the stone, and it may be useful (more than indirectly and at-a-distance useful) to him to be cut; but yet this usefulness will not justify the most skilful surgeon in the world, by force to make him endure the pain and hazard of cutting; because he has no commission, no right without the patient's own consent to do so. Nor is it a good argument, cutting will be useful to him, therefore there is a right somewhere to cut him, whether he will or no. Much less will there be an argument for any right, if there be only a possibility that it may prove useful indirectly and by accident.

Your other argument is this: if force or punishment be of necessary use, 'then it must be acknowledged, that there is a right somewhere to use it; unless we will say (what without impiety cannot be said) that the wise and benign disposer and governor of all things has not furnished mankind with competent means for the promoting his own honour in the world, and the good of souls'. If your way of arguing be true, it is demonstration[10] that force is not of necessary use. For I argue thus, in your form: We must acknowledge force not to be of necessary use, 'unless we will say (what without impiety cannot be said) that the wise disposer and governor of all things did not, for above three hundred years after Christ, furnish his church with competent means for promoting his own honour in the world, and the good of souls'. It is for you to consider whether these arguments be conclusive or no. This I am sure, the one is as conclusive as the other. But if your supposed usefulness places a right somewhere to use it, pray tell me in whose hands it places it in Turkey, Persia, or China, or any country where Christians of different churches live under a heathen or Mahometan sovereign? And if you cannot tell me in whose hands it places it there (as I believe you will find it pretty hard to do); there are then (it seems) some places where (upon your supposition of the necessary usefulness of force) 'the wise and benign governor and disposer of all things has not furnished men with competent means for promoting his own honour and the good of souls'; unless you will grant that the 'wise and benign disposer and governor of all things has, for the promoting of his honour and the good of souls, placed a power in Mahometan or heathen princes to punish Christians, to bring them to consider reasons and arguments proper to convince them'. But this is the advantage of so fine an invention, as that of force doing some service indirectly and at a distance; which usefulness, if we may believe you, places a right in Mahometan or pagan princes' hands to use force upon Christians; for fear lest mankind in those countries should be unfurnished with means for the promoting God's honour and the good of souls.

...

---

[10] Demonstrable.

You endeavour to prove, against the author, that civil society is not instituted only for civil ends, i.e. the procuring, preserving, and advancing men's civil interests. Your words are:

> I must say that our author does but beg the question, when he affirms that the commonwealth is constituted only for the procuring, preserving, and advancing of the civil interests of the members of it. That commonwealths are instituted for these ends, no man will deny. But if there be any other ends besides these, attainable by the civil society and government, there is no reason to affirm that these are the only ends for which they are designed. Doubtless commonwealths are instituted for the attaining of all the benefits which political government can yield. And therefore, if the spiritual and eternal interests of men may any way be procured or advanced by political government, the procuring and advancing those interests must in all reason be reckoned among the ends of civil societies, and so, consequently, fall within the compass of the magistrate's jurisdiction.

I have set down your words at large, to let the reader see that you of all men had the least reason to tell the author he does but beg the question; unless you mean to justify yourself by the pretence of his example. You argue thus: 'If there be any other ends attainable by civil society, then civil interests are not the only ends for which commonwealths are instituted.' And how do you prove there be other ends? Why thus, 'Doubtless commonwealths are instituted for the attaining of all the benefits which political government can yield.' Which is as clear a demonstration, as 'doubtless' can make it to be. The question is, whether civil society be instituted only for civil ends? You say, no; and your proof is, because doubtless it is instituted for other ends. If I now say, doubtless this is a good argument; is not everyone bound without more ado to admit it for such? If not, doubtless you are in danger to be thought to beg the question.

But notwithstanding you say here that the author begs the question, in the following page you tell us, 'That the author offers three considerations which seem to him abundantly to demonstrate that the civil power neither can, nor ought in any manner to be extended to the salvation of souls.' He does not then beg the question. For the question being, 'Whether civil interest be the only end of civil society', he gives this reason for the negative, 'That civil power has nothing to do with the salvation of souls'; and offers three considerations for the proof of it. For it will always be a good consequence that, if the civil power has nothing to do with the salvation of souls, 'then civil interest is the only end of civil society'. And the reason of it is plain: because a man having no other interest but either in this world or the world to come, if the end of civil society reach not to a man's interest in the other world (all which is comprehended in the salvation of his soul), it is plain that the sole end of civil society is civil interest, under which the author comprehends the good things of this world.

And now let us examine the truth of your main position, viz. 'That civil society is instituted for the attaining all the benefits that it may any way yield.' Which, if true, then this position must be true, viz. 'That all societies whatsoever are instituted for the attaining all the benefits that they may any way yield', there being nothing peculiar to civil society in the case, why that society should be instituted for the attaining all the benefits it can any way yield, and other societies not. By which argument it will follow, that all societies are instituted for one and the same end, i.e. 'for the attaining all the benefits that they can any way yield'. By which account there will be no difference between church and state; a commonwealth and an army; or between a family, and the East India Company; all which have hitherto been thought distinct sorts of societies instituted for different ends. If your hypothesis hold good, one of the ends of the family must be to preach the Gospel, and administer the sacraments; and one business of an army to teach languages, and propagate religion; because these are benefits some way or other attainable by those societies; unless you take want of commission and authority to be a sufficient impediment; and that will be so too in other cases.

It is a benefit to have true knowledge and philosophy embraced and assented to, in any civil society or government. But will you say, therefore, that it is a benefit to the society, or one of the ends of government, that all who are not peripatetics[11] should be punished, to make men find out the truth and profess it? This indeed might be thought a fit way to make some men embrace the peripatetic philosophy, but not a proper way to find the truth. For perhaps the peripatetic philosophy may not be true; perhaps a great many may have not time nor parts to study it; and perhaps a great many who have studied it cannot be convinced of the truth of it: and therefore it cannot be a benefit to the commonwealth, nor one of

---

[11] Aristotelians.

the ends of it, that these members of the society should be disturbed, and diseased[12] to no purpose, when they are guilty of no fault.

For just the same reason, it cannot be a benefit to civil society, that men should be punished in Denmark, for not being Lutherans; in Geneva, for not being Calvinists; and in Vienna, for not being papists, as a means to make them find out the true religion. For so, upon your grounds, men must be treated in those places, as well as in England, for not being of the Church of England. And then I beseech you, consider the great benefit will accrue to men in society by this method; and I suppose it will be a hard thing for you to prove, that ever civil governments were instituted to punish men for not being of this or that sect in religion: however by accident, indirectly and at a distance, it may be an occasion to one perhaps of a thousand, or a hundred, to study that controversy, which is all you expect from it. If it be a benefit, pray tell me what benefit it is. A civil benefit it cannot be. For men's civil interests are disturbed, injured, and impaired by it. And what spiritual benefit can that be to any multitude of men, to be punished for dissenting from a false or erroneous profession, I would have you find out: unless it be a spiritual benefit to be in danger to be driven into a wrong way. For if in all differing sects, [all but] one[13] is in the wrong, it is a hundred to one but that from which one dissents, and is punished for dissenting from, is the wrong.

I grant it is past doubt that the nature of man is so covetous of good, that no one would have excluded from any action he does, or from any institution he is concerned in, any manner of good or benefit that it might any way yield. And if this be your meaning, it will not be denied you. But then you speak very improperly, or rather very mistakenly, if you call such benefits as may any way (i.e. indirectly and at a distance, or by accident) be attained by civil or any other society, the ends for which it is instituted. Nothing can 'in reason be reckoned amongst the ends of any society', but what may in reason be supposed to be designed by those who enter into it. Now nobody can in reason suppose that anyone entered into civil society for the procuring, securing, or advancing the salvation of his soul, when he, for that end, needed not the force of civil society. 'The procuring, therefore, securing, and advancing the spiritual and eternal interest of men, cannot in reason be reckoned amongst the ends of civil

---

[12] Troubled or inconvenienced.
[13] The phrase 'all but one' better fits the sense and is found in later editions of Locke's *Works*.

societies', though perhaps it might so fall out, that in some particular instance, some man's spiritual interest might be advanced by your or any other way of applying civil force. A nobleman, whose chapel is decayed or fallen, may make use of his dining-room for praying and preaching. Yet whatever benefit were attainable by this use of the room, nobody can in reason reckon this among the ends for which it was built; no more than the accidental breeding of some bird in any part of it (though it were a benefit it yielded) could in reason be reckoned among the ends of building the house.

But, say you,

> doubtless commonwealths are instituted for the attaining of all the benefits which political government can yield; and therefore if the spiritual and eternal interests of men may any way be procured or advanced by political government, the procuring and advancing those interests, must in all reason be reckoned amongst the ends of civil society, and so consequently fall within the compass of the magistrate's jurisdiction.

Upon the same grounds, I thus reason: Doubtless churches are instituted for the attaining of all the benefits which ecclesiastical government can yield; and therefore, if the temporal and secular interests of men may any way be procured or advanced by ecclesiastical polity, the procuring and advancing those interests must in all reason be reckoned among the ends of religious societies, and so consequently fall within the compass of churchmen's jurisdiction. The Church of Rome has openly made its advantage of 'secular interests to be procured or advanced, indirectly, and at a distance, and in *ordine ad spiritualia*';[14] all which ways, if I mistake not English, are comprehended under your 'any way'. But I do not remember that any of the reformed churches have hitherto directly professed it. But there is a time for all things. And if the commonwealth once invades the spiritual ends of the church, by meddling with the salvation of souls, which she has always been so tender of, who can deny that the church should have liberty to make herself some amends by reprisals?

But, Sir, however you and I may argue from wrong suppositions, yet unless the Apostle (Ephesians 4), where he reckons up the church-officers which Christ has instituted in his church, had told us they were

---

[14] Refers to the church's (alleged) right to control secular things that are necessary to spiritual ends.

for some other ends than 'for the perfecting of the saints, for the work of the ministry, for the edifying of the body of Christ'; the advancing of their secular interests will scarce be allowed to be their business, or within the compass of their jurisdiction. Nor till it can be shown that civil society is instituted for spiritual ends, or that the magistrate has commission to interpose his authority, or use force in matters of religion; your supposition 'of spiritual benefits indirectly and at a distance attainable' by political government, will never prove the advancing of those interests by force to be the magistrate's business, 'and to fall within the compass of his jurisdiction'. And until then, the force of the arguments which the author has brought against it ... will hold good.

Commonwealths, or civil societies and governments, if you will believe the judicious Mr Hooker, are, as St Peter calls them (1 Peter 2: 13) *anthropine ktisis*, the contrivance and institution of man; and he shows there for what end, viz. 'for the punishment of evil-doers, and the praise of them that do well'. I do not find anywhere that it is for the punishment of those who are not in church-communion with the magistrate, to make them study controversies in religion, or hearken to those who will tell them, 'they have mistaken their way, and offer to show them the right one'. You must show them such a commission, if you say it is from God. And in all societies instituted by man, the ends of them can be no other than what the institutors appointed, which I am sure could not be their spiritual and eternal interest. For they could not stipulate[15] about these one with another, nor submit this interest to the power of the society, or any sovereign they should set over it. There are nations in the West Indies which have no other end of their society, but their mutual defence against their common enemies. In these, their captain or prince is sovereign commander in time of war; but in time of peace, neither he nor anybody else has any authority over any of the society. You cannot deny but other, even temporal ends, are attainable by these commonwealths, if they had been otherwise instituted and appointed to these ends. But all your saying, 'doubtless commonwealths are instituted for the attaining of all the benefits which they can yield', will not give authority to any one, or more, in such a society, by political government or force, to procure directly or indirectly other benefits than that for which it was instituted: and therefore there it falls not within the compass of those princes'

---

[15] Make contractual agreements.

jurisdiction to punish anyone of the society for injuring another, because he has no commission so to do; whatever reason you may think there is, that that should be reckoned amongst the ends of their society.

But to conclude: your argument has that defect in it which turns it upon yourself. And that is, that the procuring and advancing the spiritual and eternal interests of souls, your way, is not a benefit to the society: and so upon your own supposition, 'the procuring and advancing the spiritual interest of souls, any way, cannot be one of the ends of civil society'; unless the procuring and advancing the spiritual interest of souls, in a way proper to do more harm than good towards the salvation of souls, be to be accounted such a benefit as to be one of the ends of civil societies. For that yours is such a way, I have proved already. So that were it hard to prove that political government, whose only instrument is force, could no way by force (however applied) more advance than hinder the spiritual and eternal interest of men; yet having proved it against your particular new way of applying force, I have sufficiently vindicated the author's doctrine from anything you have said against it. Which is enough for my present purpose ...

# From *A Third Letter concerning Toleration in Defence of the Argument of the Letter concerning Toleration, Briefly Considered and Answered* (1691)

…

Where I say that 'force may indirectly and at a distance do some service, etc.' you say you do not understand what I mean by 'doing service at a distance towards the bringing men to salvation, or to embrace truth, unless perhaps it be what others, in propriety of speech, call by accident'. But I make little doubt but all other men that read the place, do well enough understand what I mean by those words; even such as do not understand what it is to 'do service by accident'. And if by doing service by accident, you mean doing it but seldom and beside the intention of the agent, I assure you that is not the thing that I mean when I say force may indirectly and at a distance do some service. For in that use of force which I defend, the effect is both intended by him that uses it, and withal, I doubt not, so often attained as abundantly to manifest the usefulness of it.

'But be it what it will,' say you, 'it is such a service as cannot be ascribed to the direct and proper efficacy of force. And so,' say you,

> force indirectly and at a distance may do some service. I grant it: Make your best of it. What do you conclude from thence? That therefore the magistrate may make use of it? That I deny. That such an indirect and at a distance usefulness will authorize the civil power in the use of it, that will never be proved.

It seems then you grant at last, that force may, indirectly and at a distance, do some service in the matter we are speaking of. But where, I beseech you, do I affirm that 'therefore the magistrate may make use of it'? Methinks you might remember that I assert force to be generally necessary, as well as useful, to bring erring persons to the way of truth: and that accordingly, I ground the magistrate's authority to use force for that purpose upon the necessity as well as usefulness of it. Now whether such an indirect and at a distance usefulness (as you are pleased to call it) together with a general necessity of force, will not authorize the Civil Power in the use of it, you will perhaps be better able to judge when you have answered a plain question or two.

That force does some service toward the making of scholars and artists, I suppose you will easily grant. Give me leave therefore to ask, how it does it? I supposed you will say, not by its direct and proper efficacy (for force is no more capable to work learning or arts than the belief of the true religion in men, by its direct and proper efficacy), but by prevailing upon those who are designed for scholars or artists to receive instruction, and to apply themselves to the use of those means and helps which are proper to make them what they are designed to be: that is, it does it indirectly, and at a distance. Well then, if all the usefulness of force towards the bringing scholars or apprentices to the learning or skill they are designed to attain be only an indirect and at a distance usefulness: I pray, what is it that warrants and authorizes schoolmasters, tutors, or masters, to use force upon their scholars or apprentices to bring them to learning or to the skill of their arts and trades, if such an indirect and at a distance usefulness of force, together with that necessity of it which experience discovers, will not do it? I believe you will acknowledge that even such a usefulness, together with that necessity, will serve the turn in these cases. But then I would fain know why the same kind of usefulness, joined with the like necessity, will not as well do it in the case before us. I confess I see no reason why it should not: nor do I believe you can assign any.

...

You say further: 'As force applied your way is apt to make the inconsiderate consider, so force applied another way is apt to make the lascivious chaste, etc. Thus you see castration may indirectly, and at a distance, be serviceable towards the salvation of men's souls. But will you say, from such usefulness as this, that therefore the magistrate has a right to do it, and may by force make his subjects eunuchs for the Kingdom of Heaven?' Where again I must tell you, that unless you will say castration is necessary, as well as apt, to make the lascivious chaste, this will afford you no advantage. Now I suppose you will not say castration is necessary, because I hope you acknowledge that marriage, and that grace which God denies to none who seriously ask it, are sufficient for that purpose.

But, however, this is not a like case. For if castration makes any lascivious person chaste, it does it by taking away the part upon which the power of offending depends: whereas the force which I think may be used in order to the curing men of destructive errors concerning the way of salvation, does not destroy the possibility of erring by taking away or any way disabling the offending part, but leaves men's brains safe in their skulls. Indeed, if I had said that to cure men of damnable or dangerous errors it is useful to knock out their brains, the case had been exactly parallel (as far as usefulness goes). But since I say no such thing, I hope no man that has any brains will say it is.

...

You add, 'When you can show any commission in Scripture, for the use of force to compel men to hear, any more than to embrace the doctrine of others that differ from them, we shall have reason to submit to it, and the magistrate have some ground to set up this new way of persecution.' To which I answer: though no force can compel men to embrace (if by that you mean, to believe) the doctrine of others that differ from them, yet some force may induce those who would not otherwise to hear what may and ought to move them to embrace the truth. And if the magistrate has commission to use convenient force or penalties for that purpose, his doing it will not be the setting up a new way of persecution, but the discharging of an old duty. I call it so because it is as old as the law of nature, in which the magistrate's commission lies, as has been shown already. For the Scripture does not properly give it to him, but presupposes it (and speaks of him as antecedently entrusted with it) as it does also the law of nature, which is God's law as well as the Scripture.

...

... I shall, without more ado, address myself to manifest the consistency and practicableness of my new method (as you will have it) in the way you yourself prescribe me, viz. by telling the world plainly and directly,

(1) Who are to be punished.
(2) For what.
(3) With what punishments.
(4) How long.
(5) What advantage to true religion it would be, if magistrates everywhere did so punish.
(6) And lastly, whence the magistrate had commission to do so.

Which when I have done, and by settling these points have framed the parts of my new engine, set it together and showed that it will work, without doing more harm than good in the world, you tell me you think then men may be content to submit to it. Only before I do this, I crave leave to take some notice of one of the conditions you are pleased to lay upon me. For you require me to do it, not only 'plainly and intelligently, without keeping in the uncertainty of general expressions' (which is reasonable enough) but likewise 'without supposing all along my church in the right' and my 'religion the true'.

Now as to this latter condition, I confess I do not see how you can oblige me to it. For if my church be in the right, and my religion be the true, why may I not all along suppose it to be so?

You say 'this can no more be allowed to me in this case, whatever' my 'church or religion be, than it can be to a papist or a Lutheran, a Presbyterian or an Anabaptist; nay no more to me, than it can be allowed to a Jew or a Mahometan'. No, Sir? Not whatever my church or religion be? That seems somewhat hard. And methinks you might have given us some reason for what you say: for certainly it is not so self-evident as to need no proof. But I think it is no hard matter to guess at your reason, though you did not think fit expressly to own it. For it is obvious enough that there can be no other reason for this assertion of yours, but either the equal truth, or at least the equal certainty (or uncertainty) of all religions. For whoever considers your assertion must see that, to make it good, you will be obliged to maintain one of these two things: either (1) that no religion is the true religion, in opposition to other religions: which makes all religions true, or all false, and so either way indifferent, or (2) that though some one religion be the true religion, yet no man can have any more reason than another man of another religion may have, to believe his to be the true religion: which makes all religions equally certain (or uncertain; whether you please) and so renders it vain and idle to enquire after the true religion, and only a piece of good luck if any man be of it, and such good luck as he can never know that he has, until he comes into the other world. Whichever of these two principles you will own, I know not. But certainly one or the other of them lies at the bottom with you, and is the lurking supposition upon which you build all that you say.

But as unreasonable as this condition is, I see no need to have to decline it, nor any occasion you had to impose it upon me. For certainly the making what you call my new method consistent and practicable does no way oblige me to suppose all along my religion the true, as you imagine. No, Sir: it is enough for that purpose to suppose that there is one true religion, and but one, and that that true Religion may be known by those who profess it to be the only true religion, and may also be manifested to be such, by them to others, so far at least as to oblige them to receive it and to leave without excuse if they do not. Indeed if either of the two principles but now mentioned be true, i.e. if all religions be equally true, and so indifferent, or all be equally certain (or uncertain), then without more ado the cause is yours. For then it is plain there can be no reason why any man, in respect to his salvation, should change his religion: and so there can be no room for using any manner of force to bring men to consider what may reasonably move them to change.

But if, on the contrary, there be one true religion, and no more; and that may be known to be the only true religion by those who are of it; and may by them be manifested to others, in such sort as has been said: then it is altogether as plain, that it may be very reasonable and necessary for some men to change their religion, and that it may be made to appear to them to be so. And then if such men will not consider what is offered, to convince them of the reasonableness and necessity of doing it, it may be very fit and reasonable, for anything you have said to the contrary, in order to the bringing them to consideration, to require them under convenient penalties to forsake their false religions and to embrace the true. Now as these things are all I need to suppose, so I shall take leave to suppose them, till you show good reason why I should not.

And now I come to give an account of the particulars mentioned; which I think may be done in a very few words so plainly and intelligibly, upon these supposals, as to enable any reader to see, without any more help, to how little purpose you multiply words about these matters. Here therefore I am to tell the world,

(1) *Who are to be punished.* And those, according to the whole tenor of my answer, are no other but such, as having sufficient evidence tendered to them of the true religion, do yet reject it; whether utterly refusing to consider that evidence, or not considering it as they ought, viz. with such care and diligence as the matter deserves and requires, and with honest and unbiased minds. And what difficulty there is in this, I cannot imagine. For there is nothing more evident than that those who do so reject the true religion are culpable, and deserve to be punished. And it is easy enough to know when men so reject the true religion. For that requires no more than that we know that that religion was tendered to them with sufficient evidence of the truth of it. And that it may be tendered to men with such evidence, and that it may be known when it is so tendered, these things, you know, I take leave here to suppose. Now if the persons I describe do really deserve to be punished; and may be known to be such as I describe them; then as they deserve to be punished; so they may be punished. Which is all that needs to be said upon this head, to show the consistency and practicableness of this method. And what do you anywhere say against this?

(2) *For what.* By which I perceive you mean two things. For sometimes you speak of the fault, and sometimes of the end for which men are to be punished. (And sometimes you plainly confound them.) Now if it be enquired for what fault men are to be punished, I answer: for rejecting the true religion, after sufficient evidence tendered them of the truth of it; which certainly is a fault, and deserves punishment. But if you enquire for what end such as do so reject the true religion are to be punished: I say, to bring them to embrace the true religion; and in order to that, to bring them to consider, and that carefully and impartially, the evidence which is offered to convince them of the truth of it; which are undeniably just and excellent ends and which, through God's blessing, have often been procured, and may yet be procured by convenient penalties inflicted for that purpose. Nor do I know of anything you say against any part of this, which is not already answered.

(3) *With what punishments.* Now here, having in my answer declared that I take the severities so often mentioned (which either destroy men,

or make them miserable) to be utterly unapt and improper (for reasons there given) to bring men to embrace the truth which must save them, I do not presume to determine (nor have you shown any cause why I should) just how far, within those bounds that force extends itself, which is really serviceable to that end; but content myself to say,

> that so much force, or such penalties as are ordinarily sufficient to prevail with men of common discretion, and not desperately perverse and obstinate, to weigh matters of religion carefully and impartially, and without which ordinarily they will not do this; so much force, or such penalties, may fitly and reasonably be used for the promoting true religion in the world, and the salvation of souls.

And what just exception this is liable to, I do not understand.

For when I speak of men of common discretion, and not desperately perverse and obstinate, who perhaps may well enough deserve that name, though they be not wont to be sent to Bedlam.

And if the penalties I speak of be intended for the curing men's unreasonable prejudices and refractoriness against the true religion, then the reason why the desperately perverse and obstinate are not to be regarded in measuring these penalties is very apparent. For as remedies are not provided for the incurable, so in the preparing and tempering them, regard is to be had only to those for whom they are designed.

Perhaps it may be needful here (to prevent a little cavil) to note, that there are degrees of perverseness and obstinacy, and that men may be perverse and obstinate without being desperately so: and that therefore some perverse and obstinate persons may be thought curable, though such as are desperately so cannot. (As there are likewise degrees of carelessness in men of their salvation, as well as of concern for it: so that such as have some concern for their salvation, may yet be careless of it to a great degree. And therefore if those who have any concern for their salvation deserve regard and pity, then so may some careless persons, though those who have no concern for their salvation, deserve not to be considered …) And as those medicines are thought safe and advisable which do ordinarily cure, though not always (as none do), so those penalties or punishments which are ordinarily found sufficient (as well as necessary) for the ends for which they are designed, may fitly and reasonably be used for the compassing those ends.

Now I do not see what more can be required to justify the rule here given. For if you demand that it should express what penalties, particularly, are such as it says may fitly and reasonably be used: this, you must give me leave to tell you, is a very unreasonable demand. For what rule is there that expresses the particulars which agree with it? A rule is intended for a common measure, by which particulars are to be examined, and therefore must necessarily be general. And those to whom it is given, are supposed to be able to apply it, and to judge of particulars by it. Nay, it is often seen that they are better able to do this than those who give it. And so it is in the present case: the rule here laid down is that by which I suppose governors and lawgivers ought to examine the penalties they use, for the promoting the true religion and the salvation of souls. But certainly no man doubts but their prudence and experience enables them to use and apply it better than other men, and to judge more exactly what penalties do agree with it, and what do not. And therefore I think you must excuse me if I do not take upon me to teach them what it becomes me rather to learn from them.

(4) *How long are they to be punished.* And of this the account is very easy. For certainly nothing is more reasonable than that men should be subject to punishment as long as they continue to offend. And as long as men reject the true religion, tendered them with sufficient evidence of the truth of it, so long, it is certain, they offend: because it is impossible for any man innocently to reject the true religion so tendered to him. For whoever rejects that religion so tendered does either apprehend and perceive the truth of it, or he does not. If he does, I know not what greater crime any man can be guilty of. If he does not perceive the truth of it, there is no account to be given of that, but either that he shuts his eyes against evidence which is offered him and will not at all consider it; or that he does not consider it as he ought, viz. with such care as is requisite, and with a sincere desire to learn the truth – either of which does manifestly involve him in guilt.

To say here that a man who has the true religion proposed to him with sufficient evidence of its truth may consider it as he ought, or do his utmost in considering, and yet not perceive the truth of it, is neither more nor less than to say that sufficient evidence is not sufficient evidence. For what does any man mean by sufficient evidence, but such as will certainly win assent wherever it is duly considered?

It is plain enough, therefore, that as long as men reject the true religion duly proposed to them, so long they offend and deserve punishment. And therefore it is but just, that so long they should be left liable to it.

But because my design does rather oblige me to consider how long men may need punishment, than how long it may be just to punish them, therefore I shall add, that as long as men refuse to embrace the true religion, so long penalties are necessary for them to dispose them to consider and embrace it. And that therefore, as justice allows, so charity requires, that they be kept subject to penalties until they embrace the true religion.

Thus far you proceed in your enquiry. But you demand that I should also tell the world,

(5) *What advantage to true religion it would be, if magistrates everywhere did so punish.* Where by the magistrates so punishing, if you speak to the purpose, you must mean their punishing men for rejecting the true religion (so tendered to them as has been said) in order to the bringing them to consider and embrace it. Now before we can suppose magistrates everywhere so to punish, we must suppose the true religion to be everywhere the national religion. And if this were the case, I think it is evident enough what advantage to true religion it would be if magistrates everywhere did so punish. For then we might reasonably hope that all false religions would soon vanish, and the true become once more the only religion in the world: whereas if magistrates should not so punish, it were much to be feared (especially considering what has already happened) that on the contrary, false religions, and atheism, as more agreeable to the soul, would daily take deeper root and propagate themselves, until there were no room left for the true religion (which is but a foreign plant) in any corner of the world.

(6) *And lastly, whence the magistrate had commission to do so.* But of this I have spoken already, and need not here repeat what has been said, to show that the magistrate receives his commission to punish as has been expressed from God whose minister he is.

Thus, in answer to your demand, I have given a plain account of the particulars you mention. And I shall now leave the world to judge whether what you call a new sort of discipline, and my new method, be an impracticable chimera, as you are pleased to say it is.

And now, having seen and examined, as you say, the main of my treatise, you tell me you think you might here end without going any farther. And so, Sir, I think you might, for anything you have said against the rest of it. But that I may not think myself or any of my arguments neglected, you promise to go over the remainder. And so there is no help for it, but I must wait upon you.

But you must excuse me, if I do not here prove over again that what I take to be the author's fourth proposition is really his proposition, and that his last proposition is wholly built upon that.

You say the business of my next paragraph is to prove 'that if force be useful, then somebody must certainly have a right to use it', and that 'the first argument I go about to prove it by is this: that usefulness is as good an argument to prove there is somewhere a right to use it, as uselessness is to prove nobody such a right': whereas neither is that my proposition, nor this my argument. For my words are these:

> If there be so great use and necessity of outward force (duly tempered and applied) for the promoting true religion, and the salvation of souls, as I have endeavoured to show there is: this is as good an argument to prove that there is somewhere a right to use such force for that purpose, as the utter uselessness of force (if that could be made out) would be to prove that nobody has any such right.

Where everyone sees that I do not infer a right to use force from the usefulness of it, barely (as you make me) but from the necessity as well as [the] usefulness of it. For though the utter uselessness of force (if it could be made out) would, as I here acknowledge, be a good argument to prove that nobody has any right to use it, yet I never thought that the bare usefulness of it was sufficient to prove that there is a right somewhere to use it. But if force be both useful and necessary, that, I think, is a good proof of it, and that is the thing I insist upon.

You might therefore have spared the pains you have taken to prove that usefulness of punishment cannot give a commission to punish, or that useful punishment from every hand is not lawful: for I never asserted the contrary. But because some perhaps may think that there is more in the instance you here make use of than what you intend to prove by it, it may not be amiss briefly to show there is not.

That instance is this: you say

> a man may have the stone, and it may be useful (more than indir-
> ectly and at a distance useful) to him to be cut; but yet this useful-
> ness will not justify the most skilful surgeon in the world, by force
> to make him endure the pain and hazard of cutting; because he has
> no commission, no right, without the patient's own consent to do
> so. Nor is it a good argument: Cutting will be useful to him; there-
> fore there is a right somewhere to cut him, whether he will or no.

Now that this instance does not come up to the point in question between us, is very evident. For (1) it is to be considered that the stone does not always kill, though it be not cured; but men do often live to a great age with it, and die at last of other distempers. But aversion to the true religion is certainly and inevitably mortal to the soul, if not cured, and so of absolute necessity to be cured. And yet if we should suppose the stone as certainly destructive of this temporal life, as that aversion is of men's salvation: even so, the necessity of curing it would be as much less than the necessity of curing that aversion, as this temporal life falls short in value of that which is eternal. And (2) it may be considered that cutting for the stone is not always necessary in order to the cure; and that even where it is most so, it is withal hazardous by your own confession, and may kill as well as cure, and that without any fault of the patient.

But the penalties I speak of, as they are altogether necessary (without extraordinary grace) to cure that pernicious and otherwise intractable aversion; so they can no way endanger or hurt the soul, but by the fault of him that undergoes them. And if these things be true; if there be no such necessity that persons troubled with the stone should be cured of it, as there is that such as are possessed with an aversion to the true religion should be cured of that aversion; and if cutting for the stone be neither so necessary nor yet so safe a means of curing as moderate penalties are in the other case: then how reasonable soever you may suppose that it should be left to the patient's choice whether he shall be cut or not, and how true soever it may be that the most skilful surgeon in the world has no com-mission, no right, without the patient's own consent, by force to make him endure the pain and hazard of cutting, the magistrate may nevertheless have a right to use penalties to cure men of their aversion to the true reli-gion: for it is plain enough, these things may very well stand together.

This may suffice to show how short this instance falls of the case before us. However I shall add that though, as things now stand, no surgeon has any right to cut his calculous patient, without his consent, yet if the magistrate should by a public law appoint and authorize a competent number of the most skilful in that art, to visit such as labour under the disease, and to cut those (whether they consent or not) whose lives they unanimously judge it impossible to save otherwise: I am apt to think you would find it hard to prove that in so doing he exceeded the bounds of his power. And I am sure it would be as hard to prove that those artists would have no right, in that case, to cut such persons.

. . .

Though it be very true that the author offers three considerations to prove that the civil power neither can, nor ought, in any manner to be extended to the salvation of souls, yet it may be true also that he does but beg the question, when he affirms that the commonwealth is constituted only for the procuring, preserving, and advancing the civil interests of the members of it. For certainly this affirmation, and that which he goes about to prove by those considerations, are not the same thing.

But you say the author does not beg the question. For that being, whether civil interest be the only end of civil society, he gives this reason for the negative: that civil power has nothing to do with the salvation of souls. But, in my opinion, you would have come nearer the truth if you had said (just the reverse) that the question being, whether civil power has anything to do with the salvation of souls, the author gives this reason for the negative, that civil interest is the only end of civil society. For the very truth of the matter is this: the question being whether the magistrate has any right to use any kind of force or penalties to bring men to the true religion, the author holds the negative, and in order to the proving it advances this principle, that the commonwealth is constituted only for the procuring, preserving, and advancing men's civil interests; or, as you express it, that civil interest is the only end of civil society. Consequently to which, he affirms that civil power has nothing to do with the salvation of souls, and thence infers the point he undertook to prove, viz. that the magistrate has no right to use any kind of force or penalties to bring men to the true religion, in order to the salvation of their souls. Now this I acknowledge to be a very good way of proving the conclusion, if that principle be true.

But that I think no man is bound to grant, and I suppose I have shown sufficient reason why I think so. And therefore because our author assumes that principle, without proving it, I said, and do now again say, that he does but beg the question. It is true, he offers three considerations afterwards, to prove the same thing which he designed to support by that principle. But what is that to the business? Will it follow from thence that he does not beg the question, when he takes that for a principle which his adversaries are as far from granting as they are from granting the conclusion he intends to establish by it? This you will never be able to show.

'And now,' say you, 'let us examine the truth of your main position, viz. that civil society is instituted for the attaining all the benefits that it may any way yield.' But what if this which you call my main position be no position at all of mine? That which I say is 'That commonwealths, or civil societies, are instituted for the attaining of all the benefits which political government can yield, or for all the ends which are attainable by civil society and government' (not by 'the civil society', as you make it, where you pretend to set down my words). Now I suppose there is some difference between 'civil society', and 'a civil society' or commonwealth. 'A civil society' all men understand to be a collection or multitude of men living together under the same political laws and government. But civil society is nothing else but men's living so together: that is, it is not a civil society, but that which makes a collection of men a civil society.

Neither do I say that commonwealths or civil societies are instituted for the attaining of all the benefits they can yield (as you insinuate), which is very improper: for civil societies do only attain and enjoy the benefits which civil society or government yields. And accordingly, I say they are instituted for attaining of all the benefits which civil society or political government can yield.

And this I took to be so plain a truth, that I thought it no great boldness to usher it in with a 'doubtless'. And I confess I am still so much of the same mind, that I can hardly believe that any man, who has not a very urgent occasion, will make any question of it. For if what has hitherto been universally acknowledged be true, viz. that no power is given in vain, but to be used upon occasion, I think a very little logic may serve a man to draw this conclusion from it, that all societies are instructed for the attaining all the good or all the benefits they are enabled to attain, because if you except any of those benefits, you will be obliged to admit that the power of attaining them was given in vain. Nor will it follow from hence that all societies are instituted for one and the same end (as you imagine it will) unless you suppose all societies enabled, by the powers they are endued with, to attain the same end: which I believe no man hitherto did ever affirm. And therefore, notwithstanding this position, there may be still as great a difference as you please between church and state; a commonwealth and an army; or between a family and the East India Company. Which several societies, as they are instituted for different ends, so are they likewise furnished with different powers, proportionate to their respective ends.

...

It is therefore manifest that the thing here to be considered is not whether the magistrate be 'likely to be more concerned for other men's souls, or to take more care of them than themselves'; nor, whether he be 'commonly more careful of his own soul, than other men are of theirs'; nor, whether he be 'less exposed', in matters of religion, 'to prejudices, humours, and crafty seducers than other men'; nor yet, whether he be not 'more in danger to be in the wrong than other men, in regard that he never meets with that great and only antidote of mine' (as you call it) 'against error, which I here call molestation'. But the point on which this matter turns is only this: whether the salvation of souls be not better provided for if the magistrate be obliged to procure, as much as in him lies, that every man take such care as he ought of his soul, than if he be not so obliged, but the care of every man's soul be left to himself alone: which certainly any man of common sense may easily determine. For as you will not (I suppose) deny, but God has more amply provided for the salvation of your own soul by obliging your neighbour as well as yourself to take care of it; though it is possible your neighbour may not be 'more concerned' for it than yourself, or may not be 'more careful' of his own soul than you are of yours, or may be no less 'exposed', in matters of religion, to 'prejudices' etc. than you are. Because if you are yourself wanting to your own soul, it is more likely that you will be brought to take care of it if your neighbour be obliged to admonish and exhort you to it than if he be not, though it may fall out that he will not do what he is obliged to do in that case. So I think it cannot be denied but the salvation of all men's souls is better provided for if, besides the obligation which every man has to take care of his own soul (and that which every man's neighbour has likewise to do it), the magistrate also be entrusted and obliged to see that no man neglect his soul, than it would be if every man were left to himself in this matter ... Which is enough to show that it is every man's true interest that the care of his soul should not be left to himself alone, but that the magistrate should be so far entrusted with it as I contend he is ...

# From *A Third Letter for Toleration* (1692)

## Chapter I [untitled]

…

I suppose you will grant me that anything laid upon the magistrate as a duty is some way or other practicable. Now the magistrate being obliged to use force in matters of religion, but yet so as to bring men only to the true religion, he will not be in any capacity to perform this part of his duty unless the religion he is thus to promote be what he can certainly know, or else what it is sufficient for him to believe, to be the true. Either his knowledge or his opinion must point out that religion to him, which he is by force to promote; or else he may promiscuously and indifferently promote any religion, and punish men at a venture, to bring them from that they are in to any other. This last I think nobody has been so wild as to say.

If therefore it must be either his knowledge or his persuasion that must guide the magistrate herein, and keep him within the bounds of his duty; if the magistrates of the world cannot know, certainly know, the true religion to be the true religion, but it be of a nature to exercise their faith (for where vision, knowledge, and certainty is, there faith is done away); then that which gives them the last determination herein must be their own belief, their own persuasion.

To you and me the Christian religion is the true, and that is built (to mention no other articles of it) on this, that Jesus Christ was put to death at Jerusalem, and rose again from the dead. Now do you or I know this? I do not ask with what assurance we believe it, for that in the highest degree not being knowledge is not what we now inquire after. Can any magistrate demonstrate to himself, and if he can to himself, he does ill not to do it to others, not only all the articles of his church but the fundamental ones of the Christian religion? For whatever is not capable of demonstration (as such remote matters of fact are not) is not, unless it be self-evident, capable to produce knowledge, how well grounded and great soever the assurance of faith may be wherewith it is received; but faith it is still, and not knowledge; persuasion, and not certainty. This is the highest the nature of the thing will permit us to go in matters of revealed religion, which are therefore called matters of faith: a persuasion of our own minds, short of knowledge, is the last result that determines us in such truths. It is all God requires in the Gospel for men to be saved; and it would be strange if there were more required of the magistrate, for the direction of another in the way to salvation, than is required of him for his own salvation. Knowledge then, properly so called, not being to be had of the truths necessary to salvation, the magistrate must be content with faith and persuasion for the rule of that truth he will recommend and enforce upon others; as well as of that whereon he will venture his own eternal condition.

If therefore it be the magistrate's duty to use force to bring men to the true religion, it can be only to that religion which he believes to be true; so that if force be at all to be used by the magistrate in matters of religion, it can only be for the promoting that religion which he only believes to be true, or none at all. I grant that a strong assurance of any truth, settled upon prevalent and well-grounded arguments of probability, is often called knowledge in popular ways of talking; but being here to distinguish between knowledge and belief, to what degrees of confidence soever raised, their boundaries must be kept, and their names not confounded. I know not what greater pledge a man can give of a full persuasion of the truth of anything, than his venturing his soul upon it, as he does who sincerely embraces any religion, and receives it for true. But to what degree soever of assurance his faith may rise, it still comes short of knowledge. Nor can anyone now, I think, arrive to greater evidence of the truth of the Christian religion than the first converts in the time of our Saviour and the Apostles had, of whom yet nothing more was required but to believe.

But supposing all the truths of the Christian religion necessary to salvation could be so known to the magistrate that, in his use of force for the bringing men to embrace these, he could be guided by infallible certainty;

yet I fear this would not serve your turn, nor authorize the magistrate to use force to bring men in England or anywhere else, into the communion of the national church, in which ceremonies of human institution were imposed, which could not be known nor (being confessed things in their own nature indifferent) so much as thought necessary to salvation.

But of this I shall have occasion to speak in another place; all the use I make of it here is to show that the cross in baptism, kneeling at the sacrament, and such-like things, being impossible to be known necessary to salvation, a certain knowledge of the truth of the articles of faith of any church could not authorize the magistrate to compel men to embrace the communion of that church, wherein anything were made necessary to communion, which he did not know was necessary to salvation.

By what has been already said, I suppose it is evident that if the magistrate be to use force only for promoting the true religion, he can have no other guide but his own persuasion of what is the true religion, and must be led by that in his use of force or else not use it at all in matters of religion. If you take the latter of these consequences, you and I are agreed; if the former, you must allow all magistrates, of whatsoever religion, the use of force to bring men to theirs, and so be involved in all those ill consequences which you cannot it seems admit, and hoped to decline by your useless distinction of force to be used, not for any, but for the true religion.

'It is the duty,' you say, 'of the magistrate to use force for promoting the true religion.' And in several places you tell us, he is obliged to it. Persuade magistrates in general of this, and then tell me how any magistrate shall be restrained from the use of force for the promoting what he thinks to be the true? For he being persuaded that it is his duty to use force to promote the true religion, and being also persuaded his is the true religion, what shall stop his hand? Must he forbear the use of force till he be got beyond believing, into a certain knowledge that all he requires men to embrace is necessary to salvation? If that be it you will stand to, you have my consent, and I think there will be no need of any other toleration. But if the believing his religion to be the true be sufficient for the magistrate to use force for the promoting of it, will it be so only to the magistrates of the religion that you profess? And must all other magistrates sit still and not do their duty till they have your permission? If it be your magistrate's duty to use force for the promoting the religion he believes to be the true, it will be every magistrate's duty to use force for the promoting what he believes to be the true, and he sins if he does not receive and promote it as if it were true.

...

You tell us too, that the magistrate may impose creeds and ceremonies: indeed you say sound creeds, and decent ceremonies, but that helps not your cause; for who must be judge of that 'sound' and that 'decent'? If the imposer, then those words signify nothing at all, but that the magistrate may impose those creeds and ceremonies which he thinks sound and decent, which is in effect such as he thinks fit. Indeed you telling us a little above, in the same page, that it is 'a vice not to worship God in ways prescribed by those to whom God has left the ordering of such matters', you seem to make other judges of what is sound and decent, and the magistrate but the executor of their decrees, with the assistance of his coactive power. A pretty foundation to establish creeds and ceremonies on, that God has left the ordering of them to those who cannot order them! But still the same difficulty returns; for, after they have prescribed, must the magistrate judge them to be sound and decent, or must he impose them though he judge them not sound or decent? If he must judge them so himself, we are but where we were; if he must impose them when prescribed, though he judge them not sound nor decent, it is a pretty sort of drudgery put on the magistrate. And how far is this short of implicit faith? But if he must not judge what is sound and decent, he must judge at least who are those to whom God has left the ordering of such matters; and then the King of France is ready again with his dragoons for the sound doctrine and decent ceremonies of his prescribers in the Council of Trent;[1] and that upon this ground, with as good right as any other as for the prescriptions of any others. Do not mistake me again, Sir; I do not say he judges as right; but I do say, that whilst he judges the Council of Trent or the clergy of Rome to be those to whom God has left the ordering of those matters, he has as much right to follow their decrees, as any other to follow the judgement of any other set of mortal men whom he believes to be so.

...

---

[1] The Council of Trent (1545–63) was a general council of the Catholic Church that was convened to define its dogmatic teachings in opposition to Protestant reformers. Locke implies that it prescribed to the Catholic King of France what he should judge about disputed doctrinal matters.

All the stress of your hypothesis for the necessity of force lies on this: That the majority of mankind are not prevailed on by preaching, and therefore the goodness and wisdom of God are obliged to furnish them some more effectual means, as you think. But who told you that the majority of mankind should ever be brought into the strait way and narrow gate? Or that force in your moderate degree was the necessary and competent, i.e. the just, fit means to do it, neither over nor under, but that that only, and nothing but that could do it? If to vindicate his wisdom and goodness God must furnish mankind with other means, as long as the majority, yet unwrought upon, shall give any forward demander occasion to ask, 'What other means is there left?' He must also, after your 'moderate penalties' have left the greater part of mankind unprevailed on, be bound to furnish mankind with higher degrees of force upon this man's demand: and those degrees of force proving ineffectual to the majority to make them truly and sincerely Christians, God must be bound to furnish the world again with a new supply of miracles upon the demand of another wise controller, who having set his heart upon miracles, as you have yours on force, will demand what other means is there left but miracles? For it is like this last gent[leman] would take it very much amiss of you, if you should not allow this to be a good and unquestionable way of arguing; or if you should deny that, after the utmost force had been used, miracles might not do some service at least, indirectly and at a distance, towards the bringing men to embrace the truth. And if you cannot prove that miracles may not thus do some service, he will conclude just as you do, that the cause is his.

Let us try your method a little farther. Suppose that when neither the gentlest admonitions nor the most earnest entreaties will prevail, something else is to be done as the only means left. What is it must be done? What is this necessary competent means that you tell us of? It is to 'lay briars and thorns in their way'. This therefore being supposed necessary, you say 'there must somewhere be a right to use it'. Let it be so. Suppose I tell you that right is in God, who certainly has a power to lay briars and thorns in the way of those who are got into a wrong one, whenever he has graciously pleased that other means besides instructions and admonitions should be used to reduce them. And we may as well expect that those thorns and briars laid in their way by God's providence, without telling them for what end, should work upon them as effectually, though indirectly and at a distance, as those laid in their way by the magistrate, without telling them for what end. God alone knows where it is necessary, and on whom it will be useful, which no man being capable of knowing, no man, though he has coercive power in his hand, can be supposed to be authorized to use it by the commission he has to do good, on whomsoever you shall judge it to be of great and even necessary use: no more than your judging it to be of great and even necessary use would authorize anyone, who had got one of the incision-knives of the hospital in his hand, to cut those for the stone with it, whom he could not know needed cutting or that cutting would do them any good, when the master of the hospital had given him no express order to use his incision-knife in that operation; nor was it known to any but the master, who needed, and on whom it would be useful; nor would he fail to use it himself wherever he found it necessary.

Be force of as great and necessary use as you please; let it be so the competent means for the promoting the honour of God in the world, and the good of souls, that the right to use it must necessarily be somewhere. This right cannot possibly be where you would have it, in the civil sovereigns, and that for the very reason you give, viz. because it must be 'where the power of compelling resides'. For since civil sovereigns cannot compel themselves, nor can the compelling power of one civil sovereign reach another civil sovereign, it will not in the hands of the civil sovereigns reach the most considerable part of mankind, and those who, both for their own and their subjects' good, have most need of it. Besides, if it go along with the power of compelling, it must be in the hands of all civil sovereigns alike; which, by this as well as several other reasons I have given, being unavoidable to be so, this right will be so far from useful, that whatever efficacy force has, it will be employed to the doing more harm than good; since the greatest part of civil sovereigns being of false religions, force will be employed for the promoting of those.

But let us grant what you can never prove, that though all civil sovereigns have compelling power, yet only those of the true religion have a right to use force in matters of religion: your own argument of mankind being unfurnished (which is impiety to say) with competent means for the promoting the honour of God, and the good of souls, still presses you. For the compelling power of each civil sovereign not reaching beyond his own dominions, the right of using force in the hands only of the orthodox civil sovereigns leaves the rest, which is the far greater part of the world, destitute of this your necessary 'and competent means for promoting the honour of God in the world, and the good of souls'.

...

I confess I mistook when I said that cutting, being judged useful, could not authorize even a skilful surgeon to cut a man without any farther commission, for it should have been thus: that though a man has the instruments in his hand, and force enough to cut with, and cutting be judged by you of great and even necessary use in the stone; yet this, without any farther commission, will not authorize anyone to use his strength and knife in cutting, who knows not who has the stone, nor has any light or measures to judge to whom cutting may be necessary or useful.

But let us see what you say in answer to my instance: (1) 'That the stone does not always kill, though it be not cured; but men do often live to a great age with it, and die at last of other distempers. But aversion to the true religion is certainly and inevitably mortal to the soul, if not cured, and so of absolute necessity to be cured.' Is it of absolute necessity to be cured in all? If so, will you not here again think it requisite that the wise and benign disposer and governor of all things should furnish competent means for what is of absolute necessity? For will it not be impiety to say that God has so left mankind unfurnished of competent, i.e. sufficient, means for what is absolutely necessary? For it is plain, in your account, men have not been furnished with sufficient means for what is of absolute necessity to be cured in all, if in any of them it be left uncured. For as you allow none to be sufficient evidence, but what certainly gains assent, so by the same rule you cannot call that sufficient means, which does not work the cure. It is in vain to say the means were sufficient, had it not been for their own fault, when that fault of theirs is the very thing to be cured.

You go on: 'and yet if we should suppose the stone as certainly destructive of this temporal life as that aversion is of men's eternal salvation: even so, the necessity of curing it would be as much less than the necessity of curing that aversion, as this temporal life falls short in value of that which is eternal'. This is built upon a supposition that the necessity of the means is increased by the value of the end, which being in this case the salvation of men's souls, that is of infinite concernment to them, you conclude salvation absolutely necessary: which makes you say that aversion, etc. being inevitably mortal to the soul, is of absolute necessity to be cured. Nothing is of absolute necessity but God. Whatsoever else can be said to be of necessity, is so only relatively in respect to something else; and therefore nothing can indefinitely thus be said to be of absolute necessity, where the thing it relates to is not absolutely necessary. We may say, wisdom and power in God are absolutely necessary, because God himself is absolutely necessary; but we cannot crudely say, the curing in men their aversion to the true religion is absolutely necessary, because it is not absolutely necessary that men should be saved. But this is very proper and true to be said, that curing this aversion is absolutely necessary in all that shall be saved. But I fear that would not serve your turn, though it be certain, that your absolute necessity in this case reaches no farther than this, that to be cured of this aversion is absolutely necessary to salvation, and salvation is absolutely necessary to happiness; but neither of them, nor the happiness itself of any man, can be said to be absolutely necessary.

This mistake makes you say, that supposing 'the stone certainly destructive of this temporal life, yet the necessity of curing it would be as much less than the necessity of curing that aversion, as this temporal life falls short in value of that which is eternal'. Which is quite otherwise: for if the stone will certainly kill a man without cutting, it is as absolutely necessary to cut a man for the stone for the saving of his life, as it is to cure the aversion for the saving of his soul. Nay, if you have but eggs to fry, fire is as absolutely necessary as either of the other, though the value of the end be in these cases infinitely different; for in one of them you lose only your dinner, in the other your life, and in the other your soul. But yet, in these cases, fire, cutting, and curing that aversion, are each of them absolutely and equally necessary to their respective ends, because those ends cannot be attained without them.

You say farther: 'Cutting for the stone is not always necessary in order to the cure: but the penalties you speak of are altogether necessary (without extraordinary grace) to cure that pernicious and otherwise untractable aversion.' Let it be so; but do the surgeons know who has this stone, this aversion, so that it will certainly destroy him, unless he be cut? Will you undertake to tell when the aversion is such in any man, that it is incurable by preaching, exhortation, and entreaty, if his spiritual physician will be instant with him in season and out of season; but certainly curable, if moderate force be made use of? Till you are sure of the former of these, you can never say your moderate force is necessary: till you are sure of the latter, you can never say it is competent means. What you will determine concerning extraordinary grace, and when God bestows that, I leave you to consider and speak clearly of it at your leisure.

You add that, even where 'cutting for the stone is necessary, it is withal hazardous by my confession. But your penalties can no way endanger or hurt the soul, but by the fault of him that undergoes them.' If the magistrate use force to bring men to the true religion, he must judge which is the true religion; and he can judge no other to be it but that which he believes to be the true religion, which is his own religion. But for the magistrate to use force to bring men to his own religion has so much danger in it to men's souls that, by your own confession, none but an atheist will say that magistrates may use force to bring men to their own religion.

This I suppose is enough to make good all that I aimed at in my instance of cutting for the stone, which was that though it were judged useful, and I add now necessary to cut men for the stone, yet that was not enough to authorize a surgeon to cut a man, but he must have, besides that general one of doing good, some more special commission; and that which I there mentioned, was the patient's consent.

...

[Your] case in short is this: men are apt to be misled by their passions, lusts, and other men, in the choice of their religion. For this great evil you propose a remedy, which is that men (for you must remember you are here speaking of the people putting this power into the magistrate's hand) should choose some of their fellow men, and give them a power by force to guard them, that they might not be alienated from the truth by their own passions, lusts, or by other men. So it was in the first scheme; or, as you have it now, to punish them whenever they rejected the true religion, and that proposed with sufficient evidence of the truth of it. A pretty remedy, and manifestly effectual at first sight, that because men were all promiscuously apt to be misled in their judgement or choice of their religion by passion, lust, and other men, therefore they should choose some amongst themselves, who might, they and their successors, men made just like themselves, punish them that rejected the true religion.

'If the blind lead the blind, both shall fall into the ditch', says our Saviour.[2] If men, apt to be misled by their passions and lusts, will guard

---

[2] Matthew 15: 14; Luke 6: 39.

themselves from falling into error by punishments laid on them, by men as apt to be misled by passions and lusts as themselves, how are they safer from falling into error? Now hear the infallible remedy for this inconvenience, and admire: the men to whom they have given this power must not use it, till they find those who gave it them in an error. A friend, to whom I showed this expedient, answered: This is none, for why is not a man as fit to judge for himself when he is in an error, as another to judge for him, who is as liable to error himself? I answered: This power however in the other can do him no harm, but may indirectly and at a distance do him good; because the magistrate who has this power to punish him must never use it but when he is in the right, and he that is punished is in the wrong. But, said my friend, who shall be judge whether he be in the right or no? For men in an error think themselves in the right, and that as confidently as those who are most so. To which I replied, nobody must be judge; but the magistrate may know when he is in the right. And so may the subject too, said my friend, as well as the magistrate, and therefore it was as good still to be free from a punishment that gives a man no more security from error than he had without it.

Besides, said he, who must be judge whether the magistrate knows or no? For he may mistake, and think it to be knowledge and certainty, when it is but opinion and belief. It is no matter, for that in this scheme, replied I, the magistrate, we are told, may know which is the true religion, and he must not use force but to bring men to the true religion; and if he does, God will one day call him to an account for it, and so all is safe. As safe as beating the air can make a thing, replied my friend, for if believing, being assured, confidently being persuaded that they know that the religion they profess is true, or anything else short of true knowledge, will serve the turn, all magistrates will have this power alike, and so men will be well guarded, or recovered from false religions, by putting it into the magistrate's hand to punish them when they have alienated themselves from it.

If the magistrate be not to punish men but when he knows, i.e. is infallibly certain (for so is a man in what he knows) that his national religion is all true, and knows also that it has been proposed to those he punishes with sufficient evidence of the truth of it, it would have been as good this power had never been given him, since he will never be in a condition to exercise it; and at best it was given him to no purpose, since those who gave it him were one with another as little indisposed to consider impartially, examine diligently, study, find, and infallibly know the truth, as he. But, said he at parting, to talk thus of the magistrate's punishing men that reject the true religion, without telling us who those magistrates are who have a power to judge which is the true religion, is to put this power in all magistrates' hands alike, or none; for to say he only is to be judge which is the true religion, [and] who is of it, is but to begin the round of inquiries again, which can at last end nowhere but in every-one's supposing his own to be it. But, said he, if you will continue to talk on thus, there is nothing more to be done with you, but to pity or laugh at you; and so he left me.

I assure you, Sir, I urged this part of your hypothesis with all the advantage I thought your answer afforded me; and if I have erred in it or there be any way to get out of the strait (if force must in your way be used) either of the magistrate's punishing men for rejecting the true reli-gion, without judging which is the true religion; or else that the magis-trate should judge which is the true religion; which way ever of the two you shall determine it, I see not what advantage it can be to the people, to keep them from choosing amiss, that this power of punishing them shall be put into the magistrate's hands.

...

## Chapter II: *Of the magistrate's commission to use force in matters of religion*

Though in the foregoing chapter, on examining your doctrine concern-ing the magistrates who may or who may not use force in matters of religion, we have in several places happened to take notice of the com-mission whereby you authorize magistrates to act; yet we shall in this chapter more particularly consider that commission. You tell us, 'to use force in matters of religion, is a duty of the magistrate as old as the law of nature, in which the magistrate's commission lies: for the Scripture does not properly give it him, but supposes it'. And more at large you give us an account of the magistrate's commission in these words:

> It is true indeed, the author and finisher of our faith has given the
> magistrate no new power or commission; nor was there any need
> that he should (if himself had any temporal power to give) for he
> found him already, even by the law of nature, the minister of God to

the people for good, and bearing the sword not in vain, i.e. invested with coactive power, and obliged to use it for all the good purposes which it might serve, and for which it should be found needful; even for the restraining of false and corrupt religion.

...

Christ, you say, 'has given no new power or commission to the magistrate': and for this you give several reasons.

(1) 'There was no need that he should.' Yet it seems strange that the Christian magistrates alone should have an exercise of coactive power in matters of religion, and yet our Saviour should say nothing of it, but leave them to that commission which was common to them with all other magistrates. The Christian religion in cases of less moment is not wanting in its rules; and I know not whether you will not charge the New Testament with a great defect, if that law alone which teaches the only true religion, that law which all magistrates who are of the true religion receive and embrace, should say nothing at all of so necessary and important a duty to those who alone are in a capacity to discharge it, but leave them only to that general law of nature, which others who are not qualified to use this force have in common with them.

This at least seems needful, if a new commission does not, that the Christian magistrates should have been instructed what degree of force they should use, and been limited to your moderate penalties; since, for above these twelve hundred years, though they have readily enough found out your commission to use force, they never found out your 'moderate' use of it, which is that alone which you assure us is useful and necessary.

(2) You say: 'If our Saviour had any temporal power to give', whereby you seem to give this as a reason why he gave not the civil magistrate power to use force in matters of religion, that he had it not to give. You tell us in the same paragraph that 'he is the king of kings'; and he tells us himself 'That all power is given unto him in heaven and in earth' (Matthew 28: 18). So that he could have given what power, to whom, and to what purpose he had pleased: and concerning this there needs no 'if'.

(3) 'For he found him already by the law of nature invested with coactive power, and obliged to use it for all the good purposes which it

might serve, and for which it should be found needful.' He found also fathers, husbands, masters, invested with their distinct powers by the same law and under the same obligation; and yet he thought it needful to prescribe to them in the use of those powers. But there was no need he should do so to the civil magistrates in the use of their power in matters of religion because, though fathers, husbands, masters, were liable to excess in the use of theirs, yet Christian magistrates were not, as appears by their having always kept to those moderate measures, which you assure us to be the only necessary and useful.

And what at last is their commission? 'Even that of charity, which obliges all men to seek and promote the good of others, especially their spiritual and eternal good, by such means as their several places and relations enable them to use, especially magistrates as magistrates.' This duty of charity is well discharged by the magistrate as magistrate, is it not, in bringing men to an outward profession of any, even of the true religion, and leaving them there? But, Sir, I ask you who must be judge what is for the spiritual and eternal good of his subjects, the magistrate himself or no? If not he himself, who for him? Or can it be done without anyone's judging at all? If he, the magistrate, must judge everywhere himself what is for the spiritual and eternal good of his subjects, as I see no help for it, if the magistrate be everywhere by the law of nature obliged to promote their spiritual and eternal good; is not the true religion like to find great advantage in the world by the use of force in the magistrate's hands? And is not this a plain demonstration that God has by the law of nature given commission to the magistrate to use force for the promoting the true religion, since (as it is evident) the execution of such a commission will do so much more harm than good?

To show that your indirect and at a distance usefulness, with a general necessity of force, authorizes the civil power in the use of it, you use the following words:

> That force does some service towards the making of scholars and artists, I suppose you will easily grant. Give me leave therefore to ask, how it does it? I suppose you will say, not by its direct and proper efficacy (for force is no more capable to work learning or arts than the belief of the true religion in men, by its direct and proper efficacy), but by prevailing upon those who are designed for scholars

or artists to receive instruction, and to apply themselves to the use of those means and helps which are proper to make them what they are designed to be: that is, it does it indirectly and at a distance. Well then, if all the usefulness of the force towards the bringing scholars or apprentices to the learning or skill they are designed to attain be only an indirect and at a distance usefulness; I pray, what is it that warrants and authorizes schoolmasters, tutors, or masters, to use force upon their scholars or apprentices, to bring them to learning or the skill of their arts and trade, if such an indirect and at a distance usefulness of force, together with that necessity of it which experience discovers, will not do it? I believe you will acknowledge that even such a usefulness, together with that necessity, will serve the turn in these cases. But then I would fain know, why the same kind of usefulness, joined with the like necessity, will not as well do it in the case before us?

... I answer, neither your indirect and at a distance usefulness, nor the necessity you suppose of it. For I do not think you will say that any schoolmaster has a power to teach, much less to use force on anyone's child without the consent and authority of the father. But a father, you will say, has a power to use force to correct his child to bring him to learning or skill in that trade he is designed to; and to this the father is authorized by the usefulness and necessity of force. This I deny, that the mere supposed usefulness and necessity of force authorize the father to use it; for then whenever he judged it useful and necessary for his son, to prevail with him to apply himself to any trade, he might use force upon him to that purpose; which I think neither you nor anybody else will say a father has a right to do on his idle and perhaps married son at thirty or forty years old.

There is then something else in the case; and whatever it be that authorizes the father to use force upon his child, to make him a proficient in it, authorizes him also to choose that trade, art, or science he would have him a proficient in: for the father can no longer use force upon his son, to make him attain any art or trade, than he can prescribe to him the art or trade he is to attain. Put your parallel now if you please: the father by the usefulness and necessity of force is authorized to use it upon his child to make him attain any art or science; therefore the magistrate is authorized to use force to bring men to the true religion, because it is useful and necessary. Thus far you have used it, and you think it does well.

But let us go on with the parallel: this usefulness and necessity of force authorizes the father to use it, to make his son apply himself to the use of the means and helps which are proper to make him what he is designed to be, no longer than it authorizes the father to design what his son shall be and to choose for him the art or trade he shall be of; and so the usefulness and necessity you suppose in force to bring men to any church, cannot authorize the magistrate to use force any farther, than he has a right to choose for anyone what church or religion he shall be of. So that if you will stick to this argument, and allow the parallel between a magistrate and a father, and the right they have to use force for the instructing of their subjects in religion, and children in arts, you must either allow the magistrate to have power to choose what religion his subjects shall be of, which you have denied, or else that he has no power to use force to make them use means to be of it.

A father, being entrusted with the care and provision for his child, is as well bound in duty, as fitted by natural love and tenderness, to supply the defects of his tender age. When it is born the child cannot move itself for the ease and help of natural necessities, the parents' hands must supply that inability, and feed, cleanse, and swaddle it. Age having given more strength, and the exercise of the limbs, the parents are discharged from the trouble of putting meat into the mouth of the child, clothing or unclothing, or carrying him in their arms. The same duty and affection which required such kind of helps to the infant, makes them extend their thoughts to other cares for him when he is grown a little bigger; it is not only a present support, but a future comfortable subsistence begins to be thought on: to this some art or science is necessary, but the child's ignorance and want of prospect makes him unable to choose. And hence the father has a power to choose for him, that the flexible and docile part of life may not be squandered away, and the time of instruction and improvement be lost for want of direction. The trade or art being chosen by the father, it is the exercise and industry of the child must acquire it to himself; but industry usually wanting in children the spur which reason and foresight gives to the endeavours of grown men, the father's rod and correction is fain to supply that want, to make him apply himself to the use of those means and helps which are proper to make him what he is designed to be. But when the child is once come to the state of manhood, and to be the possessor and free disposer of his goods and estate, he is then discharged from this discipline of his parents, and they have no longer any right to choose any art, science, or course of life for him, or by force to make him apply himself to the use of those means which are proper to make him be what he designs to be.

Thus the want of knowledge to choose a fit calling, and want of knowledge of the necessity of pains and industry to attain skill in it, puts a power into the parents' hands to use force where it is necessary to procure the application and diligence of their children in that which their parents have thought fit to set them to. But it gives this power to the parents only, and to no other, whilst they live; and if they die whilst their children need it, to their substitutes; and there it is safely placed: for since their want of knowledge during their nonage makes them want direction, and want of reason often makes them need punishment and force to excite their endeavours, and keep them intent to the use of those means that lead to the end they are directed to; the tenderness and love of parents will engage them to use it only for their good, and generally to quit it too, when by the title of manhood they come to be above the direction and discipline of children. But how does this prove that the magistrate has any right to force men to 'apply themselves to the use of those means and helps which are proper to make them of any religion', more than it proves that the magistrate has a right to choose for them what religion they shall be of? To your question therefore, 'what is it that warrants and authorizes schoolmasters, tutors, and masters to use force upon their scholars or apprentices?' I answer: a commission from the father or mother, or those who supply their places; for without that, no indirect or at a distance usefulness, or supposed necessity, could authorize them.

But then you will ask, is it not this usefulness and necessity that gives this power to the father and mother? I grant it. 'I would fain know then,' say you, 'why the same usefulness, joined with the like necessity, will not as well do in the case before us?' And I, Sir, will as readily tell you: because the understanding of the parents is to supply the want of it in the minority of their children; and therefore they have a right not only to use force to make their children apply themselves to the means of acquiring any art or trade, but to choose also the trade or calling they shall be of. But when being come out of the state of minority, they are supposed of years of discretion to choose what they will design themselves to be, they are also at liberty to judge what application and industry they will use for the attaining of it; and then how negligent soever they are in the use of the means, how averse soever to instruction or application, they are past the correction of a schoolmaster, and their parents can no longer choose or design for them what they shall be, nor 'use force to prevail with them to apply themselves to the use of those means and helps which are proper to make them what they are designed to be'. He that imagines a father or tutor may send his son to school at thirty or forty years old, and order him to be whipped there, or that any indirect and at a distance usefulness will authorize him to be so used, will be thought fitter to be sent thither himself and there to receive due correction.

When you have considered it is otherwise in the case of the magistrate using force your way in matters of religion; that there his understanding is not to supply the defect of understanding in his subjects, and that only for a time; that he cannot choose for any of his subjects what religion he shall be of, as you yourself confess; and that this power of the magistrate, if it be (as is claimed by you) over men of all ages, parts, and endowments; you will perhaps 'see some reason why it should not do in the case before us, as well as in that of schoolmasters and tutors, though you believe [I] cannot assign any'. But, Sir, will your indirect and at a distance usefulness, together with your supposed necessity, authorize the master of the shoemakers' company to take anyone who comes in his hands, and punish him for not being of the shoemakers' company, and not coming to their guild, when he, who has a right to choose of what trade and company he will be, thinks it not his interest to be a shoemaker? Nor can he or anybody else imagine that this force, this punishment, is used to make him a good shoemaker, when it is seen and avowed that the punishments cease, and they are free from it who enter themselves of the company, whether they are really shoemakers, or in earnest apply themselves to be so or no. How much it differs from this, that the magistrate should punish men for not being of his church, who choose not to be of it, and when they are once entered into the communion of it, are punished no more, though they are as ignorant, unskilful, and unpractised in the religion of it as before: how much, I say, this differs from the case I proposed, I leave you to consider. For after all your pretences of using force for the salvation of souls, and consequently to make men really Christians, you are fain to allow, and you give reasons for it, that force is used only to those who are out of your church; but whoever are once in it are free from force, whether they be really Christians and apply themselves to those things which are for the salvation of their souls, or no.

As to what you say, that whether they choose it or no, they ought to choose it, for your magistrate's religion is the true religion, that is the question between you and them: but be that as it will, if force be to be used in the case, I have proved that be the magistrate's religion true or false, he, whilst he believes it to be true, is under an obligation to use force as if it were true.

But since you think your instance of children so weighty and pressing, give me leave to return you your question: I ask you then, are not parents as much authorized to teach their children their religion, as they are to teach them their trade, when they have designed them to it? May they not as lawfully correct them to make them learn their catechism, or the principles of their religion, as they may to make them learn Clenard's grammar?[3] Or may they not use force to make them go to Mass, or whatever they believe to be the worship of the true religion, as to go to school, or to learn any art or trade? If they may, as I think you will not deny, unless you will say that none but orthodox parents may teach their children any religion; if they may, I say then, pray tell me a reason, if your arguments from the discipline of children be good, why the magistrate may not use force to bring men to his religion, as well as parents may use force to instruct children and bring them up in theirs? When you have considered this, you will perhaps find some difference between the state of children and grown men, between those under tutelage, and those who are free and at their own disposal; and be inclined to think that those reasons which subject children in their nonage to the use of force, may not, nor do, concern men at years of discretion.

You tell us farther,

> that commonwealths are instituted for the attaining of all the benefits which political government can yield: and therefore if the spiritual and eternal interests of men may any way be procured or advanced by political government, the procuring and advancing those interests must in all reason be received amongst the ends of civil society, and so consequently fall within the compass of the magistrate's jurisdiction.

Concerning the extent of the magistrate's jurisdiction, and the ends of civil society, whether the author or you have begged the question ... I shall leave it to the readers to judge and bring the matter, if you please,

---

[3] A standard textbook of Greek grammar.

to a shorter issue. The question is, whether the magistrate has any power to interpose force in matters of religion, or for the salvation of souls? The argument against it is, that civil societies are not constituted for that end, and the magistrate cannot use force for ends for which the commonwealth was not constituted.

The end of a commonwealth constituted can be supposed no other than what men in the constitution of, and entering into it, proposed; and that could be nothing but protection from such injuries from other men, which they desiring to avoid, nothing but force could prevent or remedy; all things but this being as well attainable by men living in neighbourhood without the bounds of a commonwealth, they could propose to themselves no other thing but this in quitting their natural liberty, and putting themselves under the umpirage of a civil sovereign, who therefore had the force of all the members of the commonwealth put into his hands, to make his decrees to this end be obeyed. Now since no man or society of men can by their opinions in religion, or ways of worship, do any man who differed from them any injury, which he could not avoid or redress, if he desired it, without the help of force; the punishing any opinion in religion, or ways of worship by the force given the magistrate, could not be intended by those who constituted or entered into the commonwealth; and so could be no end of it, but quite the contrary. For force from a stronger hand to bring a man to a religion, which another thinks the true, being an injury which in the state of nature everyone would avoid, protection from such injury is one of the ends of a commonwealth, and so every man has a right to toleration.

If you will say that commonwealths are not voluntary societies constituted by men, and by men freely entered into, I shall desire you to prove it.

In the meantime allowing it you for good, that commonwealths are constituted by God for ends which he has appointed, without the consent and contrivance of men: if you say that one of those ends is the propagation of the true religion and the salvation of men's souls, I shall desire you to show me any such end expressly appointed by God in revelation; which since, as you confess, you cannot do, you have recourse to the general law of nature; and what is that? The law of reason, whereby everyone is commissioned to do good. And the propagating the true religion for the salvation of men's souls being doing good, you say, the civil sovereigns are commissioned and required by that law to use their force for those ends.

But since by this law all civil sovereigns are commissioned and obliged alike to use their coactive power for the propagating the true religion and the salvation of souls; and it is not possible for them to execute such a commission, or obey that law, but by using force to bring men to that religion which they judge the true; by which use of force, much more harm than good would be done towards the propagating the true religion in the world, as I have showed elsewhere. Therefore no such commission, whose execution would do more harm than good, more hinder than promote the end for which it is supposed given, can be a commission from God by the law of nature. And this I suppose may satisfy you about the end of civil societies or commonwealths, and answer what you say concerning the ends attainable by them.

But that you may not think the great position of yours, which is so often ushered in with 'doubtless' (for which you imagine you have sufficient warrant in a misapplied school-maxim), is passed over too slightly and is not sufficiently answered, I shall give you that farther satisfaction.

You say: 'civil societies are instituted for the attaining all the benefits which civil society or political government can yield', and the reason you give for it [is]: 'because it has hitherto been universally acknowledged that no power is given in vain', and therefore 'if I except any of those benefits, I shall be obliged to admit that the power of attaining them was given in vain'. And if I do admit it, no harm will follow in human affairs: or if I may borrow an elegant expression of yours out of the foregoing leaf, 'the fortune of Europe does not turn upon it'. In the voluntary institution and bestowing of power, there is no absurdity or inconvenience at all that power, sufficient for several ends, should be limited by those that give the power only to one or some part of them. The power which a general commanding a potent army has may be enough to take more towns than one from the enemy, or to suppress a domestic sedition; and yet the power of attaining those benefits, which is in his hand, will not authorize him to employ the force of the army therein, if he be commissioned only to besiege and take one certain place. So it is in a commonwealth. The power that is in the civil sovereign is the force of all the subjects of the commonwealth, which supposing it sufficient for other ends than the preserving the members of the commonwealth in peace from injury and violence, yet if those who gave him that power, limited the application of it to that sole end, no opinion of any other benefits attainable by it can authorize him to use it otherwise.

Our Saviour tells us expressly that 'all power was given him in heaven and earth' (Matthew 27: 11). By which power I imagine you will not say that the 'spiritual and eternal interest' of those men whom you think need the help of political force, and of all other men too, could not any way be procured or advanced; and yet if you will hear him in another place, you will find this power (which being all power, could certainly have wrought on all men) limited to a certain number. He says, 'thou hast given him (i.e. thy son) power over all flesh, that he should give eternal life to as many as thou hast given him' (John 17: 2). Whether your universally acknowledged maxim of logic be true enough to authorize you to say that any part of this power was given him in vain, and to enable you to draw consequences from it, you were best see.

But were your maxim so true that it proved that, since it might 'indirectly and at a distance' do some service towards the 'procuring or advancing the spiritual interest' of some few subjects of a commonwealth, therefore force was to be employed to that end; yet that will scarce make good this doctrine of yours:

> doubtless, commonwealths are instituted for the attaining all those benefits which political government can yield; therefore, if the spiritual and eternal interests of men may any way be procured or advanced by political government, the procuring and advancing those interests must in all reason be reckoned among the ends of civil societies, and so consequently fall within the compass of the magistrate's jurisdiction.

For granting it true that 'commonwealths are instituted for the attaining all those benefits which political government can yield', it does not follow 'that the procuring and advancing the spiritual and eternal interest' of some few members of the commonwealth by an application of power, which indirectly and at a distance, or by accident, may do some service that way, whilst at the same time it prejudices a far greater number in their civil interests, can with reason be reckoned among the ends of civil society.

'That commonwealths are instituted for those ends, viz. for the procuring, preserving, and advancing men's civil interests,' you say, 'no man will deny.' To sacrifice therefore these civil interests of a great number of people, which are the allowed ends of the commonwealths, to the uncertain expectation of some service to be done indirectly and at a distance to a far less number, as experience has always showed those really converted to the true religion by force to be, if any at all, cannot be one of the ends of the commonwealth. Though the advancing of the spiritual and eternal interest be of infinite advantage to the persons who receive that benefit, yet if it can be thought a benefit to the commonwealth when it is procured them with the diminishing or destroying the civil interests of great numbers of their fellow citizens, then the ravaging of an enemy, the plague, or a famine, may be said to bring a benefit to the commonwealth, for either of these may indirectly and at a distance do some service towards the advancing or procuring the spiritual and eternal interest of some of those who suffer in it.

... [Y]ou except against my want of exactness, in setting down your opinion I am arguing against. Had it been any way to take off the force of what you say, or that the reader could have been misled by my words in any part of the question I was arguing against, you had had reason to complain: if not, you had done better to have entertained the reader with a clearer answer to my argument than spent your ink and his time needlessly, to show such niceness.

My argument is as good against your tenet in your own words, as in mine which you except against. Your words are: 'doubtless commonwealths are instituted for the attaining all the benefits which political government can yield; and therefore if the spiritual and eternal interest of men may any way be procured or advanced by political government, the procuring and advancing those interests must in all reason be reckoned amongst the ends of civil societies'.

To which I answered, that if this be so,

> [t]hen this position must be true, viz. that all societies whatsoever are instituted for the attaining all the benefits that they may any way yield: there being nothing peculiar to civil society in the case, why that society should be instituted for the attaining all the benefits it can any way yield, and other societies not. By which argument it will follow that all societies are instituted for one and the same end, i.e. for the attaining all the benefits that they can any way yield. By which account there will be no difference between church and state, a commonwealth and an army, or between a family and the East India Company; all which have hitherto been thought distinct sorts of societies, instituted for different ends. If your hypothesis hold good, one of the ends of the family must be to preach the Gospel,

and administer the sacraments; and one business of an army to teach languages and propagate religion; because these are benefits some way or other attainable by those societies: unless you take want of commission and authority to be a sufficient impediment: and that will be so in other cases.

To which you reply:

> Nor will it follow from hence that all societies are instituted for one and the same end (as you imagine it will), unless you suppose all societies enabled by the power they are endued with to attain the same end, which I believe no man hitherto did ever affirm. And therefore, notwithstanding this position, there may be still as great a difference as you please between church and state, a commonwealth and an army, or between a family and the East India Company. Which several societies, as they are instituted for different ends, so they are likewise furnished with different powers proportionate to their respective ends.

In which the reason you give to destroy my inference, I am to thank you; for, if you understood the force of it, it being the very same I bring to show that my inference from your way of arguing is good. I say, that from your way of reasoning about the ends of government, 'It would follow that all societies were instituted for one and the same end; unless you take want of commission and authority to be a sufficient impediment.' And you tell me here it will not follow, 'unless I suppose all societies enabled by the power they are endued with, to attain the same end'; which in other words is, unless I suppose all who have in their hands the force of any society to have all of them the same commission.

The natural force of all the members of any society, or of those who by the society can be procured to assist it, is in one sense called the power of that society. This power or force is generally put into some one or few persons' hands with direction and authority how to use it; and this in another sense is called also the power of the society: and this is the power you here speak of, and in these following words, viz. 'Several societies, as they are instituted for different ends; so likewise are they furnished with different powers proportionate to their respective ends.' The power therefore of any society in this sense, is nothing but the authority and direction given to those that have the management of the force or natural power of the society, how and to what ends to use it, by which commission the ends of societies are known and distinguished. So that all societies wherein those who are entrusted with the management of the force or natural power of the society, have commission and authority to use the force or natural power of the society to attain the same benefits, are instituted for the same end. And therefore, if in all societies those who have the management of the force or natural power of the society, are commissioned or authorized to use that force to attain all the benefits attainable by it, all societies are instituted to the same end: and so what I said will still be true, viz.

> That a family and an army, a commonwealth and a church, have all the same end. And if your hypothesis hold good, one of the ends of a family must be to preach the Gospel, and administer the sacraments; and one business of an army to teach languages, and propagate religion, because these are benefits some way or other attainable by those societies; unless you take want of commission and authority to be a sufficient impediment: and that will be so too in other cases.

To which you have said nothing but what does confirm it, which you will a little better see, when you have considered that any benefit attainable by force or natural power of a society, does not prove the society to be instituted for that end; till you also show that those to whom the management of the force of the society is entrusted, are commissioned to use it to that end.

...

## Chapter III: *Who are to be punished by your scheme*

...

You promised you would tell the world [who was to be punished], plainly and directly, and though you tell us you cannot imagine what difficulty there is in this your account of who are to be punished, yet there are some things in it that make it to my apprehension not very plain and direct. For first they must be only those who have the true religion tendered them with sufficient evidence; wherein there appears some difficulty to me, who shall be judge what is the true religion: and for that, in every country it is most probable the magistrate will be. If you think of any other, pray tell us.

Next there seems some difficulty to know, who shall be judge what is sufficient evidence. For where a man is to be punished by law, he must be convicted of being guilty; which since in this case he cannot be, unless it be proved he has had the true religion tendered to him with sufficient evidence, it is necessary that somebody there must be judge what is the true religion, and what is sufficient evidence; and others to prove it has been so tendered. If you were to be of the jury, we know what would be your verdict concerning sufficient evidence, by these words of yours:

> To say that a man who has the true religion proposed to him with sufficient evidence of its truth, may consider it as he ought, or do his utmost in considering and yet not perceive the truth of it, is neither more nor less than to say that sufficient evidence is not sufficient: for what does any man mean by sufficient evidence, but such as will certainly win assent wherever it is duly considered?

Upon which his conforming or not conforming would without any farther questions determine the point. But whether the rest of the jury could upon this be able ever to bring in any man guilty, and so liable to punishment, is a question. For if sufficient evidence be only that which certainly wins assent, wherever a man does his utmost in considering; it will be very hard to prove that a man who rejects the true religion has had it tendered with sufficient evidence, because it will be very hard to prove he has not done his utmost in considering it. So that, notwithstanding all you have here said, to punish any man by your method is not yet so very practicable.

But you clear all in your following words, which say, 'there is nothing more evident than that those who reject the true religion are culpable, and deserve to be punished'. By whom? By men: that is so far from being evident, as you talk, that it will require better proofs than I have yet seen for it. Next you say, 'It is easy enough to know when men reject the true religion.' Yes, when the true religion is known, and agreed on what shall be taken to be so in judicial proceedings, which can scarce be till it is agreed who shall determine what is true religion, and what not. Suppose a penalty should in the university be laid on those who rejected the true peripatetic doctrine, could that law be executed on anyone, unless it were agreed who should be judge what was the true peripatetic doctrine? If you say it may be known out of Aristotle's writings, then I answer, that it would be a more reasonable law to lay the penalty on anyone who rejected the doctrine contained in the books allowed to be Aristotle's, and printed under his name. You may apply this to the true religion, and the books of the Scripture, if you please: though, after all, there must be a judge agreed on to determine what doctrines are contained in either of those writings, before the law can be practicable.

But you go on to prove that 'it is easy to know when men reject the true religion': for, say you, 'that requires no more than that we know that that religion was tendered to them with sufficient evidence of the truth of it. And that it may be tendered to men with such evidence, and that it may be known when it is so tendered, these things', you say, you 'take leave here to suppose'. You suppose then more than can be allowed you. For that it can be judicially known that the true religion has been tendered to anyone with sufficient evidence, is what I deny, and that for reasons above-mentioned, which, were there no other difficulty in it, were sufficient to show the impracticableness of your method.

You conclude this paragraph thus, 'which is all that needs be said upon this head to show the consistency and practicableness of this method: and what do you anywhere say against this?' Whether I say anything or no against it, I will bring a friend of yours that will say that dissenters ought to be punished for being out of the communion of the Church of England. I will ask you now, how it can be proved that such a one is guilty of rejecting the one only true religion? Perhaps it is because he scruples the cross in baptism, or godfathers and godmothers as they are used, or kneeling at the Lord's Supper; perhaps it is because he cannot pronounce all damned that believe not all Athanasius's Creed;[4] or cannot join with some of those repetitions in our Common-prayer, thinking them to come within the prohibition of our Saviour; each of which shuts a man out from the communion of the Church of England, as much as if he denied Jesus Christ to be the Son of God. Now, Sir, I beseech you, how can it be known, that ever sufficient evidence was tendered to such a dissenter to prove that what he rejects is a part of that one only true religion, which unless he be of, he cannot be saved? Or indeed how can it be known, that any dissenter rejects that one only true religion, when being punished barely for not conforming, he is never asked, what part it is he dissents from or rejects? And so it may be some of those things which I imagine will always want

---

[4] A statement of the Christian faith, attributed to St Athanasius (293–373), which specified orthodox belief about the Trinity in opposition to Arians.

sufficient evidence to prove them to be parts of that only one true religion, without the hearty embracing whereof no man can be saved.

## Chapter IV: *What degrees of punishment?*

How much soever you have endeavoured to reform the doctrine of persecution to make it serve your turn, and give it the colour of care and zeal for the true religion in the country where alone you are concerned it should be made use of; yet you have laboured in vain, and done no more but given the old engine a new varnish to set it off the better, and make it look less frightful. For, by what has been said in the foregoing chapters, I think it will appear, that if any magistrate have power to punish men in matters of religion, all have, and that dissenters from the national religion must be punished everywhere or nowhere. The horrid cruelties that in all ages, and of late in our view, have been committed under the name, and upon the account of religion, give so just an offence and abhorrence to all who have any remains, not only of religion, but humanity left, that the world is ashamed to own it. This objection therefore, as much as words or professions can do, you have laboured to fence against; and to exempt your design from the suspicion of any severities, you take care in every page almost to let us hear of moderate force, moderate penalties; but all in vain. And I doubt not but when this part too is examined, it will appear that as you neither have, nor can limit the power of punishing to any distinct sort of magistrates, nor exempt from punishment the dissenters from any national religion; so neither have, nor can you, limit the punishment to any degree short of the highest, if you will use punishments at all in matters of religion.

...

For I ask you, to what purpose do you use any degree of force? Is it to prevail with men to do something that is in their power, or that is not? The latter I suppose you will not say, until your love of force is so increased, that you shall think it necessary to be made use of to produce impossibilities: if force then be to be used only to bring men to do what is in their power, what is the necessity you assign of it? Only this, as I remember, viz. that 'when gentle admonitions and earnest entreaties will not prevail, what other means is there left but force?'. And I upon the same ground reply: If lesser degrees of force will not prevail, what other means is there left but greater? If the lowest degree of force be necessary where gentler means will not prevail, because there is no other means left, higher degrees of force are necessary, where lower will not prevail, for the same reason. Unless you will say all degrees of force work alike; and that lower penalties prevail as much on men as greater, and will equally bring them to do what is in their power. If so, a philip on the forehead, or a farthing mulct,[5] may be penalty enough to bring men to what you propose. But if you shall laugh at these, as being for their smallness insufficient, and therefore will think it necessary to increase them; I say, wherever experience shows any degree of force to be insufficient to prevail, there will be still the same necessity to increase it. For wherever the end is necessary, and force is the means, the only means left to procure it, both which you suppose in our case, there it will be found always necessary to increase the degrees of force, where the lower prove ineffectual, as well until you come to the highest as when you begin with the lowest.

. . .

If one man will not be wrought on by as little force as another, must not greater degrees of force be used to him? Shall the magistrate who is obliged to do what lies in him, be excused for letting him be damned, without the use of all the means that were in his power? And will it be sufficient for him to plead, that though he did not all that lay in him, yet he did what ordinarily prevailed or what prevailed on several others? Force, if that be the remedy, must be proportioned to the opposition. If the dose that has frequently wrought on others will not purge a man whose life lies on it, must it not therefore be made sufficient and effectual, because it will be more than what is called ordinary? Or can anyone say the physician has done his duty, who lets his patient in an extraordinary case perish in the use of only moderate remedies, and pronounces him incurable, before he has tried the utmost he can with the powerfullest remedies which are in his reach?

. . .

. . . Now the magistrate has all your rules about the measures of punishments to be used and may, confidently and safely, go to work to establish it by a law; for he having these marks to guide him, that they must be

---

[5] A light tap, or a negligible fine.

great enough ordinarily to 'prevail with those who are not idiots or madmen, nor desperately perverse and obstinate'; great enough ordinarily to prevail with men to hear, consider, and embrace the true religion, and yet not so great as 'might tempt persons, who have any concern for their eternal salvation, to renounce a religion which they believe to be true, or profess one which they do not believe to be so': do you not think you have sufficiently instructed him in your meaning, and enabled him to find the just temper of his punishments according to your scheme, neither too much, nor too little? But however you may be satisfied with them, I suppose others, when it comes to be put in practice, will by these measures, which are all I can find in your scheme, be scarce able to find what are the punishments you would have used.

In Eutopia there is a medicine called *hiera picra,*[6] which it is supposed would cure a troublesome disease of that country; but it is not to be given but in the dose prescribed by the law, and in adjusting the dose lies all the skill. For, if you give too much, it heightens the distemper, and spreads the mortal contagion; and if too little, it does no good at all. With this difficulty the law-makers have been perplexed these many ages, and could not light on the right dose that would work the cure, till lately there came an undertaker who would show them how they could not mistake. He bid them then prescribe so much, as would ordinarily be effectual upon all that were not idiots or madmen, or in whom the humour was not desperately perverse and obstinate, to produce the end for which it was designed; but not so much as would make a man in health, who had any concern for his life, fall into a mortal disease. These were good words, and he was rewarded for them. But when by them they came to fix the dose, they could not tell whether it ought to be a grain, a dram, or an ounce, or a whole pound, any more than before; and so the dose of their hiera picra, notwithstanding this gentleman's pains, is as uncertain, and that sovereign remedy as useless as ever it was.

...

You tell us that where this only true religion, viz. of the Church of England, is received, other religions ought 'to be discouraged in some measure'. A pretty expression for undoing, imprisonment, banishment; for those have been some of the discouragements given to dissenters

---

[6] A purgative used in traditional medicine.

here in England. You will again, no doubt, cry aloud, that you tell me you condemn these as much as I do. If you heartily condemn them, I wonder you should say so little to discourage them; I wonder you are so silent in representing to the magistrate the unlawfulness and danger of using them in a discourse where you are treating of the magistrate's power and duty in matters of religion; especially this being the side on which, as far as we may guess by experience, their prudence is aptest to err. But your modesty, you know, leaves all to the magistrates' prudence and experience on that side, though you over and over again encourage them not to neglect their duty in the use of force, to which you set no bounds.

...

## Chapter V: *How long your punishments are to continue*

...

It is certainly very reasonable that men should be subject to punishment from those they offend as long as they continue to offend. But it will not from hence follow, that those who offend God are always subject to punishment from men. For if they be, why does not the magistrate punish envy, hatred, and malice, and all uncharitableness? If you answer, because they are not capable of judicial proofs: I think I may say it is as easy to prove a man guilty of envy, hatred, or uncharitableness, as it is to prove him guilty of 'rejecting the true religion tendered him with sufficient evidence of the truth of it'. But if it be his duty to punish all offences against God, why does the magistrate never punish lying, which is an offence against God, and is an offence capable of being judicially proved? It is plain therefore that it is not the sense of all mankind, that it is the magistrate's duty to punish all offences against God; and where it is not his duty to use force, you will grant the magistrate is not to use it in matters of religion; because where it is necessary, it is his duty to use it. But where it is not necessary, you yourself say, it is not lawful. It would be convenient therefore for you to reform your proposition from that loose generality it now is in, and then prove it, before it can be allowed you to be to your purpose; though it be ever so true, that 'you know not a greater crime a man can be guilty of than rejecting the true religion'.

You go on with your proof, that so long as men reject the true religion, etc. so long they offend, and consequently may justly be punished: 'Because,' say you,

> it is impossible for any man innocently to reject the true religion so tendered to him. For whoever rejects that religion so tendered, does either apprehend and perceive the truth of it, or he does not. If he does, I know not what greater crime any man can be guilty of. If he does not perceive the truth of it, there is no account to be given of that, but either that he shuts his eyes against the evidence which is offered him, and will not at all consider it; or that he does not consider it as he ought, viz. with such care as is requisite, and with a sincere desire to learn the truth; either of which does manifestly involve him in guilt. To say here that a man who has the true religion proposed to him with sufficient evidence of its truth, may consider it as he ought,

or do his utmost in considering, 'and yet not perceive the truth of it; is neither more nor less, than to say, that sufficient evidence is not sufficient evidence. For what does any man mean by sufficient evidence, but such as will certainly win assent wherever it is duly considered?'

I shall not trouble myself here to examine when 'requisite care', 'duly considered', and such other words, which bring one back to the same place from whence one set out, are cast up, whether all this fine reasoning will amount to anything but begging what is in the question: but shall only tell you, that what you say here and in other places about sufficient evidence is built upon this, that the evidence wherewith a man proposes the true religion, he may know to be such, as will not fail to gain the assent of whosoever does what lies in him in considering it. This is the supposition, without which all your talk of sufficient evidence will do you no service, try it where you will. But it is a supposition that is far enough from carrying with it sufficient evidence to make it be admitted without proof.

Whatever gains any man's assent, one may be sure had sufficient evidence in respect of that man. But that is far enough from proving it evidence sufficient to prevail on another, let him consider it as long and as much as he can. The tempers of men's minds; the principles settled there by time and education, beyond the power of the man himself to alter them; the different capacities of men's understandings, and the strange ideas they are often filled with, are so various and uncertain, that it is impossible to find that evidence (especially in things of a mixed disquisition, depending on so long a train of consequences, as some points of the true religion may), which one can confidently say will be sufficient for all men. It is demonstration that 31,876 is the product of 9,467,172 divided by 297, and yet I challenge you to find one man of a thousand, to whom you can tender this proposition with demonstrative or sufficient evidence to convince him of the truth of it in a dark room; or ever to make this evidence appear to a man, that cannot write and read, so as to make him embrace it as a truth, if another, whom he hath more confidence in, tells him it is not so. All the demonstrative evidence the thing has, all the tender you can make of it, all the consideration he can employ about it, will never be able to discover to him that evidence which shall convince him it is true, unless you will at threescore and ten, for that may be the case, have him neglect his calling, go to school, and learn to write and read, and cast accounts, which he may never be able to attain to.

You speak more than once of men's being brought to lay aside their prejudices to make them consider as they ought, and judge right of matters in religion, and I grant without doing so they cannot. But it is impossible for force to make them do it, unless it could show them which are prejudices in their minds, and distinguish them from the truths there. Who is there almost that has not prejudices, that he does not know to be so; and what can force do in that case? It can no more remove them, to make way for truth, than it can remove one truth to make way for another; or rather remove an established truth, or that which is looked on as an unquestionable principle (for so are often men's prejudices), to make way for a truth not yet known, nor appearing to be one. It is not everyone knows, or can bring himself to Descartes' way of doubting,[7] and strip his thoughts of all opinions, until he brings them to self-evident principles, and then upon them builds all his future tenets.

Do not think all the world, who are not of your church, abandon themselves to an utter carelessness of their future state. You cannot but allow there are many Turks who sincerely seek truth, to whom yet you could never bring evidence sufficient to convince them of the truth of the Christian religion, whilst they looked on it as a principle not to be questioned that the Alcoran[8] was of divine revelation. This possibly you

---

[7] Refers to the method used by Descartes, in the first of his *Meditations on First Philosophy* (1641), to doubt all previously held beliefs and to begin completely afresh.
[8] Qur'an.

will tell me is a prejudice, and so it is: but yet if this man shall tell you it is no more a prejudice in him, than it is a prejudice in anyone amongst Christians, who having not examined it, lays it down as an unquestionable principle of his religion that the Scripture is the word of God; what will you answer to him? And yet it would shake a great many Christians in their religion if they should lay by that prejudice, and suspend their judgement of it, until they had made it out to themselves with evidence sufficient to convince one who is not prejudiced in favour of it: and it would require more time, books, languages, learning, and skill than falls to most men's share, to establish them therein; if you will not allow them, in this so distinguishing and fundamental a point, to rely on the learning, knowledge, and judgement of some persons whom they have in reverence or admiration. This though you blame it as an ill way, yet you can allow in one of your own religion, even to that degree that he may be ignorant of the grounds of his religion. And why then may you not allow it to a Turk, not as a good way or as having led him to the truth; but as a way as fit for him, as for one of your church to acquiesce in; and as fit to exempt him from your force as to exempt anyone of your church from it?

To prevent your commenting on this, in which you have shown so much dexterity, give me leave to tell you, that for all this I do not think all religions equally true or equally certain. But this, I say, is impossible for you, or me, or any man, to know, whether another has done his duty in examining the evidence on both sides, when he embraces that side of the question, which we (perhaps upon other views) judge false: and therefore we can have no right to punish or persecute him for it. In this, whether and how far anyone is faulty, must be left to the searcher of hearts, the great and righteous judge of all men, who knows all their circumstances, all the powers and workings of their minds; where it is they sincerely follow, and by what default they at any time miss truth: and he, we are sure, will judge uprightly.

But when one man shall think himself a competent judge, that the true religion is proposed with evidence sufficient for another; and thence shall take upon him to punish him as an offender, because he embraces not (upon evidence that he, the proposer, judges sufficient) the religion that he judges true; he had need be able to look into the thoughts of men, and know their several abilities; unless he will make his own understanding and faculties to be the measure of those of all mankind; which if they be no higher elevated, no larger in their comprehension, no more discerning, than those of some men, he will not only be unfit to be a judge in that, but in almost any case whatsoever.

…

[Chapters VI–VIII omitted.]

## Chapter IX: *Of the usefulness of force in matters of religion*

…

[W]hatever privilege or power you claim upon your supposing yours to be the true religion, is equally due to another (who supposes his to be the true religion), upon the same claim: and therefore that is no more to be allowed to you than to him. For whose is really the true religion, yours or his, being the matter in contest between you, your supposing can no more determine it on your side than his supposing on his; unless you can think you have a right to judge in your own cause. You believe yours to be the true religion, so does he believe his; you say you are certain of it, so says he, he is: you think you have 'arguments proper and sufficient' to convince him, if he would consider them; the same thinks he of his. If this claim, which is equally on both sides, be allowed to either without any proof; it is plain he, in whose favour it is allowed, is allowed to be judge in his own cause, which nobody can have a right to be, who is not at least infallible. If you come to arguments and proofs, which you must do, before it can be determined whose is the true religion, it is plain your supposition is not allowed.

In our present case, in using punishments in religion, your suppos-ing yours to be the true religion gives you or your magistrate no more advantage over a papist, Presbyterian, or Mahometan, or more reason to punish either of them for his religion, than the same supposition in a papist, Presbyterian, or Mahometan, gives any of them or a magistrate of their religion advantage over you, or reason to punish you for your religion; and therefore this supposition, to any purpose or privilege of using force, is no more to be allowed to you than to anyone of any other religion. This the words, 'in this case', which I there used, would have satisfied any other to have been my meaning: but whether your charity made you not to take notice of them, or the joy of such an advantage as this not to understand them, this is certain. You were resolved not to lose the opportunity such a place as this afforded you, of showing your gift, in commenting and guessing shrewdly at a man's reasons, when he does not think fit expressly to own them himself.

I must own you are a very lucky hand at it; and as you do it here upon the same ground, so it is just with the same success, as you in another place have exercised your logic on my saying something to the same purpose as I do here. But, Sir, if you will add but one more to your plentiful stock of distinctions, and observe the difference there is between the ground of anyone's supposing his religion is true, and the privilege he may pretend to by supposing it true, you will never stumble at this again; but you will find, that though upon the former of these accounts, men of all religions cannot be equally allowed to suppose their religions true, yet, in reference to the latter, the supposition may and ought to be allowed or denied equally to all men. And the reason of it is plain, viz. because the assurance wherewith one man supposes his religion to be true, being no more an argument of its truth to another, than vice versa; neither of them can claim by the assurance wherewith he supposes his religion the true, any prerogative or power over the other, which the other has not by the same title an equal claim to over him.

...

... '[T]here is one true religion, and but one', we are agreed. But what you say in the next place, that 'that one true religion may be known by those who profess it', will need a little examination. As, first, it will be necessary to inquire what you mean by 'known'; whether you mean by it knowledge properly so called, as contra-distinguished to belief; or only the assurance of a firm belief? If the latter, I leave you your supposition to make your use of it, only with this desire, that to avoid mistakes, when you do make any use of it, you would call it 'believing'. If you mean that the true religion may be known with the certainty of knowledge properly so called; I ask you farther, whether that true religion be to be known by the light of nature, or needed a divine revelation to discover it? If you say (as I suppose you will) the latter, then I ask whether the making out of that to be a divine revelation, depends not upon particular matters of fact, whereof you were no eyewitness, but were done many ages before you were born? And if so, by what principles of science they can be known to any man now living?

The articles of my religion, and of a great many such other short-sighted people as I am, are articles of faith, which we think there are so good grounds to believe that we are persuaded to venture our eternal happiness on that belief; and hope to be of that number of whom our Saviour said, 'Blessed are they that have not seen, and yet have believed.'[9] But we neither think that God requires, nor has given us faculties capable of knowing in this world, several of those truths which are to be believed to salvation. If you have a religion, all whose general truths are either self-evident, or capable of demonstration (for matters of fact are not capable of being any way known but to the bystanders), you will do well to let it be known for the ending of controversies, and banishing of error concerning any of those points out of the world. For whatever may be known, besides matter of fact, is capable of demonstration; and when you have demonstrated to anyone any point in religion, you shall have my consent to punish him if he do not assent to it. But yet let me tell you, there are many truths even in mathematics, the evidence whereof one man seeing, is able to demonstrate to himself, and so may know them: which evidence yet he not being able to make another see (which is to demonstrate to him), he cannot make known to him, though his scholar be willing and with all his power applies himself to learn it.

But granting your supposition, 'that the one true religion may be known by those who profess it to be the only true religion'; will it follow from hence, that because it is knowable to be the true religion, therefore the magistrate who professes it actually knows it to be so? Without which knowledge, upon your principles, he cannot use force to bring men to it. But if you are but at hand to assure him which is the true religion, for which he ought to use force, he is bound to believe you; and that will do as well as if he examined and knew himself, or perhaps better. For you seem not well satisfied with what the magistrates have lately done, without your leave, concerning religion in England.[10] And I confess the easiest way to remove all difficulties in the case, is for you to be the magistrate's infallible guide in matters of religion.

...

If you can make it practicable that the magistrate should punish men for rejecting the true religion, without judging which is the true religion; or

9 John 20: 29.
10 In 1689 the *Toleration Act* removed some restrictions on dissenters' practices.

if true religion could appear in person, take the magistrate's seat, and there judge all that rejected her, something might be done. But the mischief of it is, it is a man that must condemn, men must punish; and men cannot do this but by judging who is guilty of the crime which they punish. An oracle, or an interpreter of the law of nature, who speaks as clearly, tells the magistrate he may and ought to punish those 'who reject the true religion, tendered with sufficient evidence'; the magistrate is satisfied of his authority, and believes this commission to be good. Now I would know how possibly he can execute it, without making himself the judge first what is the true religion, unless the law of nature at the same time delivered into his hands the Thirty-Nine Articles of the one only true religion, and another book wherein all the ceremonies and outward worship of it are contained. But it being certain that the law of nature has not done this; and as certain that the articles, ceremonies, and discipline of this one only true religion, have been often varied in several ages and countries, since the magistrate's commission by the law of nature was first given: there is no remedy left but that the magistrate must judge what is the true religion, if he must punish them who reject it. Suppose the magistrate be commissioned to punish those who depart from right reason; the magistrate can yet never punish anyone, unless he be judge what is right reason; and then judging that murder, theft, adultery, narrow cart-wheels, or want of bows and arrows in a man's house, are against right reason, he may make laws to punish men guilty of those, as rejecting right reason.

...

## Chapter X: *Of the necessity of force in matters of religion*

...

Where men cannot live together without mutual injuries, not to be avoided without force, reason has taught them to seek a remedy in government, which always places power somewhere in the society to restrain and punish such injuries; which power, whether placed in the community itself or some chosen by the community to govern it, must still be in the hands of men; and where (as in society of civilized and settled nations) the form of the government places this power out of the community itself, it is unavoidable that out of men (such as they are) some should be made magistrates, and have coercive power of force put into their hands to govern and direct the society for the public good; without which force, so placed in the hands of men, there could be no civil society, nor the ends for which it is instituted to any degree attained. And thus government is the will of God.

It is the will of God also, that men should be saved; but to this, it is not necessary that force or coactive power should be put into men's hands; because God can and has provided other means to bring men to salvation: to which you indeed suppose, but can never prove, force necessary.

The passions, humours, liableness to prejudices and errors, common to magistrates with other men, do not render force in their hands so dangerous and unuseful to the ends of society, which is the public peace, as to the ends of religion, which is the salvation of men's souls. For though men of all ranks could be content to have their own humours, passions, and prejudices satisfied, yet when they come to make laws, which are to direct their force in civil matters, they are driven to oppose their laws to the humours, passions, and prejudices of men in general, whereby their own come to be restrained. For if law-makers, in making of laws, did not direct them against the irregular humours, prejudices, and passions of men, which are apt to mislead them; if they did not endeavour, with their best judgement, to bring men from their humours and passions, to the obedience and practice of right reason, the society could not subsist; and so they themselves would be in danger to lose their station in it, and be exposed to the unrestrained humours, passions, and violence of others. And hence it comes, that be men as humoursome, passionate, and prejudiced as they will, they are still by their own interest obliged to make use of their best skill, and with their most unprejudiced and sedatest thoughts, take care of the government, and endeavour to preserve the commonwealth; and therefore, notwithstanding their humours and passions, their liableness to error and prejudice, they do provide pretty well for the support of society, and the power in their hands is of use to the maintenance of it.

But in matters of religion it is quite otherwise: you had told us, about the latter end of your *Argument*[11] how liable men were in choosing their religion to be misled by humour, passion, and prejudice; and therefore it was not fit that in a business of such concernment they should be left

---

[11] Proast's *Argument of the Letter Concerning Toleration* ... (p. 54).

to themselves; and hence, in this matter of religion, you would have them subjected to the coactive power of the magistrate. But this contrivance is visibly of no advantage to the true religion, nor can serve at all to secure men from a wrong choice. For the magistrates, by their humours, prejudices, and passions, which they are born to like other men, being as liable and likely to be misled in the choice of their religion as any of their brethren, as constant experience has always shown; what advantage could it be to mankind, for the salvation of their souls, that the magistrates of the world should have power to use force to bring men to that religion which they, each of them, by whatsoever humour, passion, or prejudice influenced, had chosen to themselves as the true? For whatsoever you did, I think with reverence we may say that God foresaw, that whatever commission one magistrate had by the law of nature, all magistrates had; and that commission, if there were any such, could be only to use their coactive power to bring men to the religion they believed to be true, whether it were really the true or no; and therefore I shall, without taking away government out of the world, or so much as questioning it, still think this a reasonable question: 'What if God, foreseeing this force would be in the hands of men, as passionate, as humoursome, as liable to prejudice and error, as the rest of their brethren; did not think it a proper means, in such hands, to bring men into the right way?'

...

[I]f ... the religion of dissenters from the true be a fault to be punished by the magistrate, who is to judge who are guilty of that fault? Must it be the magistrate everywhere; or the magistrate in some countries, and not in others; or the magistrate nowhere? If the magistrate nowhere is to be judge who are dissenters from the true religion, he can nowhere punish them. If he be to be everywhere judge, then the King of France, or the Great Turk, must punish those whom they judge dissenters from the true religion, as well as other potentates. If some magistrates have a right to judge, and others not: that yet, I fear, how absurd soever it be, should I grant it, will not do your business. For besides that they will hardly agree to make you their infallible umpire in the case, to determine who of them have, and who have not this right to judge which is the true religion; or if they should, and you should declare the King of England had that right (viz. whilst he complied to support the orthodoxy, ecclesiastical polity, and those ceremonies which you approve of); but that the King of

France, and the Great Turk, had it not; and so could have no right to use force on those they judged dissenters from the true religion, you ought to bethink yourself what you will reply to one that should use your own words ...

...

For if you were to argue with a papist, or a Presbyterian, in the case, what privilege have you to tell him that his reason and conscience is perverted, more than he has to tell you that yours is so? Unless it be this insupportable presumption, that your reason and conscience ought to be the measure of all reason and conscience in all others; which how you can claim without pretending to infallibility, is not easy to discern.

...

There are propositions extant in geometry, with their demonstrations annexed, and that with such sufficient evidence to some men of deep thought and penetration as to make them see the demonstration, and give assent to the truth: whilst there are many others, and those no novices in mathematics, who, with all the consideration and attention they can use, are never able to attain unto it. It is so in other parts of truth. That which has evidence enough to make one man certain, has not enough to make another so much as guess it to be true, though he has spared no endeavour or application in examining it. And therefore, if the magistrate be to punish none but those who reject the true religion, when it has been offered with sufficient evidence, I imagine he will not have many to punish if he will, as he ought, distinguish between the innocent and the guilty.

...

By this time, Sir, I suppose you see upon what grounds I think you have not cleared those difficulties which were charged by me on your method; and my reader will see what reason there was for those imputations, which, with so loud an outcry, you laid upon me of unfair dealing; since there is not one of them which cannot be made good to be contained either in your book, or in your hypothesis; and so clearly, that I could not imagine that a man who had so far considered government as to engage in print, in such a controversy as this, could miss seeing it as soon as mentioned to him. One of them which very much offends you, and makes you so often tell me what I say is impertinent, and nothing to

the purpose, and sometimes to use warmer expressions, is, that I argue
against a power in the magistrate to bring men to his own religion: for I
could not imagine that, to a man of any thought, it could need proving,
that if there were a commission given to all magistrates by the law of
nature, which obliged them to use force to bring men to the true religion, it was not possible for them to put this commission in execution,
without being judges what was the true religion; and then there needed
no great quickness to perceive that every magistrate, when your commission came to be put in execution, would, one as well as another, find
himself obliged to use force to bring men to that which he believed to be
the true religion.

# From *A Second Letter to the Author of the Three Letters for Toleration* (1704)

...

As to 'using force in matters of religion' (which are your words, not mine), if you mean by it the using force to bring men to any other religion besides the true, I am so far from owning the question to be whether the magistrate has a right to use force for such a purpose, that I have always thought it out of question that no man in the world, magistrate or other, can have any right to use either force or any other means that you can name to bring men to any false religion, how much soever he may persuade himself that it is the true.

It is not therefore from any alteration, but from the true state of the question, that I 'take occasion', as you complain without cause, 'to lay load on [you], for charging [me] with the absurdities of a power in the magistrates to punish men to bring them to their religion'. But it seems, having little to say against what I do assert, you find it necessary yourself to alter the question, and to make the world believe that I assert what I do not, that you may have something before you which you can confute. And so you undertake to prove, that 'if upon [my] grounds the magistrate be obliged to use force to bring men to the true religion, it will necessarily follow that every magistrate who believes his religion to be true is obliged to use force to bring men to his'.

Now because this undertaking is so necessary for you, and your whole cause seems to depend upon the success of it, I shall the more carefully consider how well you perform it. But before I do this, it will be fit to let you know, in what sense I grant your inference, and in what sense I deny it. Now that every magistrate, who upon just and sufficient grounds believes his religion to be true, is obliged to use some moderate penalties (which is all the force I ever contended for) to bring men to his religion, I freely grant; because that must needs be the true religion, since no other can upon such grounds be believed to be true. But that any magistrate, who upon weak and deceitful grounds believes a false religion to be true (and he can never do it upon better grounds), is obliged to use the same (or any other) means to bring men to his religion, this I flatly deny; nor can it by any rules of reasoning be inferred from what I assert. But I shall now consider how you attempt to do it.

You suppose, you say, that I will grant you (what he must be a hard man indeed that will not grant) 'that anything laid upon the magistrate as a duty is some way or other practicable. Now,' you go on,

> the magistrate being obliged to use force in matters of religion, but yet so as to bring men only to the true religion, he will not be in any capacity to perform this part of his duty, unless the religion he is thus to promote be what he can certainly know, or else what it is sufficient for him to believe to be the true. Either his knowledge or his opinion must point out that religion to him, which he is by force to promote.

Where if by knowing, or knowledge, you mean the effect of strict demonstration, and by believing, or opinion, any sort of assent or persuasion, how slightly soever grounded: then I must deny the sufficiency of your division, because there is a third sort of degree or persuasion, which though not grounded upon strict demonstration, yet in firmness and stability does far exceed that which is built upon slight appearance of probability, being grounded upon such clear and solid proof as leaves no reasonable doubt in an attentive and unbiased mind: so that it approaches very near to that which is produced by demonstration, and is therefore, as it respects religion, very frequently and familiarly called in Scripture, not faith or belief only, but knowledge, and in diverse places, full assurance; as might easily be shown, if that were needful. Now this kind of persuasion, this knowledge, this full assurance, men may and ought to have of the true religion; but they can never have it of a false one. And this it is, that must point out that religion to the magistrate, which he is to promote by the method I contend for.

And hence appears the impertinency of all your discourse concerning the difference between faith and knowledge, where the thing you were concerned to make out, if you would speak to the purpose, was no other but this: that there are as clear and as solid grounds for the belief of false religions as there are for the belief of the true: or, that men may both as firmly and as rationally believe and embrace false religions as they can the true. This, I confess, is a point which, when you have well cleared and established it, will do your business; but nothing else will. And therefore your talk of the difference between faith and knowledge, however it may amuse such as are prone to admire all that you say, will never enable you, before better judges, from the duty of every magistrate to use moderate penalties for the promoting of the true religion to infer the same obligation to lie upon every magistrate in respect to his religion, whatever it be. Because there is (as I believe all judicious men will acknowledge, till you have proved the contrary) this perceptual advantage on the side of the true religion, that it may and ought to be believed upon clear and solid grounds, such as will appear the more so, the more they are examined, whereas no other religion can be believed but upon such appearances only as will not bear a just examination.

...

You go on: 'By what has been already said' (which has been already sufficiently considered) 'I suppose it is evident that if the magistrate be to use force only for promoting the true religion, he can have no other guide but his own persuasion of what is the true religion, and he must be led by that in his use of force.' Where if by the word 'guide' you mean the magistrate's next guide, subordinate to his principal guide, which is no other but God himself by his laws; I readily grant you this consequence. But how you will oblige me by it to allow, as you say I must, 'all magistrates, of whatsoever religion, the use of force to bring men to theirs', I do not see. For though the magistrate can have no other next, subordinate guide in this matter, but his own persuasion of what is the true religion, yet he is accountable to his principal guide and supreme judge for his very persuasion, as well as for all that he does in pursuance of it. For, if he be not some way wanting to himself and to his duty, he may and will get a well-grounded and right persuasion of what is the true religion, which will be a true and faithful guide to him. But if, through his own fault, a wrong persuasion gets the guidance of him, he alone must answer both for that persuasion, and for all that he does by the direction of it. And no principle of mine will oblige me to allow of his miscarriages.

You proceed further:

> Persuade magistrates in general of this [that it is their duty to use force for the promoting the true religion] and then tell me how any magistrate shall be restrained from the use of force, for the promoting what he thinks to be the true? For he being persuaded that it is his duty to use force to promote the true religion, and being also persuaded his is the true religion, what shall stop his hand?

To which I answer: nothing that I know, but the hand of the Almighty, if he think fit to do it. And this is all the answer I need to give you. But if you will needs have more, *Respondebit pro me meus Aristoteles.*[1] That old conductor of human understanding, among a great many observations which have remained unquestioned to this day, has this for one: That if but one absurdity be granted, a thousand will follow. And if they will follow, who can help it? But though I cannot answer that question, yet I can tell you who is to answer both for the first absurdity, and for all the rest that follow from it, namely, not any man that holds nothing but truth, for from mere truth nothing but truth will follow: but he alone who admits the first absurdity.

Now I do indeed assert that as every magistrate is obliged to embrace and profess the true religion himself, as far as he has the means of knowing it, so likewise to provide that it be duly proposed to his subjects; and withal to require their receiving and professing it, under such moderate penalties as shall be judged most likely to prevail with them to lay aside all prejudice, and to consider fairly what it has to say for itself, that so they may be induced to give it that reception which it deserves and requires. And seeing no hurt, but a great deal of good, that would follow if this were done by all the magistrates in the world, I see no reason to doubt of the truth of this assertion. But if any magistrate, who owns this to be his duty, does withal admit a false religion to be the true, I grant that his conscience, so debauched, will require him to do that for the promoting his false religion, which ought to be done for none but the true. And if the greater part of the magistrates of the world should be acted by

---

[1] 'My Aristotle will reply for me.' An undergraduate's examination answer. The following reference to Aristotle as the 'old' conductor of human understanding strongly suggests that Proast knew or at least guessed at Locke's identity (as author of the *Essay Concerning Human Understanding*).

such consciences, I grant likewise that whatever hurt would be done, by so abusing the means of promoting the true religion, would spread itself so much the wider.

But what will you draw from all this? Or what is the true spring and cause of this miscarriage, and the harm done by it? Is it the persuasion that all magistrates are bound to lay some moderate penalties upon the refusers of the true religion, duly tendered to them? No, certainly: for if all magistrates did so, no harm but undoubtedly a great deal of good would flow from it; but the embracing false religions instead of the true. For it is that alone that works and produces the noxious miscarriage; whilst the other persuasion does only occasion it, by the unlucky accident of its being joined with false religions. But can you, from that persuasion's thus accidentally occasioning the miscarriage, conclude it to be false, and that no man can own it without allowing all magistrates, of whatsoever religion, the use of force to bring men to theirs? If you think you may, I suppose it is no hard matter to convince you that you cannot.

For I doubt not but you will grant that there are some men in the world (and how great a part of mankind they may be, neither do you nor I know) who believe some things which are really forbidden by God, and very heinous sins, to be commanded by him and to belong to their duty. Such was that wretched person … who thought himself commanded by God (Deuteronomy 13: 6, 8, 9, 10) to kill his father for persuading him to receive the Communion kneeling. Now there is nothing more manifest than that to preach that every man is bound, as he expects to be saved, to endeavour to do his whole duty, may occasion some men (and God alone knows how many) to commit those sins which they take to be part of their duty. If therefore you conclude well in the other case, you must, by parity of reason, conclude here also, that the doctrine mentioned, viz. that every man is bound to endeavour to do his whole duty, is false; and that no man can preach it, without allowing all men to do whatever they believe to be part of their duty. For if no doctrine that may occasion sin where it is received can be true or be preached, without allowing men to sin, then the doctrine mentioned must needs be false; and no man can preach it, without allowing all men to do whatever they believe to be part of their duty, though some should believe some of the greatest sins to be so. But if this be no good consequence, neither can that be such, which you take so much pains to fix upon me.

You tell me indeed, from the *Discourse Concerning Conscience*, written by a 'very judicious and reverend Prelate',[2] as you justly call him, that 'where a man is mistaken in his judgement, even in that case it is always a sin to act against it'. A truth which I never denied or questioned. But it had been more to your purpose if that excellent author had anywhere told us (what I assure myself he has not, nor ever will) that it is *never* a sin for a man to act according to his judgement. For if that were true, it would necessarily follow that an erroneous conscience discharges men from the obligation even of the most sacred of divine laws; so that in following such a conscience, they act innocently and contract no guilt or blame, though the things they do be never so plainly and strictly forbidden by God. And so the wretch before mentioned did not sin, if he killed his father (as I suppose he did) because his mistake of the sense of Deuteronomy 13 took off the obligation, as to him, of the fifth and sixth Commandments. And if this be good divinity, then I must acknowledge that whoever asserts that every magistrate is bound to promote the true religion by moderate penalties, must allow every magistrate to use the same means for the promoting his own religion, how false or impious soever it be.

But if this be by no means to be admitted; but those sacred laws must be acknowledged to retain their obliging force, notwithstanding whatever errors men may suffer to possess their minds, which I hope you acknowledge, as well as I: then I suppose you will admit that that abandoned miscreant was as much as ever obliged, by the fifth and sixth Commandments, to love and reverence his father and, instead of killing him, to do all he could to cherish and preserve his life, even while his mistake of the sense of that other text of Scripture obliged him (as much as a mistake could do) to kill him. And if so, I see not how you will avoid admitting likewise, that how firmly soever any magistrate may believe his own false religion to be the true, and how much soever that erroneous belief or persuasion may be thought to oblige him to use the means which are proper for the promoting the true religion for the promoting his own, he is nevertheless at the same time most strictly forbidden by the first Table of the Divine Law to use (I say not force only, but) any means at all for the promoting his own religion: so that he will sin very heinously in doing it, though he does but act according to his judgement ...

---

[2] Locke's reference was to John Sharp, Archbishop of York, author of *A Discourse Concerning Conscience* (1678).

# From *A Fourth Letter for Toleration* (1704)

...

[Y]ou grant that every magistrate, without knowing that his religion is true, is obliged, upon his believing it to be true, to use force to bring men to it; indeed you add, 'who believes it to be true upon just and sufficient grounds'. So you have got a distinction, and that always sets off a disputant, though many times it is of no use to his argument. For here let me ask you, who must be judge whether the grounds, upon which he believes his religion to be true, be just and sufficient? Must the magistrate himself judge for himself or must you judge for him? A third competitor in this judgement I know not where you will find for your turn.

If every magistrate must judge for himself, whether the grounds upon which he believes his religion to be true are just and sufficient grounds, your limitation of the use of force to such only as believe upon just and sufficient grounds, bating that it is an ornament to your style and learning, might have been spared, since it leaves my inference untouched in the full latitude I have expressed it concerning every magistrate; there not being any one magistrate excluded thereby from an obligation to use force to bring men to his own religion by this your distinction. For if every magistrate, who upon just and sufficient grounds believes his religion to be true, be obliged to use force to bring men to his religion, and every magistrate be himself judge whether the grounds he believes upon be just and sufficient; it is visible every magistrate is obliged to use force to bring men to his religion; since anyone, who believes any religion to be true, cannot but judge the grounds upon which he believes it to be true are just and sufficient. For if he judged otherwise, he could not then believe it to be true.

If you say you must judge for the magistrate, then what you grant is this: that every magistrate who, upon grounds that you judge to be just and sufficient, believes his religion to be true, is obliged to use force to bring men to his religion. If this be your meaning, as it seems not much remote from it, you will do well to speak it out, that the magistrates of the world may know who to have recourse to in the difficulty you put upon them, in declaring them under an obligation to use force to bring men to the true religion; which they can neither certainly know, nor must venture to use force to bring men to, upon their own persuasion of the truth of it; when they have nothing but one of these two, viz. knowledge or belief that the religion they promote is true, to determine them.

Necessity has at last (unless you would have the magistrate act in the dark and use his force wholly at random) prevailed on you to grant that the magistrate may use force to bring men to that religion which he believes to be true; but, say you, 'his belief must be upon just and sufficient grounds'. The same necessity remaining still must prevail with you to go one step further, and tell me whether the magistrate himself must be judge, whether the grounds, upon which he believes his religion to be true, be just and sufficient; or whether you are to be judge for him. If you say the first, my inference stands good, and then this question, I think, is yielded, and at an end. If you say you are to be judge for the magistrates, I shall congratulate to the magistrates of the world the way you have found out for them to acquit themselves of their duty, if you will but please to publish it, that they may know where to find you; for in truth, Sir, I prefer you, in this case, to the pope; though you know that old gentleman at Rome has long since laid claim to all decisions of this kind, and alleges infallibility for the support of his title; which indeed will scarce be able to stand at Rome, or anywhere else, without the help of infallibility.

. . .

[Y]ou ... pretend an uncertainty of what I mean by 'knowing or knowledge, and by believing or opinion'. First, as to knowledge, I have said 'certainly know'. I have called it 'vision; knowledge and certainty; knowledge properly so called'. And for believing or opinion, I speak of believing with assurance, and say that believing in the highest degree of assurance is not knowledge. That whatever is not capable of demonstration, is not, unless it be self-evident, capable to produce knowledge, how well grounded and great soever the assurance of faith may be wherewith it is received. That I grant, that a strong assurance of any truth, settled upon prevalent and well-grounded arguments of probability, is often called knowledge in popular ways of talking; but being here to distinguish between knowledge and belief, to what degrees of confidence soever raised, their boundaries must be kept and their names not confounded; with more to the same purpose; whereby it is so plain, that by knowledge I mean the effect of strict demonstration; and by believing or opinion, I mean any degree of persuasion even to the highest degree of assurance; that I challenge you yourself to set it down in plainer and more express terms.

But nobody can blame you for not finding your adversary's meaning, let it be ever so plain, when you can find nothing to answer to it. The reason, therefore, which you allege for the denying the sufficiency of my division, is no reason at all. Your pretended reason is because there is 'a third sort or degree of persuasion; which though not grounded upon strict demonstration; yet in firmness and stability does far exceed that which is built upon slight appearances of probability', etc. Let it be so, that there is a degree of persuasion not grounded upon strict demonstration, far exceeding that which is built upon slight appearances of probability. But let me ask you what reason can this be to deny the sufficiency of my division, because there is, as you say, a third sort or degree of persuasion; when even that which you call this third sort or degree of persuasion is contained in my division. This is a specimen indeed, not of answering what I have said, but of not answering; and for such I leave it to the reader. 'A degree of persuasion, though not grounded on strict demonstration, yet in firmness and stability far exceeding that which is built upon slight appearances of probability, [you] call here a third sort or degree of persuasion.' Pray tell me which are the two other sorts; for knowledge upon strict demonstration, is not belief or persuasion, but wholly above it. Besides, if the degrees of firmness in persuasion make different sorts of persuasion, there are not only three, but three hundred sorts of persuasion; and therefore the naming of your third sort was with little ground, and to no purpose or tendency to an answer.

...

[Y]ou seem to me to build upon these two false propositions:

(1) That in the want of knowledge and certainty of which is the true religion, nothing is fit to set the magistrate upon doing his duty in employing of force to make men consider and embrace the true religion, but the highest persuasion and full assurance of its truth. Whereas his own persuasion of the truth of his own religion, in what degree soever it be, so he believes it to be true, will, if he thinks it his duty by force to promote the true, be sufficient to set him on work. Nor can it be otherwise, since his own persuasion of his own religion, which he judges so well grounded as to venture his future state upon it, cannot but be sufficient to set him upon doing what he takes to be his duty in bringing others to the same religion.

(2) Another false supposition you build upon is this, that the true religion is always embraced with the firmest assent. There is scarce anyone so little acquainted with the world, that has not met with instances of men most unmoveably confident and fully assured in a religion which was not the true. Nor is there, among the many absurd religions of the world, almost anyone that does not find votaries to lay down their lives for it; and if that be not firm persuasion and full assurance that is stronger than the love of life, and has force enough to make a man throw himself into the arms of death, it is hard to know what is firm persuasion and full assurance. Jews and Mahometans have frequently given instances of this highest degree of persuasion. And the Brahmins' religion in the East is entertained by its followers with no less assurance of its truth, since it is not unusual for some of them to throw themselves under the wheels of a mighty chariot, wherein they on solemn days draw the image of their God about in procession, there to be crushed to death, and sacrifice their lives in honour of the God they believe in.

If it be objected that those are examples of mean and common men, but the great men of the world, and the heads of societies, do not so easily give themselves up to a confirmed bigotry, I answer: the persuasion they have of the truth of their own religion is visibly strong enough to make them venture themselves, and use force to others upon the belief of it. Princes are made like other men, believe upon the like grounds that other men do, and act as warmly upon that belief, though the grounds of their persuasion be in themselves not very clear, or may appear to others to be not of the utmost solidity. Men act by the strength of their persuasion, though they do not always place their persuasion and assent on that side on which, in reality, the strength of truth lies. Reasons that are not thought of, nor heard of, nor rightly apprehended, nor duly weighed, make no impression on the mind; and truth, how richly soever stored with them, may not be assented to but lie neglected. The only difference between princes and other men herein is this, that princes are usually more positive in matters of religion but less instructed. The softness and pleasures of a court, to which they are usually abandoned when young, and affairs of state which wholly possess them when grown up, seldom allow any of them time to consider and examine that they may embrace the true religion. And here your scheme, upon your own supposition, has a fundamental error that overturns it. For your affirming that force, your way applied, is the necessary and competent means to bring men to the true religion, you leave magistrates destitute of these necessary and competent means of being brought to the true religion, though that be the readiest way, in your scheme the only way, to bring other men to it, and is contended for by you as the only method.

But further, you will perhaps be ready to reply that you do not say barely, that men may not as firmly, but that they cannot as firmly and rationally, believe and embrace false religions as they can the true. This, be it as true as it will, is of no manner of advantage to your cause. For here the question, necessary to be considered in your way of arguing, returns upon you: who must be judge whether the magistrate believes and embraces his religion rationally or no? If he himself be judge, then he does act rationally, and it must have the same operation on him as if it were the most rational in the world; if you must be judge for him, whether his belief be rational or no, why may not others judge for him as well as you? Or at least he judge for you, as well as you for him, at least till you have produced your patent of infallibility and commission of superintendency over the belief of the magistrates of the earth, and shown the commission whereby you are appointed the director of the magistrates of the world in their belief, which is or is not the true religion?

...

But perhaps you will tell me that you do not allow that magistrates, who are of false religions, should be determined by their own persuasions, which are 'built upon slight appearances of probability; but such as are grounded upon clear and solid proofs', which the true religion alone has.

In answer to this, I ask, who must be judge whether his persuasion be grounded on clear and solid proofs: the magistrate himself, or you for him? If the magistrate himself, then we are but where we were; and all that you say here, with the distinction that you have made about several sorts of persuasion, serves only to lead us about to the same place. For the magistrate, of what religion soever, must, notwithstanding all you have said, be determined by his own persuasion. If you say you must be judge of the clearness and solidity of the proofs upon which the magistrate grounds the belief of his own religion, it is time you should produce your patent and show the commission whereby you act.

There are other qualifications you assign of the proof on which you tell us 'your third sort or degree of persuasion is grounded; and that is such as leaves no reasonable doubt in an attentive and unbiased mind'; which, unless you must be judge what is a reasonable doubt, and which is an attentive and unbiased mind, will do you no manner of service. If the magistrate must be judge for himself in this case, you can have nothing to say to him; but if you must be judge, then any doubt about your religion will be unreasonable, and his not embracing and promoting your religion will be want of attention and an unbiased mind. But let me tell you, give but the same liberty of judging for the magistrate of your religion to the men of another religion, which they have as much right to as you have to judge for the magistrate of any other religion in the points mentioned; all this will return upon you. Go into France, and try whether it be not so. So that your plea for the magistrate's using force for promoting the true religion, as you have stated it, gives as much power and authority to the King of France to use it against his dissenting subjects as to any other prince in Christendom to use it against theirs; name which you please.

The fallacy in making it the magistrate's duty to promote by force the only true religion lies in this, that you allow yourself to suppose the magistrate, who is of your religion, to be well-grounded, attentive, and unbiased, and fully and firmly assured that his religion is true; but that other magistrates of other religions different from yours are not so: which, what is it but to erect yourself into a state of infallibility above all other men of different persuasions from yours, which yet they have as good a title to as yourself?

. . .

Pray tell me, is firmness of persuasion, or being of the true religion, either of them by itself sufficient to point out to the magistrate that religion which it is his duty to promote by force? For they do not always go together. If being of the true religion by itself may do it, your mentioning firmness of persuasion, grounded on solid proof that leaves no doubt, is to no purpose but to mislead your reason; for everyone that is of the true religion does not arrive at that high degree of persuasion, that full assurance which approaches that which is very near to that which is produced by demonstration. And in this sense of full assurance, which you say men may have of the true religion and can never have of a false one, your answer amounts to this: that full assurance, in him that embraces the true religion, will point out the religion he is by force to promote: where it is plain, that by fullness of assurance you do mean not the firmness of his persuasion that points out to him the religion which he is by force to promote (for any lower degree of persuasion to him that embraces the true religion would do it as certainly, and to one that embraces not the true religion, the highest degree of persuasion would even in your opinion do nothing at all); but his being of the true religion, is that which alone guides him to his duty of promoting the true religion by force.

So that to my question: how shall a magistrate who is persuaded that it is his and every magistrate's duty to promote the true religion by force, be determined in his use of force? You seem to say his firm persuasion or full assurance of the truth of the religion he so promotes must determine him; and presently, in other words, you seem to lay the stress upon his actually being of the true religion. The first of these answers is not true, for I have shown that firmness of persuasion may and does point out to magistrates false religions as well as the true: and the second is much what the same, as if to one, who should ask what should enable a man to find the right way who knows it not, it should be answered, the being in it. One of these must be your meaning, choose which you please of them.

...

You tell us, it is by the law of nature magistrates are obliged to promote the true religion by force. It must be owned that, if this be an obligation of the law of nature, very few magistrates overlook it, so forward are they to promote that religion by force which they take to be true. This being the case, I beseech you tell me what was Huaina Capac, emperor of Peru, obliged to do? Who, being persuaded of his duty to promote the true religion, was not yet within distance of knowing or so much as hearing of the Christian religion, which really is the true (so far was he from a possibility to have his belief grounded upon the solid and clear proofs of the true religion). Was he to promote the true religion by force? That he neither did nor could know anything of; so that was morally impossible for him to do. Was he to sit still in the neglect of his duty incumbent on him? That is in effect to suppose it a duty and no duty at the same time. If, upon his not knowing which is the true religion, you allow it not his duty to promote it by force, the question is at an end: you and I are agreed, that it is not the magistrate's duty by force to promote the true religion. If you hold it in that case to be his duty, what remains for him to do but to use force to promote that religion which he himself is strongly, nay, perhaps to the highest degree of firmness, persuaded is the true? Which is the granting what I contend for, that, if the magistrate be obliged to promote by force the true religion, it will thence follow, that he is obliged to promote by force that religion which he is persuaded is the true; since, as you will have it, force was given him to that end, and it is his duty to use it, and he has nothing else to determine it to that end but his own persuasion. So that one of these two things must follow, either that in that case it ceases to be his duty, or else he must promote his own religion; choose you which you please ... [here the text ends]

# Index

Apostolic succession, 10, 16, 43
Aristotle, 147, 167
assent, 52–3, 55, 72, 129, 153, 158, 165, 173, 174
atheism, xii, 21, 37, 54
Augustine, St, xv, xviii
authenticity, and sincerity, xxiii

Bagshaw, Edward, xi
Bayle, Pierre, xviii, xxvi
belief, argument from, xxi, 8, 30–1, 50–3, 55,
    64, 69–71
  defined, xiv–xvi
belief, reasons for, xiii, xxii, 57, 81, 153–5

castration, analogy with, 83, 109–10
Catholics, viii, xii, 31, 35–6
charity, 3, 4, 5, 13, 15, 16, 17, 62, 116, 135
Chillingworth, William, ix, xi
church, nature of, 9, 10, 13
  see also Apostolic succession;
        commonwealth, church and
civil interests, xvi, xx, xxi, 7, 11–15, 32, 61, 102,
    104–5, 143–4
  salvation and, 119
  see also harm
civil power, see state, powers of
Clarendon Code, viii
commonwealth, church and, 6, 15, 20–1, 26,
    28, 103, 105
conscience
  conformity and, 65–6
  erroneous, 169
  forms of worship and, 4, 70
  interest and, 94
  law and, 31, 33, 42
  rights and, xi, xii
consent, xiv, xxviii, 47, 63, 131, 136, 141

  see also social contract
consideration
  cannot be forced, 77–8, 91–6
  limited need for, xxii–xxiii, 112
  penalties and, 57–9, 65, 154, 162
  resistance to, 57, 84–5

decency, 22, 25, 126
dialogue, model of, xxvi–xxvii, 67, 156, 162
dissenters
  and Anglicans, xxii, 86, 94
  assemblies of, 40
  punishment of, 76, 77–8, 89, 93, 95–6,
        113–14, 148–9, 151
  toleration of, viii, 39

Edict of Nantes, x
  see also protestants, French persecution of
educational analogies, xxviii, 96, 109, 135–7,
        138–9
equality, xxvi, xxvii, xxix, 39, 95, 157
error, argument from, xxiv, 20, 65, 71, 79–80,
        85, 131–2, 161, 174
  defined, xiv–xvi
  Proast's reply to, xxiv, 167–8
excommunication, 12, 35

faith and knowledge, xxiv, 87, 123, 124, 158
  assurance and, 165, 171–2
Filmer, Sir Robert, xxviii
force, indirect use of, 56, 73–4, 76, 78, 82, 109,
        136, 139, 143
forms of worship, see indifferent things

grace, 86, 98, 118, 127

harm, 13, 16, 25, 26, 34, 141

heresy, 4, 14, 43–5

indifferent things, ix, xi, 11, 18, 22–5, 40, 46, 125

Jewish commonwealth, 28–30
Jews, 20, 23, 25, 41, 54, 68, 85, 86, 173
    conversion of, 68

law of nature, xx, 47, 48, 110, 133–5, 141–2, 159, 176
law, rule of, 48–9, 73, 88–9, 92, 147
liberalism, xi, xxviii, xxx
Limborch, Philip van,0448n, ix
Locke, other works
    *Essay Concerning Human Understanding,* xvii, 50–3
    *Essay on Toleration,* x
    *Reasonableness of Christianity,* xxii
    *Second Treatise,* xv, xix, xxvi, xxx, 47–9
    *Thoughts on Education,* xiii
    *Two Tracts,* xi–xii, xv
Loyola, St Ignatius, xvii
Luke, Gospel of, and conversion, 0453n, xviii, xxvi

mandate, argument from, xix–xx, 7, 71, 82–4, 99–100, 106–7, 116, 133–5, 145, 159, 163
    defined, xiv–xvi
medical analogies, xix, 16, 18–19, 21, 73, 79, 94, 100–1, 114, 118–19, 128, 129–31, 150–1
miracles, 83, 127
Muslims (Mahometans), 28, 36, 54, 68, 70, 101, 156, 173

New Testament, contrasted with Old, xiv, 25, 29

order, argument from, xxvi, 15, 39, 41–2
    defined, xii, xiii
orthodoxy, xxvii, 3, 14, 16, 26, 65, 90, 128

pagans, 13, 27, 31, 41, 54, 68, 70
parental powers, xxviii, 137–8, 140
penalties
    duration of, 115–16, 153
    moderate use of, xvii, 59, 64, 74, 93, 98–9, 114, 127, 135, 149, 165, 167
    state and, xvi
    violent use of, 4, 38, 59, 74, 113, 149
persecution, irrationality of, xv–xvi, xvii, xxx, 66, 75, 81

pluralism, xxix, xxx, 57
political theory
    Locke and, xiii, xxiv, xxx
    transnational context of, x, xxiv, xxix, 69, 70, 104, 161–2
power-seeking as motive, xvii, xxix, 3, 17, 27, 42
protestantism, xxi
protestants, French persecution of, x, 69, 75, 88, 126, 175

Rawls, John, xxv
Remonstrants, Dutch, ix, xi, xxii, 41
Reynolds brothers, xxii, 81
Rome, Church of, 83, 90, 105, 171
Rye House plot, viii

salvation
    magistrate's care for, 61, 62–4, 121–2
    personal responsibility for, 31–2, 34, 104
scepticism, xxiii, xxiv, xxvii, 111–12, 155, 166
Shaftesbury, Earl of, viii, ix, x
sincerity, xvii, xxiii, 7, 8, 11, 21, 72, 76
social contract, xv, xix–xx, xxiii, xxv, xxvii–xxviii, 106, 141, 160
Socinians, 20, 41
state
    powers of, xviii–xix, xxvi, 7, 14, 26, 32–3, 61–2, 102, 128
    distinguished from capacity, 142–3, 145–6
    *see also* civil interests; law of nature
    Proast's view of, xix, 110, 120–1

tempers, xiii, 153
toleration, the case for, *see* belief, argument from; error, argument from; mandate, argument from; order, argument from
Toleration Act (1689), 158
true religion
    claims to possess, 91–2
    imposition by state, xxiv, 116, 164
    knowledge of, 111–12, 166, 173, 176
    magistrate's judgement of, 123–6, 132–3, 135, 140, 159, 170–1, 174–5
    prevails by own light, 69, 87

Waldron, Jeremy, xiv, xvi, xxi
Walwyn, William, xii, xv, xxvii

zeal, *see* power-seeking as motive

# Cambridge texts in the history of philosophy

*Titles published in the series thus far*

Aquinas *Disputed Questions on the Virtues* (edited by E.M. Atkins and Thomas
   Williams)
Aquinas *Summa Theologiae, Questions on God* (edited by Brian Davies and Brian
   Leftow)
Aristotle *Nicomachean Ethics* (edited by Roger Crisp)
Arnauld and Nicole *Logic or the Art of Thinking* (edited by Jill Vance Buroker)
Augustine *On the Free Choice of the Will, On Grace and Free Choice, and Other Writings*
   (edited by Peter King)
Augustine *On the Trinity* (edited by Gareth Matthews)
Bacon *The New Organon* (edited by Lisa Jardine and Michael Silverthorne)
Berkeley *Philosophical Writings* (edited by Desmond M. Clarke)
Boyle *A Free Enquiry into the Vulgarly Received Notion of Nature* (edited by Edward B.
   Davis and Michael Hunter)
Bruno *Cause, Principle and Unity* and *Essays on Magic* (edited by Richard Blackwell
   and Robert de Lucca with an introduction by Alfonso Ingegno)
Cavendish *Observations upon Experimental Philosophy* (edited by Eileen O'Neill)
Cicero *On Moral Ends* (edited by Julia Annas, translated by Raphael Woolf)
Clarke *A Demonstration of the Being and Attributes of God and Other Writings* (edited by
   Ezio Vailati)
*Classic and Romantic German Aesthetics* (edited by J.M. Bernstein)
Condillac *Essay on the Origin of Human Knowledge* (edited by Hans Aarsleff)
Conway *The Principles of the Most Ancient and Modern Philosophy* (edited by Allison P.
   Coudert and Taylor Corse)
Cudworth *A Treatise Concerning Eternal and Immutable Morality* with *A Treatise of
   Freewill* (edited by Sarah Hutton)
Descartes *Meditations on First Philosophy*, with selections from the *Objections and
   Replies* (edited by John Cottingham)
Descartes *The World and Other Writings* (edited by Stephen Gaukroger)
Fichte *Attempt at a Critique of All Revelation* (edited by Allen Wood, translated by
   Garrett Green)
Fichte *Foundations of Natural Right* (edited by Frederick Neuhouser, translated by
   Michael Baur)
Fichte *The System of Ethics* (edited by Daniel Breazeale and Günter Zöller)
*Greek and Roman Aesthetics* (edited by Oleg V. Bychkov and Anne Sheppard)
Hamann *Philosophical Writings* (edited by Kenneth Haynes)
Heine *On the History of Religion and Philosophy in Germany and Other Writings* (edited
   by Terry Pinkard, translated by Howard Pollack-Milgate)
Herder *Philosophical Writings* (edited by Michael Forster)
*Hobbes and Bramhall on Liberty and Necessity* (edited by Vere Chappell)
Humboldt *On Language* (edited by Michael Losonsky, translated by Peter Heath)
Hume *Dialogues Concerning Natural Religion and Other Writings* (edited by Dorothy
   Coleman)

Hume *An Enquiry concerning Human Understanding* (edited by Stephen Buckle)

Kant *Anthropology from a Pragmatic Point of View* (edited by Robert B. Louden with an introduction by Manfred Kuehn)

Kant *Critique of Practical Reason* (edited by Mary Gregor with an introduction by Andrews Reath)

Kant *Groundwork of the Metaphysics of Morals* (edited by Mary Gregor with an introduction by Christine M. Korsgaard

Kant *Metaphysical Foundations of Natural Science* (edited by Michael Friedman)

Kant *The Metaphysics of Morals* (edited by Mary Gregor with an introduction by Roger Sullivan)

Kant *Observations on the Feeling of the Beautiful and Sublime and Other Writings* (edited by Patrick Frierson and Paul Guyer)

Kant *Prolegomena to any Future Metaphysics* (edited by Gary Hatfield)

Kant *Religion within the Boundaries of Mere Reason and Other Writings* (edited by Allen Wood and George di Giovanni with an introduction by Robert Merrihew Adams)

Kierkegaard *Concluding Unscientific Postscript* (edited by Alastair Hannay)

Kierkegaard *Fear and Trembling* (edited by C. Stephen Evans and Sylvia Walsh)

La Mettrie *Machine Man and Other Writings* (edited by Ann Thomson)

Leibniz *New Essays on Human Understanding* (edited by Peter Remnant and Jonathan Bennett)

Lessing *Philosophical and Theological Writings* (edited by H.B. Nisbet)

Locke *On Toleration* (edited by Richard Vernon)

Malebranche *Dialogues on Metaphysics and on Religion* (edited by Nicholas Jolley and David Scott)

Malebranche *The Search after Truth* (edited by Thomas M. Lennon and Paul J. Olscamp)

*Medieval Islamic Philosophical Writings* (edited by Muhammad Ali Khalidi)

*Medieval Jewish Philosophical Writings* (edited by Charles Manekin)

Melanchthon *Orations on Philosophy and Education* (edited by Sachiko Kusukawa, translated by Christine Salazar)

Mendelssohn *Philosophical Writings* (edited by Daniel O. Dahlstrom)

Newton *Philosophical Writings* (edited by Andrew Janiak)

Nietzsche *The Antichrist, Ecce Homo, Twilight of the Idols and Other Writings* (edited by Aaron Ridley and Judith Norman)

Nietzsche *Beyond Good and Evil* (edited by Rolf-Peter Horstmann and Judith Norman)

Nietzsche *The Birth of Tragedy and Other Writings* (edited by Raymond Geuss and Ronald Speirs)

Nietzsche *Daybreak* (edited by Maudemarie Clark and Brian Leiter, translated by R.J. Hollingdale)

Nietzsche *The Gay Science* (edited by Bernard Williams, translated by Josefine Nauckhoff)

Nietzsche *Human, All Too Human* (translated by R.J. Hollingdale with an introduction by Richard Schacht)

Nietzsche *Thus Spoke Zarathustra* (edited by Adrian Del Caro and Robert B. Pippin)

Nietzsche *Untimely Meditations* (edited by Daniel Breazeale, translated by R.J. Hollingdale)

Nietzsche *Writings from the Early Notebooks* (edited by Raymond Geuss and Alexander Nehamas, translated by Ladislaus Löb)

Nietzsche *Writings from the Late Notebooks* (edited by Rüdiger Bittner, translated by Kate Sturge)

Novalis *Fichte Studies* (edited by Jane Kneller)

Plato *The Symposium* (edited by M.C. Howatson and Frisbee C.C. Sheffield)

Reinhold *Letters on the Kantian Philosophy* (edited by Karl Ameriks, translated by James Hebbeler)

Schleiermacher *Hermeneutics and Criticism* (edited by Andrew Bowie)

Schleiermacher *Lectures on Philosophical Ethics* (edited by Robert Louden, translated by Louise Adey Huish)

Schleiermacher *On Religion: Speeches to its Cultured Despisers* (edited by Richard Crouter)

Schopenhauer *Prize Essay on the Freedom of the Will* (edited by Günter Zöller)

Sextus Empiricus *Against the Logicians* (edited by Richard Bett)

Sextus Empiricus *Outlines of Scepticism* (edited by Julia Annas and Jonathan Barnes)

Shaftesbury *Characteristics of Men, Manners, Opinions, Times* (edited by Lawrence Klein)

Adam Smith *The Theory of Moral Sentiments* (edited by Knud Haakonssen)

Spinoza *Theological-Political Treatise* (edited by Jonathan Israel, translated by Michael Silverthorne and Jonathan Israel)

Voltaire *Treatise on Tolerance and Other Writings* (edited by Simon Harvey)